A BOLD PLAN FOR AMERICA

14 NONPARTISAN SOLUTIONS BASED ON THE FACTS

JOHN P. BURKE

LITTLE CREEK PRESS
MINERAL POINT, WISCONSIN

Copyright © 2024 by John Burke

All rights reserved. No part of this publication may be reproduced, distributed, or transmitted in any form or by any means, including photocopying, recording, digital scanning, or other electronic or mechanical methods, without the prior written permission of the publisher, except in the case of brief quotations embodied in critical reviews and certain other noncommercial uses permitted by copyright law. For permission requests or other information, please send correspondence to the following address:

Little Creek Press
5341 Sunny Ridge Road
Mineral Point, WI 53565

ORDERING INFORMATION

Quantity sales. Special discounts are available on quantity purchases by corporations, associations, and others. For details, contact info@littlecreekpress.com

Orders by US trade bookstores and wholesalers.
Please contact Little Creek Press for details.

Printed in the United States of America

Cataloging-in-Publication Data
Names: Burke, John, author
Title: A Bold Plan for America / 14 Nonpartisan Solutions Based on the Facts
Description: Mineral Point, WI / Little Creek Press, 2024
Identifiers: LCCN: 2023911232 | ISBN: 978-1-955656-59-7
Subjects: POL000000 POLITICAL SCIENCE/American Government/General
POL040010 POLITICAL SCIENCE/American Government/Executive Branch
POL008000 POLITICAL SCIENCE/Political Process/Campaign & Elections

Book design by Little Creek Press

This book is dedicated to the founding fathers who risked their lives, their families, and their fortunes to create a country that so many of us have benefited from. They deserve better.

"I am not an advocate for frequent changes in laws and constitutions, but laws and institutions must go hand in hand with the progress of the human mind. As that becomes more developed, more enlightened, as new discoveries are made, new truths discovered and manners and opinions change, with the change of circumstances, institutions must advance also to keep pace with the times. We might as well require a man to wear still the coat which fitted him when a boy as civilized society to remain ever under the regimen of their barbarous ancestors."

—Thomas Jefferson

Table of Contents

INTRODUCTION 1

NONPARTISAN SOLUTIONS

1. CREATE A HIGH-PERFORMANCE GOVERNMENT 9
2. INITIATE CLIMATE CHANGE LEADERSHIP FAST! 21
3. REDUCE THE RISK OF NUCLEAR WAR 35
4. FIX THE HEALTH-CARE SYSTEM 45
5. REBUILD AMERICA 69
6. SAVE SOCIAL SECURITY AND EXPAND IT! 75
7. REFORM CONGRESS 87
8. RIGHT-SIZE DEFENSE SPENDING 95
9. ADMINISTER A RESPONSIBLE FOREIGN POLICY 105
10. REDUCE GUN DEATHS IN AMERICA 115
11. FIX THE LEGAL SYSTEM 129
12. EMBRACE THE IMMIGRATION ADVANTAGE 137
13. REFORM CAMPAIGN FINANCE 147
14. SIMPLIFY THE TAX CODE AND BALANCE THE BUDGET 153

CONCLUSION 169

ABOUT THE AUTHOR 173

ACKNOWLEDGMENTS 174

ENDNOTES 175

> **"And sometime, at some point, do something for your country."**
>
> —David McCullough, Pulitzer Prize-winning historian

Introduction

I am a concerned citizen. I love the United States, and it tears me apart to see the decline of our country. It tears me apart even more because that decline is self-inflicted.

I believe that our country is in the mess that we are in because our current group of leaders from both parties are more interested in their careers, their parties, and getting reelected than they are in addressing the serious long-term issues that we face as a nation.

All countries and all organizations have problems. Those that achieve long-term success have leaders who have the humility to admit that their organization has problems and the will and the open-mindedness to solve those problems.

The decline of empires and great nations is nothing new. The empire of Alexander the Great, the Roman and Byzantine Empires, the Mongol Empire, and even the British Empire came to an end because of internal decay, economic troubles, and external pressures.

Our American experiment has lasted for close to 250 years. In that time, we have made great contributions to the advancement of the world. We invented the world's most successful democracy. We were the decisive factor in ending World War I. Along with our Allies, we helped to save the civilized world during World War II, and we then helped rebuild Europe and Japan. We won the Cold War, put a man on the moon, and helped to develop the internet. The list goes on and on—we have a history that we should all be proud of.

Unfortunately, past success does not guarantee future success. The leaders of our country today are different from the leaders of yesterday. Think about it. Washington, Adams, Jefferson, Lincoln, Teddy Roosevelt, Franklin Roosevelt, and Eisenhower were leaders who cared more about the Nation than they did about themselves. Today's politician in America seems to use the following formula:

1. Raise a lot of money. The candidate who raises the most money wins more than 80 percent of the time.

2. Vilify your opponent. Instead of talking about your resume and your plan, run endless mind-numbing commercials about what an idiot your opponent is.

3. Don't talk about the issues that matter. Just pick one or two wedge issues that fire people up and focus on those. Ignore the national debt, the future of the health-care system, and the future of social security, and spend your time talking about such things as transgender bathrooms and the moral decay of the country.

4. Once elected, make decisions in the best interest of your party and your supporters, because these are the debts you need to pay off, and this is where the money is going to come from to win reelection.

5. Rinse and repeat. Resume raising money for your next election.

How is this style of politics working for us? The current state of the Union would say, not very well:

1. A mountain of debt. We are $34 trillion in debt, as I write.[1] There is no real credible plan from any of our presidential candidates or from our national leaders to address the deficit; they keep kicking the can down the road.

2. A warming planet with no clear, serious plan to address its changing climate on the only planet we have.

3. An inventory of 5,400 active and inactive nuclear weapons in our arsenal that are one miscalculation away from blowing up the world.[2] If you don't think this is possible, you probably didn't think a global pandemic could bring the world's economy to its knees.

4. A political system where you can donate as much money to political candidates as you would like, shifting the balance of power away from one person, one vote to the more money you spend, the more votes you can buy.

5. A military-industrial complex that outspends the next 10 countries in the world combined.[3]

6. A health-care system that is almost twice as expensive as any other health system in the world and produces results that rank us 55th out of 57 Western nations.[4]

7. A nation where our gun laws are so ineffective that more than 45,000 of our citizens are killed every year by guns, 85,000 are shot but don't die, and more than one million women have been shot at by a spouse or partner.[5]

8. A prison system with 629 inmates per 100,000 people in the U.S. versus the United Kingdom at 131, Canada at 104, and Germany at 70.[6]

9. A Social Security system that is not financially viable past the year 2035.[7]

10. A tax code that is thousands of pages long and "whose biggest breaks go to corporations and individuals who can afford the best lobbyists," according to the late Republican Senator Tom Coburn.[8]

I have compiled a simple scorecard to help you rate any candidate running for public office. You can determine your scorecard ratings by reviewing a candidate's website, watching a few of their speeches online, and assessing their track record in previous leadership positions.

National Leadership Scorecard	Possible Score	Leader's Score
Humility. Leaders who put the success of the Nation ahead of personal success.	20	
Is a learn-it-all, not a know-it-all. Successful leaders add knowledge in order to make the best decisions.	10	
Puts the best and the brightest in the room. Our leaders make important decisions. The best leaders gather the most intelligent people and are good listeners.	10	
Tells the truth. "There can be no democracy without the truth…" —Andrew Young, former U.S. Ambassador to the U.N.[9]	20	
Addresses important long-term issues. Our country would be far better off if our leaders talked about and had clear plans to deal with our Nation's most pressing issues.	20	
Runs an honorable campaign. Focuses on the issues, their plan, and their leadership skills. Treats their opponent with respect.	20	
TOTAL	100	

In our democracy, we elect our representatives, members of Congress, and presidents. They work for us—the citizens. Because we hire our leaders with our votes and because they work for us, we have some responsibility for the mess that we are in. If we had better citizenship in America, we would have a far better country. I have devised a simple scorecard to help all of us become better citizens. You can complete this second scorecard through an honest five-minute self-assessment.

Citizen of the United States Scorecard	Possible Score	Citizen's Score
Be educated about the issues. John Kennedy once said that "only an educated and informed people will be a free people."[10] 54 percent of Americans cannot name the three branches of Government.[11] 67 percent of Americans cannot name their representative.[12] Two of three Americans would not pass the U.S. Citizenship test.[13]	25	
Vote. 34 percent of eligible voters did not vote in the 2020 Presidential election. 54 percent of voters did not vote in the 2022 mid-term elections.[14]	25	
Respect and obey the laws. In our country no one is above the law.	10	
Pay taxes honestly. "I like to pay taxes. With them, I buy civilization." —Oliver Wendell Holmes Jr.[15]	10	
Respect differences. Value other people's views even if you disagree.	10	
Be healthy. The number one factor driving our national debt is health-care costs. We are the unhealthiest generation of Americans. Take personal responsibility for your health and that of your family.	10	
Be nice. Make Mister Rogers, the American icon for compassion and morality, proud by (a) being helpful to others, (b) being polite by saying "please" and "thank you," (c) being humble and caring more about others than you do about yourself.	10	
TOTAL	100	

As we enter the 2024 election season, we are at a crucial point in our Nation's history. Unfortunately, I fear that we are in for another democracy-busting Presidential election featuring record-breaking fundraising, a massive amount of negative ads, candidates who care more about winning than they do about the future of the country, and very little conversation about the candidates' plans to address the biggest challenges we face.

In the end, the healing of our country's internal wounds will be up to us, the ordinary citizens of the United States. On a daily basis, we cannot control what the President does or what Congress does, but we can take personal responsibility for our individual decisions and actions in our everyday lives. If you are waiting for a candidate with a magic wand who everyone in the country will get behind and will do all the work for us, it is probably not going to happen.

The future of our country is up to us, citizens of the United States!

In his letter from the Birmingham jail in August 1963, Martin Luther King Jr. wrote that the main roadblocks to achieving equal rights were "not merely for the vitriolic words and actions of the bad people but for the appalling silence of the good people."[16] As I talk to people around the country about the state of our Union, I am consistently disappointed to see that so many good people have given up. They are silent.

In 2011, I attended my son's graduation from Marquette University. The keynote speaker was David McCullough, a renowned historian and Pulitzer Prize-winning author. It was a memorable message. McCullough's final piece of advice struck me: "And sometime, at some point, do something for your country." I have been haunted by this challenge over the past 13 years. One of my good friends said to me years ago after I came out with my first book, "I am a staunch Republican. I read your book, and I agree with every one of your proposals. If you put smart people in a room, and put the facts on the board, 90 percent of the time, smart people from no matter what party will come to the same conclusions." It is my belief that my friend is a microcosm of America. It is my hope that this book can accomplish the following:

1. Provide a plan for America. There is not a candidate in the current field running for the highest office in the land with a comprehensive plan. It is embarrassing. This book is my plan for America. It is bold, it is specific, it is creative, it is nonpartisan, and it asks for shared sacrifice. This is the type of plan we should expect from any serious leader seeking the highest office in the land.

2. Educate the American people. My plan takes on 14 of our biggest challenges. It is filled with FACTS and potential solutions. This book can help you think about your country's future, it can help educate you on 14 of our biggest challenges, and it will hopefully help you to become a better citizen of the United States.

3. Help to change the direction of the country. When you look at our challenges and at the facts, it is clear to me that we need better leadership in our country, and we need to make major changes. I hope that this book will find its way to some of our leaders, and I hope that it will inspire them to think bigger about what our future could be.

4. Bring Americans together. Our leaders run elections to win, and unfortunately, a winning strategy is dividing Americans. It is my hope that this book can bring people together by presenting facts about our most challenging problems.

My National Leadership and Citizen scorecards are easy tools to evaluate candidates to improve citizen involvement in our democracy. These are simple action steps for people who have been sitting on the sidelines, frustrated and silent.

If the citizens become educated on our biggest challenges and become more demanding of our elected officials to make decisions in the best long-term interest of the country, we can indeed change the direction of the Nation. I am a firm believer in what the anthropologist Margaret Mead said many years ago. "A small group of people can change the world. Indeed it is the only thing that ever has." I hope you find the facts, along with my thoughts and opinions about the state of our Nation, worthwhile, and I hope that all of us can use this crisis to reexamine the relationship that we have with our incredible country and become worthy of the title "Citizen of the United States."

1

Create a High-Performance Government

"A leader takes people where they want to go. A GREAT leader takes people where they don't necessarily want to go, but ought to be."

—Rosalynn Carter[17]

The United States Government is not a high-performance government. "We, the people" own our Government, yet our leaders tolerate poor performance in many areas of the Government. Our Government is not ONE big organization but a fleet of smaller organizations, like the Air Force, which defends our skies; the National Park Service, which protects and promotes our most beautiful lands; the Internal Revenue Service, which collects the taxes that provides the fuel for the Government to exist; Homeland Security, which keeps us safe; the Department of Health and

Human Services, which is in charge of the health of the Nation; and the list goes on and on. Some of these organizations are exceptional. They have great leaders, a great team, clear direction, and they deliver superior performance. Other organizations within the Government have poor leadership, lack a plan, and deliver lousy performance year after year for you, the taxpayer.

Candidates who run for the highest office in the land rarely talk about the performance of the government that they are hoping to lead. The Government's performance affects your everyday life. It affects your pocketbook, your children's education, your health, and your security, to name a few. The key to creating a high-performance government is to set high standards for every organization in the government and to hold leaders accountable. All great organizations have a great team, and the citizens of the United States should expect nothing less from their Government.

Poor performance within the U.S. Government is nothing new, and it is NOT the fault of Government employees; it is a leadership issue. I believe there are two main reasons why we have poor performance in our Government:

1. WE FAIL TO ADDRESS THE BIG ISSUES IN OUR COUNTRY UNTIL THEY BECOME A CRISIS.
Our Government does little to prepare for the major problems that confront us.

I am reminded of a story I heard many years ago of the manager who sits in the office all day and makes decisions. Small easy decisions were called mice, and large, complex decisions were "big, hairy monsters." One by one, an aide brings the manager decisions to make. The aide walks in with a mouse, and the manager addresses the issue. Problem solved. The aide walks in with another mouse. The confident manager addresses the issue, and another problem is solved. Then the aide walks over to a closet, takes his key out, and opens the door. Out pops a big, hairy monster of a problem. The aide leads the big, hairy monster to the boss. The boss looks at the big, hairy monster of a problem and says, "Put it back. We will deal with it another day." **Too often, this story is the same for the Federal Government. We fail to deal with the biggest problems of the day. And then one day, we get crushed with COVID-19, crushed with the current obesity epidemic in the United States, crushed by our failing public schools in the poorest areas of our country, and crushed by an out-of-control $34 trillion in Federal debt. And we are setting ourselves up for the biggest one of them all—climate change. We know all these problems exist, but our leaders keep them in the closet because they are more interested in getting reelected than in doing their jobs.**

Columnist Robert J. Samuelson wrote an excellent editorial in *The Washington Post* in September 2018 that said:

> As a society, we have failed to confront some of the major social, political and economic realities of our time: immigration, globalization, health spending, global warming, federal budget deficits, stubborn poverty and the aging of society, among others. What almost all of these issues have in common is that the remedies they suggest are unpleasant. They demand, in the political vernacular, "sacrifice." To close federal budget deficits, taxes must go up and spending must come down. To deal with an aging society, people must work longer.... To resist global warming, fossil-fuel prices must go up—a lot—either through taxes or regulations.... There is no gentle way to do this.[18]

2. IT IS ALMOST IMPOSSIBLE TO REMOVE POOR PERFORMERS. We have a lot of great Federal Government employees who have put in many long hours of public service to help make America what it is today. Unfortunately, we also have poor performers on the team. In many government jobs—such as at the Environmental Protection Agency, the Small Business Administration, the Department of Housing and Urban Development, and the Office of Management and Budget, as well as a dozen other Federal agencies—your chances of dying on the job are higher than those of being fired, according to a *USA Today* article:

The federal government fired 0.55 percent of its workers in the budget year that ended September 30, 2011. That amounted to 1,668 out of a workforce of 2.1 million. The private sector fires about 3 percent of workers annually for poor performance. That means your chance of being fired in the private sector is six times higher than your chance of being fired if you work for the federal government. The 1,800-employee Federal Communications Commission and the 1,200-employee Federal Trade Commission didn't fire a single employee. Last year, the federal government fired none of its 3,000 meteorologists, 2,500 health insurance administrators, 1,000 optometrists, 800 historians, or 500 industrial property managers.[19]

....

Another factor affecting performance at the Federal, state, and local levels of government is unions. For example, a study carried out in 2020 by Loyola University of Chicago law professor Stephen Rushin reviewed a database of 624 police arbitration awards and found a 52 percent rate of reducing or overturning disciplinary actions against police officers.[20] Additionally, in 46 percent of the cases, police agencies were ordered to rehire officers they had fired. Seattle Mayor Jenny Durkan said, "You're putting bad cops back into the departments. If you want to really reform police departments, you have to have true accountability. And if someone uses excessive force, kills someone unlawfully, or is dishonest—if they're fired, they should stay fired."

An article in *The New York Times* updated on April 2, 2021, reporting on how police unions have become such powerful opponents to reform efforts stated, "Over the past five years, as demands for reform have mounted in the aftermath of police violence in cities like Ferguson, Missouri, Baltimore, and now Minneapolis, police unions have emerged as one of the most significant roadblocks to change. The greater the political pressure for reform, the more defiant the unions often are in resisting it—with few city officials, including liberal leaders, able to overcome their opposition."[21]

Government unions are more interested in protecting the employee than they are in creating the best government in the world by setting high standards and holding people accountable.

The late Senator John McCain (R-AZ) once said, **"The failings in our civil service are encouraged by a system that makes it very difficult to fire someone even for gross misconduct. We must do away with the current system that treats federal employment as a right and makes dismissal a near impossibility."**[22]

The American people own the Federal Government. Federal employees are supposed to work for us. At most high-performance companies, you get a warning if you do not do your job. If you continue to fail to do your job, you are fired. Without the ability to fire people, the company has no leverage with the underachievers. Over time, the problem spreads, a culture of mediocrity sets in, and many of the best employees leave. Nothing demoralizes A-players more than having to work with slackers. So, when you can't get rid of workers who are not proficient, they stay, and some of our best employees choose to leave. This is precisely what we have in certain areas of our Federal Government today. And you are the owner of the team!

President Franklin D. Roosevelt, a great friend of the American worker, felt that public employee unions were a bad idea. "Meticulous attention," Roosevelt said in 1937, "should be paid to the special relations and obligations of public servants to the public itself and to the government.... The process of collective bargaining, as usually understood, cannot be transplanted into the public service."[23]

Steve Jobs, regarded as one of the smartest people in the past 100 years, built one of the most valuable companies in the world and reinvented five businesses in his lifetime, and he thought public teachers' unions were terrible:

But it pains me because we do know how to provide a great education. We really do. We could make sure that every young child in this country got a great education. We fall far short of that.... The problem there, of course, is the unions. The unions are the worst thing that ever happened to education because it's not a meritocracy. It turns into a bureaucracy, which is exactly what has happened. The teachers can't teach, and administrators run the place, and nobody can be fired. It's terrible.[24]

Businesses need to compete in the marketplace. If someone offers a better product or price, the market forces you to react or go out of business. What government unions do is take competitiveness out of the game. Poorly performing areas of our Government can survive because public employee unions protect poor performers. The government unions win, and the people lose.

....

The next President of the United States should introduce the John McCain High-Performance Government Act of 2025 within the first 300 days of being on the job. The following four initiatives have the potential to create more change in the way our Government operates than in the past 100 years and will produce a high-performance government that our citizens deserve.

1. THE PRESIDENT SHOULD REQUIRE EVERY BUSINESS UNIT IN THE FEDERAL GOVERNMENT TO HAVE AN ACTION PLAN WITHIN THE FIRST SIX MONTHS OF HIS OR HER ADMINISTRATION. In the fall of 2019, Jim Collins (one of the foremost business thought leaders in America) visited Trek and gave a presentation to our leadership group that changed the company. Jim said something I will never forget: "How does Trek become a truly iconic company? By every one of you here, every one of your businesses, becoming a sparkling minibus of excellence."[25] We took that concept and ran with it. Today at Trek, there are 727 small business units (or minibuses), with a plan in place. It has made a massive difference at Trek and can do the same for the Federal Government. I would guess there are more than 210,000 small business units in the Federal Government. By the end of 2025, every small business unit in the Federal Government should have a plan containing the following three components:

- An overall goal that can motivate the team and add value to the citizens it serves. The President should set the goal for every team in the Federal Government to be the best in the world at whatever they do. This is how we create an amazing government. Every single part of the Federal Government should have a stated goal to become the best in the world at what they do—the best tax collection service in the world, the best health-care system in the world, the best transportation system in the world. When you start looking at small businesses within the Government through the "Best in the World Glasses," the game changes.

- A list of accomplishments and brutal facts over the past three months. You can only improve if you have the self-awareness to understand your current set of problems.

- A list of objectives and key results that will help to transform each department into the best in the world. Years ago, I read a book by John Doerr, a venture capitalist, entitled *Measure What Matters*. Doerr's key point was that every organization should have a list of objectives and key results (OKRs). As part of each small business unit's plan, every leader in the Federal Government will have OKRs, which will be updated every quarter. This style of management works. When Google started, it was the 18th search company.[26] Today, Google dominates search. What was the difference? Google used OKRs throughout the organization, while the other companies did not. OKRs throughout the Federal Government would make a massive difference.

As a citizen, ask yourself what percentage of your Government's departments have an overall goal that motivates the team? What percentage can list their accomplishments over the last 90 days, as well as their failures?

What percentage have a plan to become the best in the world at what they do? What percentage have a list of items that they are struggling with and need help? I am betting that the answer to most of these questions is zero. **There is a massive opportunity to improve the performance of every part of our Government.** The next President should ensure that every small business unit of YOUR Government has a plan, that we put the best team on the field, and that we deliver value for you, the taxpayer.

2. THE PRESIDENT SHOULD IMPLEMENT THE GREAT PLACES TO WORK SURVEY ACROSS THE FEDERAL GOVERNMENT WITHIN THE FIRST 90 DAYS OF HIS OR HER ADMINISTRATION.

The Great Place to Work Institute sends confidential surveys to employees and asks more than 50 questions to assess whether the organization is a great place to work. Based on the responses, the organization earns a score of 0 to 100. Many studies have concluded that happier employees are more productive, and organizations with higher GPTW scores consistently outperform their peers. We successfully implemented the Great Place to Work Program at Trek in 2013, which has made a massive difference—happier, more productive employees provide better service and, most importantly, deliver better overall results.

I know that GPTW can also make a massive difference in our Government. By implementing the GPTW Program, we will know how the Government ranks compared to other businesses; we will be able to compare one department to another; and we will be able to compare one leader to another. The survey also asks employees for feedback on making their small business unit a better place to work and a unit that adds more value to the customers. The feedback is gold. We have not had a President in our history who has put in place a proven process to generate employee feedback from every single employee in the Federal Government. Our next President could be the first. This one move would significantly improve the performance of our Government for no additional cost.

3. ABOLISH PUBLIC EMPLOYEE UNIONS AT THE FEDERAL LEVEL BY ISSUING AN EXECUTIVE ORDER WITHIN THE FIRST 30 DAYS OF HIS OR HER ADMINISTRATION. Those who work for the Government are already represented by the Government and should not be allowed to organize. Franklin Roosevelt was opposed to government unions at the Federal level for good reasons. You cannot have a high-performance team if the coach cannot fire the players. I am all for feedback and coaching. I am for creating a great place to work and compensating employees well, but at the end of the day, if you want a high-performance team, you need to be able to change out the players if they are not performing their job with or without a union.

4. CREATE LEVEL 5 LEADERS THROUGHOUT THE FEDERAL GOVERNMENT. In his book *Good to Great*, Jim Collins discusses the key factor separating good and great companies. That factor is Level 5 leadership, a combination of great humility and incredible will. There were 2.95 million Federal employees in 2023,[27] and I estimate that there are at least 295,000 leadership positions. The University of Michigan did a study years ago and concluded that there are two reasons why people fail at their jobs. First, people did not understand their job responsibilities; and second, they were never trained to do their job. The President could significantly increase the effectiveness of our Government's executive branch leaders by enacting the following:

- Set the expectation for anyone who is a leader in the Federal Government to be a Level 5 leader. Introduce the Level 5 Leadership Scorecard. All leaders will be graded twice a year and will know exactly where they stand.

- Create the United States Level 5 Leadership Training Academy to give every Federal employee the ability to improve their leadership skills. A great leadership program benefits not only the leaders in the company, but all employees who want to improve their skills. It has also been my experience that great leadership training not only

Level 5 Leadership Scorecard	Your Score
Humility Places goals of the team ahead of their own. Does not care who gets the credit. Learn-it-all versus know-it-all. Asks questions; great listener.	
TOTAL HUMILITY SCORE (0-5)	
Will Gets stuff done fast; acts quickly. Deals with reality; great at Plan B. Takes personal responsibility; does not blame others. Tackles the hard things; will knock down walls to deliver results.	
TOTAL WILL SCORE (0-5)	
Best team on the field Sets high standards and holds people accountable. Makes great hiring decisions. Coaches continuously up or out; moves people off the bus quickly. Has great energy and commitment to Great Place to Work.	
TOTAL TEAM SCORE (0-5)	
Vision Open to new ideas; commitment to continuous improvement. Can think outside the box. Thinks globally.	
TOTAL VISION SCORE (0-5)	
TOTAL LEVEL 5 SCORE (0-5)	

helps employees at work but has an amazing impact on their lives outside of work. The President should tap the best and the brightest leaders throughout America to develop the training program. A U.S. Level 5 Leadership Program could be up and running within six months. The more effective leaders we have in our Government, the higher our Government will perform. I worked with a team at Trek to develop a highly successful Level 5 Leadership Program. It has made a massive difference in a company with 6,000 employees. Imagine the difference a great leadership program would have for all employees of the Federal Government.

We live in a world where, over the past 20 years, virtually every product or service has improved, become more affordable, or both. In the private sector, if your product has not improved or become more affordable, you are out of business. Good government matters to every citizen in this country. I am confident that the next President of the United States could significantly improve the culture and performance of the Federal Government with very little cost by implementing the John McCain High-Performance Government Act of 2025.

2

Initiate Climate Change Leadership FAST!

"We are in the fight of our lives. And we are losing. Greenhouse gas emissions keep growing. Global temperatures keep rising. And our planet is fast approaching tipping points that will make climate chaos irreversible. We are on a highway to climate hell with our foot still on the accelerator."

—António Guterres, Secretary-General of the United Nations, remarks delivered at the opening of the 2022 United Nations Climate Change Conference (COP27), November 7, 2022[28]

When it comes to climate change, there is good news, and there is bad news. The good news is that for the first time, President Biden and Congress passed a bill in August 2022 to take the first major step in reducing our carbon emissions.[29] The Inflation Reduction Act has the potential to reduce our carbon emissions by 40 percent by the end of this decade. I think the effect of the bill is best summed up by Anand Gopal, executive director of policy at Energy Innovation: "This is a dramatically large climate bill, the biggest in U.S. history. It doesn't mean the U.S. won't need to do more to achieve its emissions goals, but it will make a meaningful difference."[30] The bad news is that we have a long way to go, and the stakes are high.

There are two key questions for every American citizen and for the next President. First, "Do you believe that climate change is real?" If your answer to the first question is yes, then the second question is straightforward. "Are we doing enough as a country?" My answer to the first question is yes; I believe climate change is real. My answer to the second question is no; I don't think we are doing enough as a country regarding climate change. I think the Inflation Reduction Act is a good first step, but if we really want to be a leader in climate change for the good of our country and to be a role model for the rest of the world, we have more work to do.

Our Nation has a rich history of being a role model for the rest of the world. We were a role model in the formation of a democracy; we tipped the balance in World War I; we helped to save the world during World War II; we led the rebuilding of the world after World War II; and we won the race to the moon, to name a few. So here we are at the fork in the road of the greatest battle humanity has ever seen. The game is about human survival, the objective is to save our planet, and the clock is ticking. This is a complicated game because we are not the only players. Every nation needs to play because we all breathe the same air, we all drink the same water, and our weather and climate are influenced by the behavior of other nations. We need to lead. We need to make friends to save the only planet that we have. We need someone willing to make the tough calls and lead us through this high-stakes crisis.

The climate crisis requires a long-term vision in a short-term, immediate-gratification world. If you put a frog in a boiling pot of water, the frog jumps out, stunned by the brutal environment. If you put a frog in a pot of water at room temperature and raise the temperature by one degree every minute, the frog sits in the boiling pot of water, gets used to the environment, and then dies because it boils to death. The United States (and the majority of the rest of the world) is the frog that was put in the pot of water at room temperature. Every year we spew more carbon into the atmosphere. Every year the climate gets worse, and strange stuff happens, like in Houston, where you have had three 500-year floods in five years,[31] or the summer of 2023 record-breaking heatwave across the Nation which has seen waters off of South Florida reach 101.1 degrees,[32] and sidewalks in Arizona send people to the hospital with third-degree burns.[33] Every year, like the frog, we get used to our environment. We talk about it and take some small actions, but we don't make the big move and jump out of the pot of water.

Here is why I think every American citizen and the next President should be concerned with where we are today:

1. THE EXPERTS ARE TELLING US THAT WE HAVE A CRISIS ON OUR HANDS, AND IT IS GETTING WORSE ... A LOT WORSE. Zeke Hausfather a research scientist at Berkeley Earth, an independent organization that analyzes environmental data, wrote an opinion piece in *The New York Times* on October 13, 2023. The article starts out with a paragraph that every American should read: "Staggering. Unnerving. Mind-boggling. Absolutely gobsmackingly bananas. As global temperatures shattered records and reached dangerous new highs over and over the past few months, my climate scientist colleagues and I have just about run out of adjectives to describe what we have seen. Data from Berkeley Earth released on Wednesday shows that September was an astounding 0.5 degree Celsius (almost a full degree Fahrenheit) hotter than the prior record, and July and August were around 0.3 degree Celsius (0.5 degree Fahrenheit) hotter. 2023 is almost certain to be the hottest year since reliable global records began in the mid-1800s and probably for the past 2,000 years (and well before that)."[34]

2. CARBON DIOXIDE LEVELS ARE RISING AND COULD WARM THE PLANET BY 4 DEGREES CELSIUS BY 2060. Researchers at the Mauna Loa Observatory in Hawaii have measured carbon dioxide (CO_2) levels in the atmosphere since 1958.[35] The first measurements showed the amount of CO_2 in the atmosphere at 315 parts per million (ppm). In 2006, the level was 380 ppm, and in May 2022, the level of carbon in the atmosphere measured 421 ppm.[36] Researchers say the amount of CO_2 in the atmosphere could double pre-industrial levels by 2060.[37] A continued increase in CO_2 will cause extreme sea level rise, more extreme storms, wildfires, drought, and food and water shortages. Scientists believe we are already in the red zone. If nothing is done, and the level of carbon continues to rise, the temperature on the planet will rise significantly in the next 50 years, and the impact will be catastrophic.

Percentage of climate scientists who agree that climate-warming trends over the past century are **likely due to human activities.**

Source: https://climate.nasa.gov/faq/17/do-scientists-agree-on-climate-change/#:~:text=Yes percent2C percent20the percent20vast percent20majority percent20of,global percent20warming percent20and percent20climate percent20change

3. THE TEMPERATURE OF OUR PLANET HAS INCREASED BY 2 DEGREES SINCE 1880.[38]

The average U.S. atmospheric temperature for 2020 was 54.4 degrees Fahrenheit (°F), 2.4 degrees above the 20th-century average, making it the fifth warmest year in 126 years of record keeping.[39] The years from 2015 to 2022 have been the hottest the world has experienced on record, per the World Meteorological Organization, with 2019 coming in second only to 2016's record-high heat.[40] Although two degrees over 140 years may not sound like a lot, consider that the average normal temperature for the human body is 98.6 °F. If you increased that to 100.6 °F, you would be sick. That is where we are as a planet today. We have a temperature of 100.6 °F, and we are sick. What is worse is that the "doctors" (global scientists) are telling us that if we don't change some of our habits, our Earth's atmospheric temperature will be the human

Global Average Temperature 1850–2021

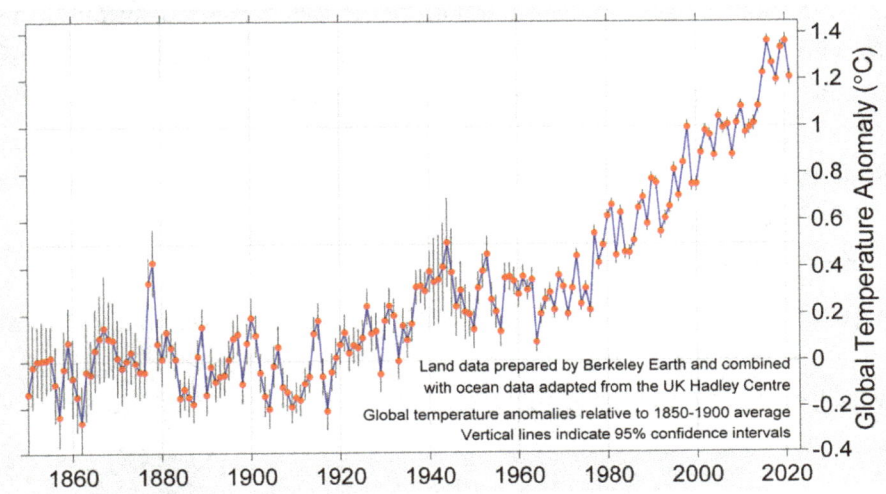

Source: https://berkeleyearth.org/global-temperature-report-for-2021/

equivalent of 105.2 °F by the year 2100. The human body dies at 108 °F. What happens when Earth's temperature rises? Heat waves, forest fires, changes in rainfall and snowfall patterns, more intense storms, a more hospitable environment for transmitting infectious diseases such as COVID-19,[41] and the extinction of various plants and animals. **Since 1970, there has been a 68 percent loss in mammal, fish, reptile, bird, and amphibian populations.**[42]

4. THE EFFECTS OF CLIMATE CHANGE ARE HAPPENING TODAY ACROSS OUR COUNTRY. Global average sea level has risen 8-9 inches (21-25 centimeters) since 1880 with nearly half of that increase coming since 1993,[43] with 2020 setting a new record of 3.6 inches above the 1993 levels. Coastal cities across America are feeling the effects of flooding and the increased intensity of hurricanes, spurred on by warmer ocean temperatures and higher sea levels. The 2020 Atlantic hurricane season had the most storms ever recorded for a single season,[44] with Hurricane Laura being the strongest and most damaging in the U.S., making landfall in southwestern Louisiana on August 27, 2020, as a Category 4 storm with 150-mile-per-hour winds and killing at least 47 people.[45] In fact, across the United States, 2020 was marked by a record 22 separate billion-dollar weather and climate disasters, costing the Nation a combined $95 billion in damages.[46] More recently, on September 28, 2022, the U.S. suffered the effects of Hurricane Ian, another Category 4 storm that battered Southwest Florida. In a matter of days, the death toll surpassed 144 people.[47] Nearly 7,000 homes were damaged in Volusia County alone.[48] At the beginning of August 2022, more than 10 inches of rain fell in Illinois, which, together with events in St. Louis and eastern Kentucky, marked the third 1-in-1,000-year rain event in the lower 48 states in about a week.[49]

In 2020, close to 9,900 wildfires burned 4.3 million acres in California, twice the previous record.[50] California fires killed 33 people in 2020, with overall economic losses of more than $19 billion and firefighting costs

Cumulative Changes in Relative Sea Level

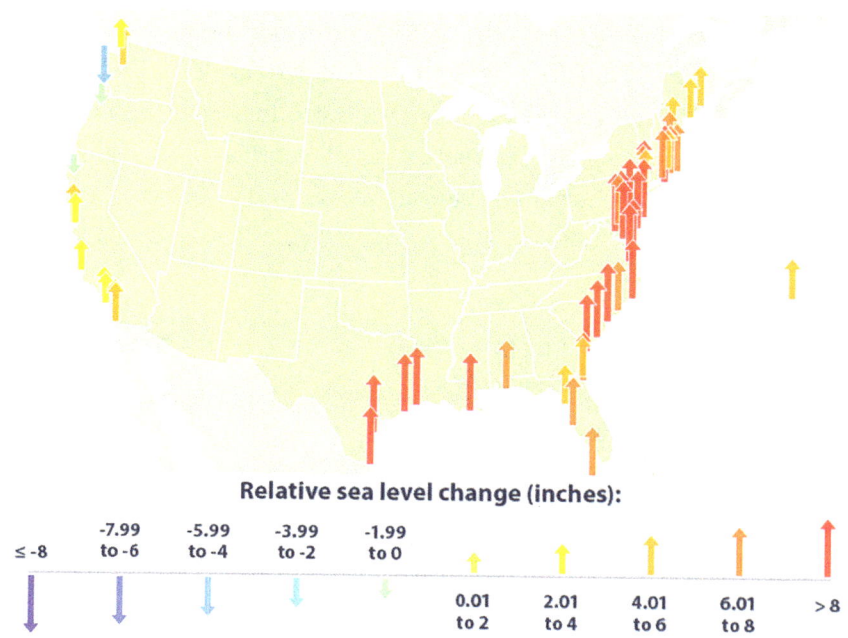

This map shows cumulative changes in relative sea level from 1960 to 2021 at tide gauge stations along U.S. coasts. Relative sea level reflects changes in sea level as well as land elevation.

Source: NOAA, 20226. Web update: July 2022

NOAA (National Oceanic and Atmospheric Administration). 2022 update to data originally published in: NOAA. 2009. Sea level variations of the United States 1854–2006. NOAA Technical Report NOS CO-OPS 053. www.tidesandcurrents.noaa.gov/publications/Tech_rpt_53.pdf.

approaching $2.1 billion.[51] Taken together, the years 2020 and 2021 burned more area within California than the previous seven years combined and only slightly less than the total burned between 1980 and 1999. Between 2015 and 2020, total insured economic losses were more than $50 billion, and over 50,000 structures—mostly homes—were destroyed.[52] Wildfires are not just in California, and they don't just happen in summer. An example is Colorado's Marshall Fire of December 30, 2021, which burned nearly 1,100 residences across several suburbs of Boulder in just a few

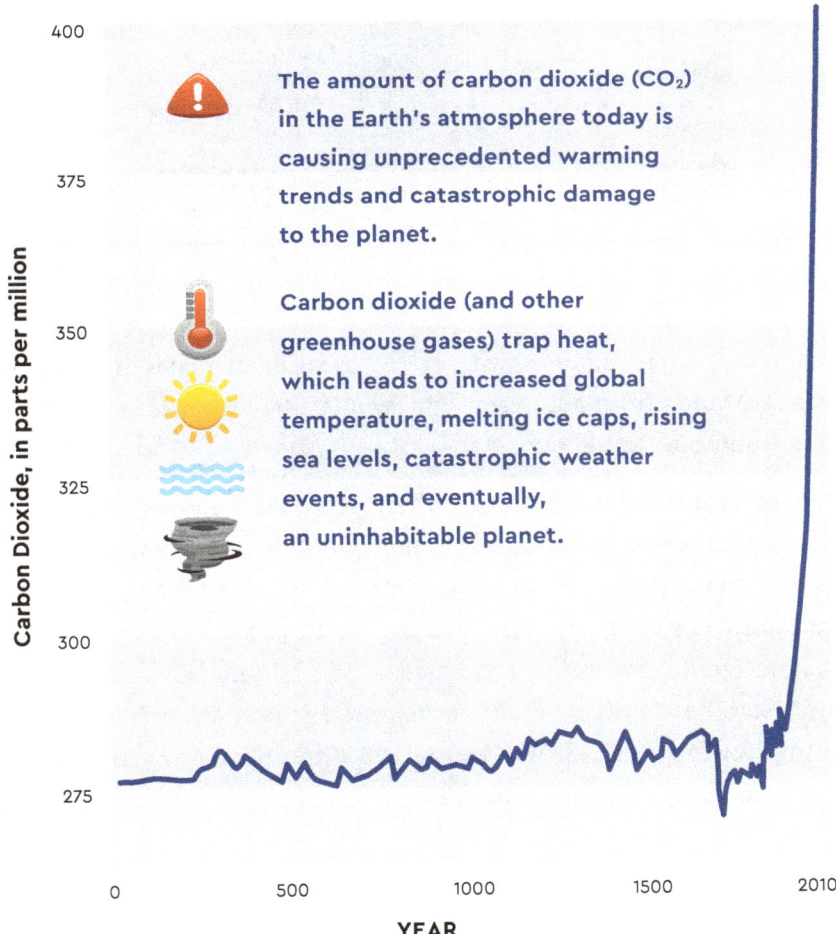

Source: Kennedy, R (Director). (2018). *Above and Beyond: NASA's Journey to Tomorrow* [Motion Picture]. United States: Fathom Events

U.S. 2023 Billion-Dollar Weather and Climate Disasters

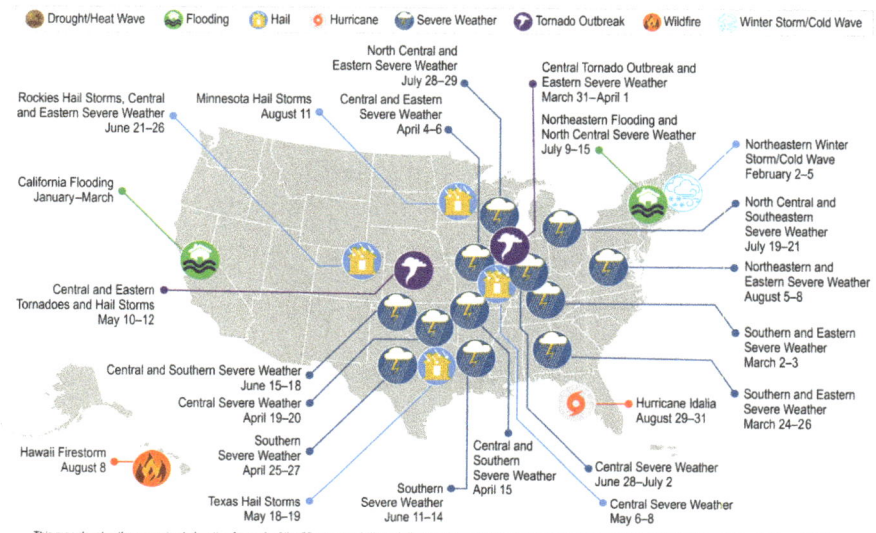

Source: NOAA National Centers for Environmental Information (NCEI) U.S. Billion-Dollar Weather and Climate Disasters (2023). https://www.ncei.noaa.gov/access/billions/, DOI: 10.25921/stkw-7w73

short hours in the middle of winter.[53] One stunned resident remarked, "It was 200 yards from a Costco—why would I have to worry about fire? It's, like, suburbia, you know?"[54]

In the first nine months of 2023, there were 24 weather and climate disasters, with losses exceeding $1 billion. On August 8, a wildfire caused massive damage to the city of Lahaina on the island of Maui, where two million tourists visit every year. The fire destroyed 2,200 buildings, and the cost to rebuild the city is estimated at $5.5 billion.[55] Records from the NOAA's National Centers for Environmental Information highlight the alarming upward trend: from 1980 to 1990, there were 35 such events; from 1991 to 2001, 59 events; and from 2002 to 2011, 84 billion-dollar loss events.[56]

5. THE UNITED STATES IS THE SECOND-LARGEST POLLUTER IN THE WORLD, EMITTING 5,981 MILLION METRIC TONS OF CARBON DIOXIDE INTO THE ATMOSPHERE IN 2020.[57] The average American citizen emits 13.0 metric tons of carbon dioxide per year compared to the average German, who emits 7.3 metric tons; the average Japanese, who releases 8.0 metric tons; and the average person in the United Kingdom, who is responsible for 4.6 metric tons, based on global 2020 statistics.[58] The carbon that we spew into the atmosphere does not just pollute our air; it affects every global citizen. As a country, we have a moral responsibility to clean up the mess that we have created.

Per-Capita CO$_2$ Emissions

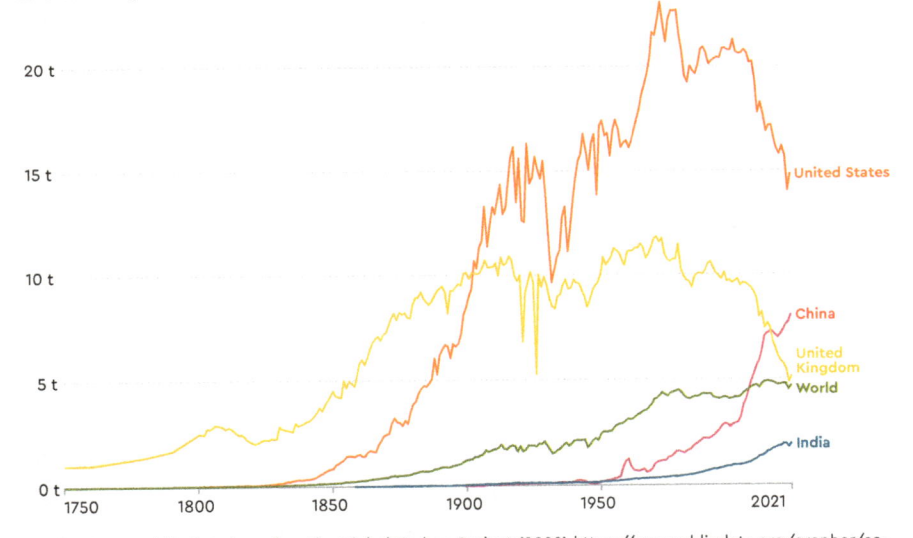

Carbon dioxide (CO₂) emissions from fossil fuels and industry. Land use change is not included.

Source: Our World in Data based on the Global Carbon Project (2022) https://ourworldindata.org/grapher/co-emissions-per-capita?tab=chart&country=USA~GBR~IND~CHN~OWID_WRL

Fossil emissions measure the quantity of carbon dioxide (CO₂) emitted from the burning of fossil fuels and directly from industrial processes such as cement and steel production. Fossil CO₂ includes emissions from coal, oil, gas, flaring, cement, steel, and other industrial processes. Fossil emissions do not include land use change, deforestation, soils, or vegetation.

6. CLIMATE CHANGE IS COSTING US A FORTUNE AND IS SUCKING UP MASSIVE RESOURCES. Over the past decade, extreme weather and the health impact of burning fossil fuels have cost the American economy at least $240 billion annually. It is estimated that the cost will increase by at least 50 percent over the next decade.[59] Florida's September 2022 Hurricane Ian alone is estimated to have cost between $53 and $74 billion.[60] The frequency and severity of hurricanes come from the warming of oceans due to greenhouse gases in the atmosphere. The massive costs of wildfires, tornadoes, and floods are going to continue to increase as we continue to pump more and more carbon into the atmosphere.

7. SCIENTISTS ARE TELLING US THAT THE ENVIRONMENT WILL FACE GREATER PRESSURE IN THE FUTURE. The world's population is projected to increase from 8 billion today to 9.8 billion by 2050.[61] In 30 years, we will have an additional 2 billion people on Earth. As Thomas Friedman writes in *Thank You for Being Late*, "The impact on the planet's natural systems and climate will become exponentially more devastating because more and more of those 9.7 billion people are moving to large urban areas and up the socioeconomic ladder … where they will drive more cars, live in more and bigger homes, consume more water and electricity, and eat more protein…" **Today, roughly 86 percent of Americans have air conditioning in their homes and apartments, compared to only 7 percent in Brazil and less than that in India.**[62] **What happens when the rest of the world starts to consume like Americans?**

8. FOREIGN POLICY AND MILITARY IMPLICATIONS. Top military officials have warned for years that climate change will have serious ramifications for the United States military.[63] Climate change leads to extreme weather events, which lead to humanitarian disasters and failed nations, which increase the likelihood of extremism and terrorism. Here's one example: Between 2006 and 2009, Syria suffered a terrible drought that scientists blame on human-induced climate change.[64] The drought, combined with government policies that hurt farmers, forced more than one million rural Syrians to flee to cities, multiplying the stresses that sparked the 2011 uprising against the Syrian Government. The continuing civil war has claimed the lives of more than 500,000 Syrians and has displaced more than half of the population and has left 12 million people food insecure, United Nations figures show.[65] Syria is the perfect example of more humanitarian disasters and stress on the U.S. military as global climate change speeds up. **Add onto this pile that a large percentage of the carbon burned on our planet comes from unstable regimes**

worldwide. Reducing our carbon emissions would mean we would lessen our dependence on foreign oil and increase global stability.

....

It is my opinion that based on the facts, the next President of the United States should take the following four steps as soon as possible:

1. MAKE CLIMATE CHANGE LEADERSHIP THE TOP PRIORITY OF THE NEW ADMINISTRATION. The climate is changing because, as global citizens, we are pouring more carbon dioxide into the atmosphere than the planet can handle. We need every country involved in the solution, and the next President should make sure that the United States is at the table taking a leadership role. Secretary-General of the United Nations António Guterres said in 2018, "What is missing—still, even after the clinching of the Paris Agreement—is leadership, a sense of urgency, and a true commitment to a decisive multilateral response."[66] The United States should provide leadership and a sense of urgency to make global climate change one of our top priorities. We only have one planet. The President should, within the first 30 days of his or her administration, host a group of business leaders (who generate the majority of the carbon) and government officials from both parties, along with environmental experts, to develop a specific list of action items to make sure the United States takes a leadership role when it comes to climate change.

2. IN THE PRESIDENT'S FIRST 90 DAYS, HE OR SHE SHOULD ASK CONGRESS TO IMPLEMENT THE BAKER-SHULTZ CARBON DIVIDENT PLAN. Former Secretary of State James Baker and the late former Secretary of State George Shultz joined with former Treasury Secretary Hank Paulson, former Walmart chairman Rob Walton, former Vice President Al Gore, leading environmental groups, and a few large oil companies, including ExxonMobil, BP, and Royal Dutch Shell, to support a simple carbon tax of $40 per metric ton. The plan has two basic parts:[67]

- The Federal Government would impose a tax on carbon dioxide emissions, beginning at $40 per metric ton, on July 1, 2025. The tax would be collected where the fossil fuels enter the economy, such as the mine, well, or port, and would increase the prices of carbon-emitting products. The tax would send a clear message to both businesses and consumers that we must reduce our carbon footprint.

- The proceeds of this tax would be significant, in the $300 billion range per year, and would be returned to the American people through a quarterly dividend. It is estimated that a family of four would receive $2,000 in the first year to offset the higher costs of products that contribute to carbon emissions. Those families reducing their carbon footprint would benefit the most, and those citizens and companies consuming the most carbon-emitting products would pay the most. American companies exporting to countries without comparable carbon programs would receive rebates to make sure that American companies are competing on a level playing field. This would also send a strong message to other nations to adopt the same carbon tax as the United States.

There are a few reasons why I believe that the Baker-Shultz Carbon Dividend Plan is the right plan to address the climate change issue. First, it is nonpartisan. Talented people from both sides of the aisle support this idea, as well as oil companies and large retailers like Walmart. Second, it is simple. One simple tax can significantly reduce the amount of carbon dioxide we pour into the atmosphere. Instead of coming up with hundreds of government programs, we can create one straightforward tax that would incentivize every American to reduce their consumption of carbon-emitting products. One simple move, and we can take a significant step forward in addressing global climate change and be an example for the rest of the world.

3. ENDORSE THE ONE TRILLION TREE CAMPAIGN. The next President should endorse and promote the simple concept of planting one trillion trees during this decade. Al Gore said, "The best available technology for pulling carbon dioxide from the air is something called a tree."[68] Planting trees is simple, effective, economical, and something everyone can do.

Trees pull carbon out of the atmosphere, and trees are a symbolic message that we are taking care of the planet.

4. TASK NASA WITH DEVELOPING TECHNOLOGY TO REMOVE CARBON FROM THE ATMOSPHERE. The global community continues to pour carbon into the atmosphere at historic levels. The Paris Agreement calls for zero new carbon into the atmosphere by 2050.[69] In the 1950s, we were terrified that the Russians were ahead of us in the race to space, so we did something about it. President Kennedy challenged the Nation to "send a man to the moon and return him to Earth before the end of the decade." The next President should challenge NASA once again to create technology that can remove a significant amount of carbon out of the atmosphere by 2034 and turn the tide on climate change. Why NASA? First, NASA knows more about the health of the planet than any other organization. Second, NASA has super-smart scientists and engineers. Third, NASA has been incredibly successful in solving difficult problems. In the first 30 days of his or her administration, the President should meet with NASA leaders to ensure they know the mission and have the tools and support to get the job done.

Twenty years from now, citizens from around the world will ask whether their leaders did enough to save the planet. I want Americans to be as proud of our leadership on climate change as we were proud of our leadership at the end of World War II and the Cold War. This is the defining issue of our generation. The Inflation Reduction Act, which President Biden passed, was the first step in America taking action to save the planet. There is more work to be done. **There will be hard work and sacrifices along the way for every American to turn the tide and lead the world on climate change. Robert Swan, the first explorer to walk to both the North and South Poles, once said, "The greatest threat to our planet is the belief that someone else will save it."[70] If we want to save the only planet we have, we all need to pitch in.**

3

Reduce the Risk of Nuclear War

"It's a near miracle that nuclear war has so far been avoided."

—Noam Chomsky, linguist and political theorist, 2012[71]

We have one problem that could destroy humanity in a matter of minutes—the real and growing possibility of nuclear war. The reality is that the threat of nuclear war is greater today than at any time since the Cuban Missile Crisis. U.N. Secretary-General António Guterres warned in August 2022, "Humanity is just one misunderstanding, one miscalculation away from nuclear annihilation," and urged the world to renew a push toward eliminating all such nuclear weapons. "Luck is not a strategy. Nor is it a shield from geopolitical tensions boiling over into nuclear conflict."[72]

Today some 13,000 nuclear weapons are thought to remain in service in the arsenal of the nine nuclear-armed states.[73] The Cold War—which, ironically, contained the threat of nuclear war—is now gone. Many people have no idea that a single strategic nuclear warhead today is 1,000 times more powerful than the bomb dropped on Hiroshima, Japan, helping to end World War II.[74] Technology is only making matters worse. Russia, China, and the United States are in a race to develop hypersonic nuclear weapons that are much more maneuverable in flight, which will make these nuclear missiles much more difficult to track and destroy than the current ballistic missiles.[75]

For some reason, news organizations and the public are more focused on issues that make for sensational short-term news—mass shootings, natural disasters, and plane crashes, to name a few. As a society, we think too short term and focus on headline news instead of on the most critical issues like the potential for a nuclear accident or a nuclear war. Nuclear weapons and the potential that someone could blow up the world should be near the top of any President's list.

Starting in 1947, members of the Bulletin of the Atomic Scientists have used the metaphoric Doomsday Clock as a symbol that represents the likelihood of a human-made global catastrophe due to unchecked scientific and technological advances. It is reevaluated every year in January. In 1947, the clock was originally set at 7 minutes to midnight. It has since been set backward 8 times and forward 17 times. In January 2020, the Bulletin of the Atomic Scientists—whose Board of Sponsors includes 13 Nobel Prize recipients—moved the Doomsday Clock from 2 minutes to 100 seconds before midnight. This announcement marked the most severe security threat in the Doomsday Clock's history, greater than during the Cuban Missile Crisis or at any time in the Cold War. The statement from the Bulletin of the Atomic Scientists said, "Humanity continues to face two simultaneous existential dangers—nuclear war and climate change—that are compounded by a threat multiplier, cyber-enabled information warfare, that undercuts society's ability to respond. The international security situation is dire, not just because these threats exist, but because world leaders have allowed the international political infrastructure for managing them to erode."[76]

In January 2022, the Bulletin of the Atomic Scientists mentioned the January 6, 2021, insurrection at the U.S. Capitol as an example that no country is immune from threats to its democracy. "Notably, the insurrectionists came close to capturing Vice President Mike Pence and the 'nuclear football' that accompanies the Vice President as the backup system for nuclear launch commands."[77] This happened in the United States of America. Russia, China, Pakistan, India, and other governments are significantly less stable than the United States, and all have nuclear weapons. The 2022 report from the Bulletin of the Atomic Scientists also cites unrest on the Korean Peninsula, Russia's invasion of Ukraine, tensions between China and the United States in the South China Sea, and the end of the U.S.-Iran nuclear agreement.[78] More recently, Russian President Putin said he would use "all available means" to defend Russian territory and that the atomic bombs the United States dropped on Japan in 1945 "created a precedent."[79]

In early October 2022, President Biden said, "For the first time since the Cuban Missile Crisis, we have a direct threat to the use of nuclear weapons if, in fact, things continue down the path they are going."[80]

Continuing an alarming downward trend, in January 2023, the Doomsday Clock was moved forward to 90 seconds (1 minute, 30 seconds) before midnight and remained unchanged in January 2024.[81]

If you don't think that the potential for a nuclear war either caused by an accident or launched by an enemy of the United States is a possibility, you probably did not think that COVID-19 could kill 6.9 million people[82] (and counting) and bring the greatest economies of the world to their knees. **The President should have the vision to recognize that the potential for a nuclear accident or nuclear war is much higher than anyone realizes. It scares the hell out of me, and it should scare the hell out of you. The President should take the lead and prioritize the elimination of the chance of a nuclear war started by the United States, and should work with the global community to eliminate nuclear weapons from the face of the earth by 2028.** Below are the reasons why we should all be concerned about the threat of nuclear war:

1. ACCIDENTS HAPPEN. In 1961, a U.S. Air Force B-52 airplane broke up midair over Goldsboro, North Carolina. It carried two Mark 39 hydrogen bombs, and each would have been 260 times more powerful than the Hiroshima bomb. Thankfully, they did not detonate.[83] During the Cold War, eight nuclear weapons were lost.[84] In 1979, President Carter's national security adviser Zbigniew Brzezinski was awakened by a phone call in the middle of the night warning of an all-out Soviet nuclear attack. He received a second call confirming the attack and informing him of the imminent nuclear destruction of the United States. Shortly before calling the President, Brzezinski received a third call canceling the alarm. It was a mistake caused by human and technical errors.[85]

> In 1961 a U.S. Air Force B-52 broke up in midair over Goldsboro, North Carolina. It was carrying two Mark 39 hydrogen bombs, and each would have been **260 times more powerful than the bomb dropped on Hiroshima.**

2. WEAPONS THAT ARE DEVELOPED END UP BEING USED. Hiram Maxim, who invented the machine gun, said, "Only a general who was a barbarian would send his men to certain death against the concentrated power of my new gun."[86]

Orville Wright had thoughts similar to Maxim's: "When my brother and I built and flew the first man-carrying flying machine, we thought that we were introducing into the world an invention which would make further wars practically impossible."[87] Just as with the machine gun, the airplane did not end war; it made war kill even more people. On March 9, 1945, more than 90,000 people were killed, and 25 percent of Tokyo was

A Trident II nuclear submarine-launched ballistic missile travels at a speed of **18,000 miles per hour** destroyed by bombs dropped from the planes that Orville Wright thought might make war impractical.[88] Today, some 3,804 nuclear warheads are deployed with operational forces around the world, and another 8,696 are in storage or waiting to be dismantled.[89] We are betting that they will not be used. History would say that we are crazy.

3. COMPUTER SYSTEMS HAVE PROBLEMS, AND WHEN YOU ARE TALKING ABOUT NUCLEAR WAR, A SYSTEMS PROBLEM COULD CAUSE THE END OF THE WORLD. A computer system failure could trigger a nuclear war. According to Martin Hellman, an expert on issues surrounding nuclear war, "In 1979 and the first half of 1980, there were 3,703 low-level false alerts in the United States alone."[90] Hellman also has written, "In 1995, Russian air defense mistook a meteorological rocket launched from Norway for a US submarine-launched ballistic missile, causing the Russian 'nuclear football'—a device which contains the codes for authorizing a nuclear attack—to be opened in front of President Boris Yeltsin. This was the first time such an event had occurred, and fortunately Yeltsin was sober enough to make the right decision."[91]

4. THE U.S. NUCLEAR WEAPONS PROGRAM COSTS A FORTUNE. According to the Congressional Budget Office (CBO), the United States military budgeted $33.6 billion on the nuclear force in 2019. The CBO's

$1.2 trillion could:

Provide a 25 percent salary increase for the 3.5 million public school teachers for six years

Send 18 million students to a two-year public college free of charge

Buy 2.8 million homes

OR **Modernize the U.S. Nuclear Arsenal**

projected cost of the U.S. nuclear force for the next 10 years is $494 billion. The CBO estimates the cost of modernizing the U.S. nuclear arsenal could reach $1.2 trillion over the next 30 years.[92]

We could use the $40 billion a year, on average, that nuclear weapons will cost us for more important projects. Colin Powell, who served as Secretary of State and Chairman of the Joint Chiefs of Staff, had 28,000 nuclear weapons under his command. **After leaving office and upon further reflection, General Powell said, "The one thing I convinced myself after all these years of exposure to the use of nuclear weapons is that they are useless."**[93] **We are currently working on a plan to spend more than $1 trillion over the next 30 years to modernize our nuclear forces. Imagine what we as a country could do with $1 trillion over the next 30 years—A LOT!**

The congressional budget's projected cost of the U.S. nuclear force for the next 10 years: **$494 BILLION**

5. THE GREATEST NUCLEAR THREAT TODAY IS NOT ONLY THE RUSSIANS BUT THE TERRORISTS. In February 2006, Oleg Khinsagov, a Russian national, was arrested for possession of 79.5 grams of weapons-grade uranium. Khinsagov intended to sell the material for $1 million.[94] This is a real story, and this stuff can happen. There is nuclear material all over the world, and the probability of a person who works in a nuclear lab with access to this material selling it to a bad guy is greater than zero. The next President should use the power of the Presidency to significantly reduce the threat of nuclear war. In the 2010 documentary *Nuclear Tipping Point*, Henry Kissinger says:

> "Once nuclear weapons are used, we will be driven to take global measures to prevent it. So some of us have said.... If we have to do it afterwards, why don't we do it now?"[95]

Stockpile of Destruction

Estimated Global Nuclear Warheads 2023 Union of Concerned Scientists story on Stockholm International Peace Research Institute (SIPRI) report

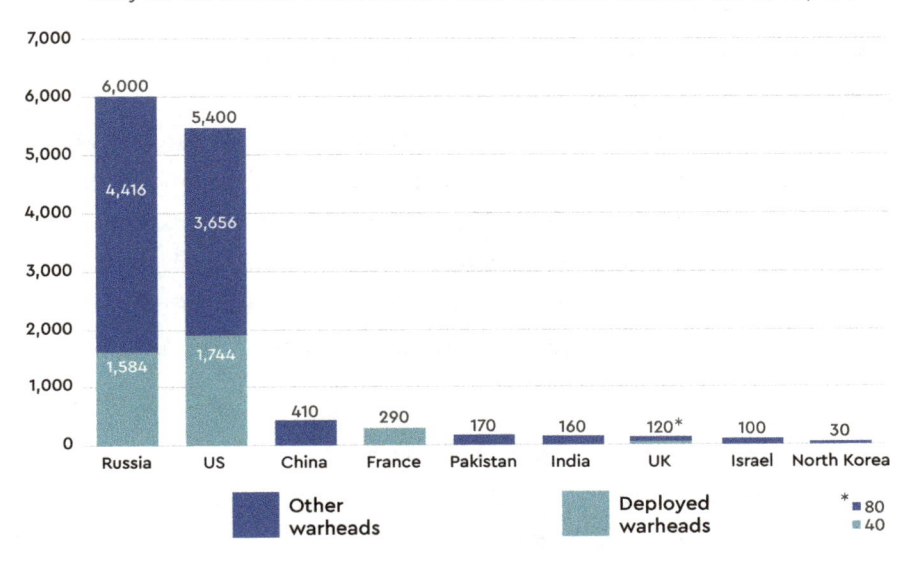

Country	Other warheads	Deployed warheads	Total
Russia	4,416	1,584	6,000
US	3,656	1,744	5,400
China			410
France			290
Pakistan			170
India			160
UK			120*
Israel			100
North Korea			30

*■ 80
■ 40

Source: "Nuclear Weapons Worldwide," Union of Concerned Scientists, accessed on February 8, 2023, https://www.ucsusa.org/nuclear-weapons/worldwide

....

It is my belief that the next President should focus on three simple steps to dramatically reduce the threat of nuclear war and set a good example for the rest of the world:

1. ON THE PRESIDENT'S FIRST DAY IN OFFICE, I WOULD RECOMMEND THAT HE OR SHE IMMEDIATELY REDUCE THE NUMBER OF DEPLOYED U.S. NUCLEAR WEAPONS FROM 1,744 TO AROUND 300. Gary Schaub Jr. and James Forsyth Jr., civilian employees of the U.S. Air Force, wrote an op-ed in *The New York Times* on May 23, 2010, in which they recommended reducing to around 300 the number of nuclear weapons to be deployed on land, sea, and airplanes.[96] I do not want the United States to mistakenly start a nuclear war. By decreasing our nuclear arsenal to around 300 active nuclear weapons, we will reduce the chances of a nuclear accident initiated by the United States by over 80 percent.

2. THE PRESIDENT SHOULD SIGN U.N. RESOLUTION 62/36, AGREEING THAT THE UNITED STATES WILL NOT USE NUCLEAR WEAPONS AS A FIRST-STRIKE OPTION and will only use our nuclear arsenal if someone detonates a nuclear warhead on U.S. land as long as every other country in the world agrees to play by the same rules. This agreement would end the possibility of nuclear war being waged over a misguided perceived threat or a misunderstood provocation. In 2008, 139 countries voted for U.N. Resolution 62/36, which would remove nuclear weapons from "high-alert, quick-launch status." Only three nations voted against the measure: the U.S., the U.K., and France.[97]

3. THE PRESIDENT SHOULD SET THE GOAL OF CREATING A NUCLEAR WEAPONS-FREE WORLD BY 2028, AND HIS OR HER ADMINISTRATION WILL TAKE A LEADERSHIP ROLE IN MAKING IT HAPPEN. We have done many incredible things in our 248 years as a nation. Why not lead the world in creating a nuclear weapons-free world? We will lead by example by reducing our nuclear arsenal on day one of the administration and signing U.N. Resolution 62/36. When the world sees that the United States has reduced its nuclear force by 80 percent and that the United States has agreed not to use a first-strike option, we will gain credibility to lead this effort. A Harvard University study in 2010 estimated that at that point, the cost of securing all nuclear weapons and nuclear materials over a four-year period would be about $10 billion.[98]

The President should propose to the leaders of the G20 that we set a global goal of eliminating nuclear weapons by 2028, create the Global Nuclear-Free Fund, and buy up all the nuclear weapons in the world. If our nuclear arsenal already costs more than $30 billion a year to maintain, I believe that as a nation, we would be better off spending $10 billion to rid the world of nuclear weapons than we would be spending an estimated $494 billion over the next 10 years to modernize weapons that we never plan to use.

It is my hope that this generation of Americans will be the first generation that significantly reduces the threat of nuclear war and takes a leadership role in negotiating a treaty that eliminates nuclear weapons from the face of the Earth.

In 1961, in a speech to the United Nations, President Kennedy warned of the devastation that would result from a nuclear war:

> Today, every inhabitant of this planet must contemplate the day when this planet may no longer be habitable. Every man, woman, and child lives under a nuclear sword of Damocles, hanging by the slenderest of threads, capable of being cut at any moment by accident or miscalculation or by madness. The weapons of war must be abolished before they abolish us.
>
> Men no longer debate whether armaments are a symptom or a cause of tension. The mere existence of modern weapons—10 million times more powerful than any that the world has ever seen, and only minutes away from any target on earth—is a source of horror, discord, and distrust. Men no longer maintain that disarmament must await the settlement of all disputes—for disarmament must be a part of any permanent settlement. And men may no longer pretend that the quest for disarmament is a sign of weakness—for in a spiraling arms race, a nation's security may well be shrinking even as its arms increase.
>
> For 15 years this organization [The United Nations] has sought the reduction and destruction of arms. Now that goal is no longer a dream—it is a practical matter of life or death. The risks inherent in disarmament pale in comparison to the risks inherent in an unlimited arms race.[99]

More than 60 years have passed since President Kennedy spoke of the threat of nuclear war. Unfortunately, we are no closer to abolishing nuclear weapons before they abolish us. The cold, hard reality is that we are further away. While there may be fewer nuclear weapons today, they are more powerful now than at any other time in history. More nations have nuclear weapons today than at any other time in history. We also face the high probability that more nations and terrorist groups will obtain nuclear weapons in the near future. We continue to play a game of nuclear roulette, and at some point in time, if we continue to do nothing to reduce the risk, the gun will go off.

It is my hope that the new President leads this generation of Americans in the quest to eliminate nuclear weapons from the face of the Earth and travels a different road than previous Presidents from both parties who have done nothing and have continually kicked the can of one of humanity's biggest problems to the next generation.

4

Fix the Health-Care System

> "The greatest asset of a nation
> is the health of its people."
>
> —William J. Mayo, MD[100]

No President has ever pledged to use the Presidency's full power to improve the health of the American people. The next President should. We spend more money than any other country in the world on health care and get horrible results. In 2021, we spent $4.3 trillion or $12,914 per person as a nation on health care, which amounts to 18.3 percent of our gross domestic product (GDP).[101] The next closest country is Germany, which spent 12.8 percent of its GDP. For all of the money we spend on health, the United States is ranked 55th out of 57 countries for overall health as surveyed in the Bloomberg 2020 Health-Efficiency Index.[102] To make matters worse, our health-care system puts 530,000 of your fellow Americans into bankruptcy every year because they cannot pay their medical bills. A survey conducted by the Kaiser Family Foundation and the *Los Angeles Times* found that "four in ten people report that their family has had either problems paying medical bills or difficulty affording premiums or out-of-pocket medical costs."[103]

As a country, our leaders have failed us when it comes to health. Our leaders have us playing the wrong game as a nation. Over the past 50 years, the conversation has been around drug prices, technology, insurance, and spending more money. The conversation is never about improving the health of the American people or extending the life span and the quality of the years that Americans live. Leaders get elected by making people feel good, and no one wants to tell voters that they are a big part of the problem. **We are raising the unhealthiest generation of Americans in history, and we are doing nothing about it.**

For all of the money we spend, Americans' average life expectancy is 76.1 years.[104] **If you live in Italy, you will live SIX years longer than if you live in the United States, and in the United States, we spend almost twice as much on health as our friends in Italy.** The Bloomberg analysis shows that Canada's system produces 3.5 years longer life expectancy than the U.S. and costs almost 60 percent less.[105]

	🇺🇸	🇨🇦
Life Expectancy (2020)	78.5	82.0
Health-care cost as a percent of GDP	17.8 percent	11.7 percent
Health-care cost per person	$12,318	$5,905[106]

If we think of the U.S. health-care system as an athletic team competing in a league, then we would be baseball's Los Angeles Dodgers, outspending almost every other team, year in and year out, but unlike the Dodgers, we end up near the bottom of the league every single year. We tolerate being the highest-paid team with some of the worst results year after year, and we do nothing serious about changing the equation.

Despite having the highest costs in the world with close to the worst results, no one is addressing the real problems of our health-care system.

World Health

Health-care comparisons around the world

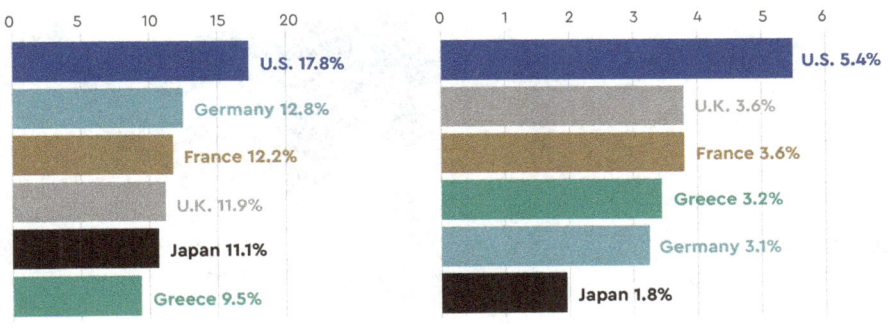

Expenditure on health care as a percentage of GDP
- U.S. 17.8%
- Germany 12.8%
- France 12.2%
- U.K. 11.9%
- Japan 11.1%
- Greece 9.5%

Infant mortality per 1,000 live births
- U.S. 5.4%
- U.K. 3.6%
- France 3.6%
- Greece 3.2%
- Germany 3.1%
- Japan 1.8%

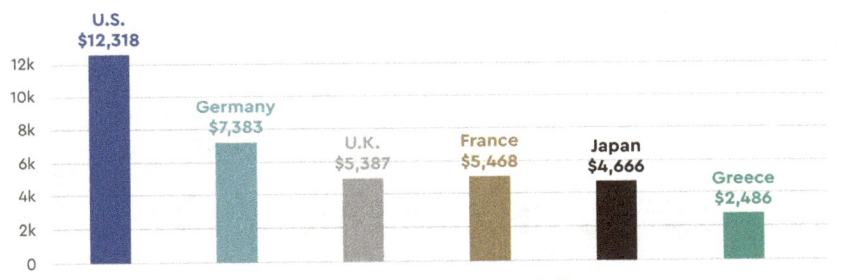

Expenditure on health care, per capita in U.S. dollars
- U.S. $12,318
- Germany $7,383
- U.K. $5,387
- France $5,468
- Japan $4,666
- Greece $2,486

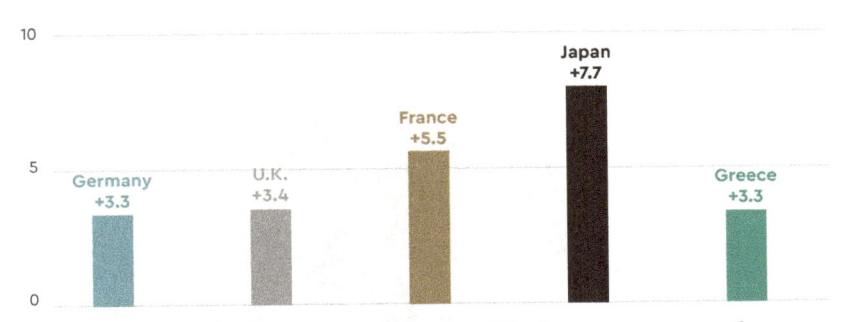

Additional years of life expectancy beyond 77, the average age of American life expectancy
- Germany +3.3
- U.K. +3.4
- France +5.5
- Japan +7.7
- Greece +3.3

Sources: OECD (2020), Health spending (indicator). doi: 10.1787/8643de7e-en (Accessed 2020) https://data.oecd.org/healthres/health-spending.htm

OECD (2020), Infant mortality rates (indicator). doi: 10.1787/83dea506-en (Accessed 2020) https://data.oecd.org/healthres/health-spending.htm

OECD (2020), Life expectancy at birth (indicator). doi: 10.1787/27e0fc9d-en (Accessed 2020) https://data.oecd.org/healthstat/life-expectancy-at-birth.htm#indicator-chart

Obesity Rate in the United States (1985–2020)

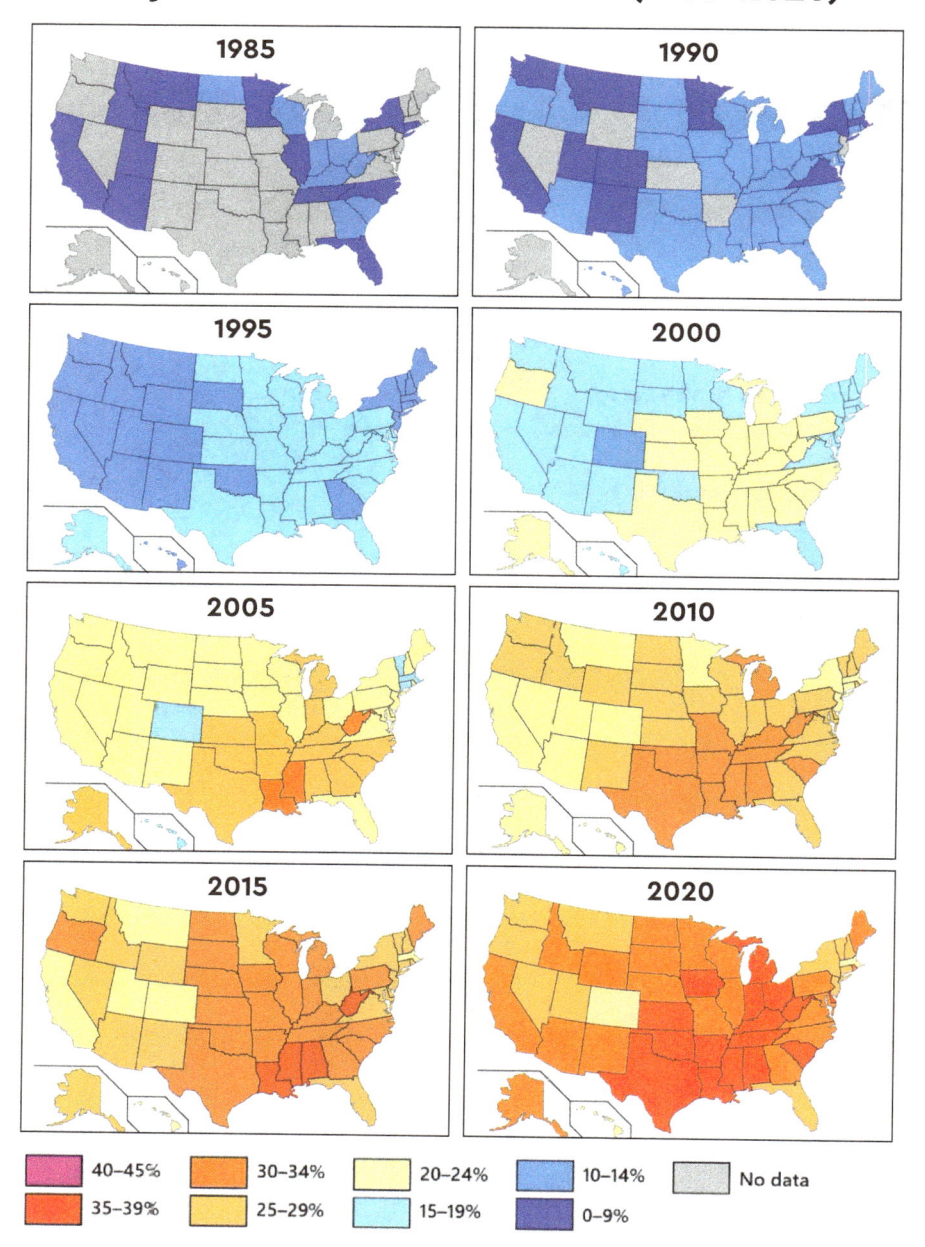

Color	Range
	40–45%
	35–39%
	30–34%
	25–29%
	20–24%
	15–19%
	10–14%
	0–9%
	No data

Source: Behavioral Risk Factor Surveillance System. https://www.themanual.com/fitness/obesity-rate-in-america-has-skyrocketed,"

*Sample size <50, the relative standard error (dividing the standard error by the prevalence) ≥30 percent, or no data in a specific year.

As President Barack Obama said, "The greatest threat to America's fiscal health is not Social Security.... It's not the investments that we've made to rescue our economy during this crisis. By a wide margin, the biggest threat to our Nation's balance sheet is the skyrocketing cost of health care. It is not even close."[107] And what have we done as a country regarding what President Obama said is the biggest threat to our Nation's balance sheet almost 12 years ago? Basically nothing.

Gary Player, a golf legend and health fanatic, lamented the health of Americans:

> America is maybe the most unhealthy nation in the world because they live on crap," Player said. "They've got the best food in the world, the best farmers and the best food but they live on crap. When [British chef] Jamie Oliver went to America he went to areas where children never had cabbage or broccoli or spinach or vegetables in their life. People giving their children a soft drink and a doughnut to go to school. No wonder academically they're affected.
>
> 55 percent of the greatest country in the world is obese? How can you compete against the Chinese? You haven't got a chance! People that are lean and mean and working hard and producing maybe 100 engineers to every two or three that you produce. Kids that are learning like crazy at school and spending hours learning. You go to Korea and those kids finish school at 7 o'clock at night because there's no sense of entitlement. It frustrates me because I happen to have 15 American grandchildren. I love America but I get so upset at the way I see the obesity. I just don't see how the healthcare system can work. I pray it does but I just don't see how it can work with this tsunami of obesity.[108]

Our health-care system is failing the American people, and our leaders have done virtually nothing to improve the situation. Here are the six key reasons why the next President should propose radical changes to our current health-care system:

1. OUR HEALTH-CARE COSTS ARE OUT OF CONTROL. We spend over $4 trillion annually on health care, more as a percentage of GDP than any other country in the Western world, and we get close to the worst results.[109]

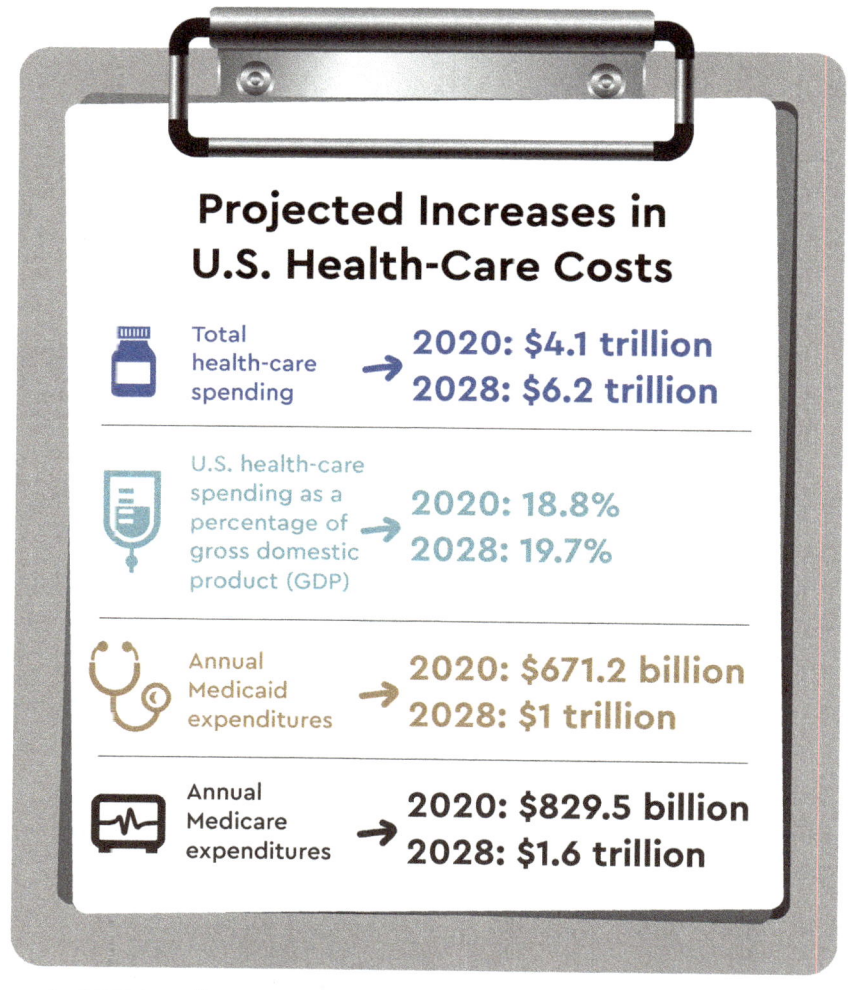

Projected Increases in U.S. Health-Care Costs

Total health-care spending	→	2020: $4.1 trillion 2028: $6.2 trillion
U.S. health-care spending as a percentage of gross domestic product (GDP)	→	2020: 18.8% 2028: 19.7%
Annual Medicaid expenditures	→	2020: $671.2 billion 2028: $1 trillion
Annual Medicare expenditures	→	2020: $829.5 billion 2028: $1.6 trillion

Sources: As of 2020, https://www.cms.gov/data-research/statistics-trends-and-reports/national-health-expenditure-data/nhe-fact-sheet#:~:text=NHE percent20grew percent209.7 percent25 percent20to percent20 percent244.1,20 percent20percent percent20of percent20total percent20NHE; https://www.spglobal.com/marketintelligence/en/news-insights/latest-news-headlines/us-healthcare-spending-to-hit-6-2-trillion-by-2028-growth-set-to-outpace-gdp-57739003

In a 2015 article in *The New Yorker* magazine, Dr. Atul Gawande—a surgeon, writer, and public-health researcher pointed to a study of more than one million Medicare patients that researched how often they were given any of 26 tests or treatments that "scientific and professional organizations have consistently determined to have no benefit or to be outright harmful." The study found that as many as 42 percent of the patients had received unnecessary tests in one year. Gawande said his mother was one of them.[110]

2. THE FUTURE PROJECTIONS FOR HEALTH-CARE SPENDING ARE OMINOUS.

Health-care spending has risen from 5 percent of our GDP in 1960 to 18 percent in 2021.[111] The average annual premium for employer-sponsored health insurance in 2022, according to the Kaiser Family Foundation, was $22,463 for a family.[112]

According to the U.S. Government, the total cost in 2020 for national health expenditures was $4.1 trillion.[113] The Government is projecting that by 2030, the total cost of health expenditures in the United States will hit $6.8 trillion.[114] Medicare faces significant financial challenges in the coming years. Our population is getting older, and the ratio of workers to enrollees is declining. "Our Government spent $900.8 billion on Medicare in 2021,[115] and the Congressional Budget Office estimates it will increase to $1.4 trillion by 2027.[116] Health costs will have a huge effect on the Federal budget in the coming years:

> Future growth in spending per beneficiary for Medicare and Medicaid—the federal government's major health care programs—will be the most important determinant of long-term trends in federal spending. Changing those programs in ways that reduce the growth of costs—which will be difficult, in part because of the complexity of health policy choices—is ultimately the nation's main long-term challenge in setting federal fiscal policy.[117]

3. THE HEALTH-CARE INDUSTRIAL COMPLEX MADE UP OF DRUG COMPANIES, HOSPITALS, AND INSURANCE COMPANIES IS NOT WORKING IN THE LONG-TERM BEST INTEREST OF THE UNITED STATES OR ITS CITIZENS. In 2010, doctors performed more than 51 million inpatient surgical procedures in U.S. hospitals, according to the National Quality Forum, or one for every six Americans.[118] No other country in the world comes even close to operating on nearly 20 percent of its citizens annually. It is crazy. For example, the United States conducts 71 percent more computerized tomography (CT) scans per capita than Germany. The cost of those CT scans through Medicare is four times as much as Germany's.[119]

If Germany has 100 patients who get a CT scan, the U.S. has 171. If the cost in Germany is $250, then in the U.S., it is $1,000, or four times as much. So a summary of the total costs looks like this:

Germany: 100 x $250 = $25,000
United States: 171 x $1,000 = $171,000

4. OUR HEALTH-CARE SYSTEM IS OVERLY INFLUENCED BY LOBBYING AND CAMPAIGN CONTRIBUTIONS. In 2013, journalist Steven Brill wrote an exposé on the exorbitant costs of health care in America. He reported that since 1998, the pharmaceutical and health care industries "have spent $5.36 billion ... on lobbying Washington." In comparison, the defense industry spent $1.53 billion on lobbying efforts during the same period. Brill said, "That's right: the health care-industrial complex spends three times what the military-industrial complex spends in Washington."[120] As shown in the following chart depicting expenditures from 1998 through mid-2022, the numbers have virtually doubled since Brill's exposé.

The health-care lobby has even infiltrated the Senate Finance Committee, which is directly involved with health-care legislation and programs. According to an analysis by the Lee Newspapers State Bureau in Montana,

Lobbyist Spending From 1998–2022

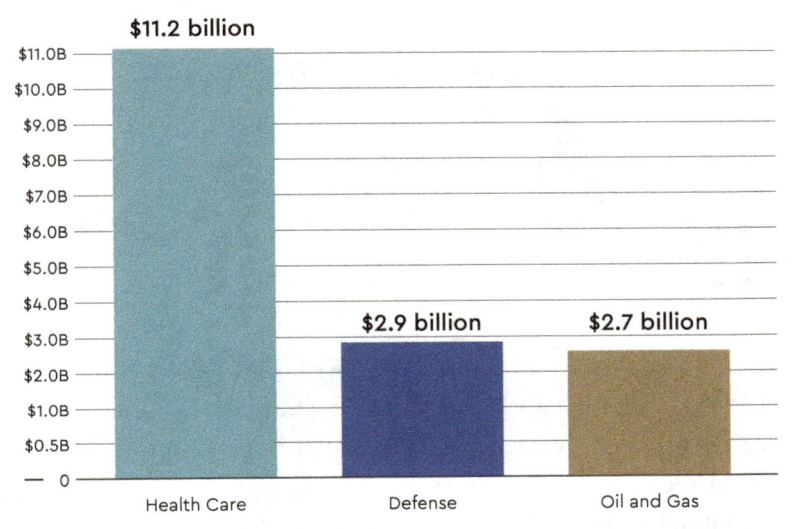

Industry	Spending
Health Care	$11.2 billion
Defense	$2.9 billion
Oil and Gas	$2.7 billion

Figures on this page are calculations by OpenSecrets based on data from the Senate Office of Public Records.

Source: Data for the most recent year was downloaded on April 24, 2023 and includes spending from January 1 to March 31. Prior years include spending from January through December.
https://www.opensecrets.org/federal-lobbying/industries

the health-care lobby made campaign contributions totaling $3.4 million from 2003 to 2008 to former Senator Max Baucus, a Montana Democrat who served as chairman of the committee. The ranking Republican committee member, Charles Grassley of Iowa, received over $2 million in campaign contributions from the health-care industry during that time.[121]

Our country has now exceeded $34 trillion in debt.[122] Yet, the leadership of our country, the people who make the decisions regarding health care, are taking massive campaign contributions from the people who benefit from the current game. The health-care industry should be embarrassed. The industry is responsible for sticking our Nation with the highest health-care costs in the world and providing some of the worst results.[123]

In 2019, **70 MILLION surgical procedures** were performed—the equivalent of one for every five Americans.[124]

5. OUR LAWS PREVENT THE U.S. GOVERNMENT FROM NEGOTIATING THE BEST PRICES FOR MEDICARE. "More than $280 billion will be spent this year on prescription drugs in the United States," wrote Steven Brill. "If we paid what other countries did for the same products, we would save $94 billion a year."[125] The Government of the people, by the people, and for the people has laws in place that restrict it from negotiating the best possible drug prices for the people. Our politicians have created a game where the insurance companies and the drug companies win, and our citizens lose. The drug companies keep the politicians in office so they can keep producing massive profits. The passage of the Inflation Reduction Act in August 2022, allowing Medicare to negotiate the price of 10 medications, begins to address this critical issue but falls way short.

6. THE HEALTH OF THE AMERICAN PEOPLE IS POOR. The numbers don't lie. The average American today weighs 30 pounds more than the average American weighed 60 years ago.[126] We eat poorly, and as a whole, we don't exercise enough. In fact, in his book *Outlive,* Dr. Peter Attia states that 77 percent of the American population does not exercise.[127] We are now the unhealthiest nation in the Western world, with over 40 percent of adults and 19 percent of our youth who are obese, according to the National Center for Health Statistics,[128] and the trend is likely to get even worse. **Medical scientists say by 2030,[129] as many as 50 percent of Americans will be obese, and nearly one of every four of us will fall**

into the category of severely obese, according to *The New York Times* columnist Jane E. Brody.[130]

Below are some sobering facts surrounding the obesity epidemic in the United States:

- According to the Centers for Disease Control (CDC), the 42 percent of American adults and nearly 20 percent of American children who are obese[131] are significantly more likely to develop high blood pressure (hypertension), high LDL cholesterol, type 2 diabetes, coronary heart disease, stroke, gallbladder disease, osteoarthritis (a breakdown of cartilage and bone within a joint), sleep apnea and breathing problems,

Health-Care Costs by Year

Year	National Health-Care Spending (Billions)	Percent Growth	Cost Per Person
1960	$27.2	NA	$146
1965	$41.9	9.0 percent	$209
1970	$74.6	13.1 percent	$355
1975	$133.3	14.4 percent	$605
1980	$255.3	15.3 percent	$1,108
1985	$442.9	9.4 percent	$1,833
1990	$721.4	11.9 percent	$2,843
1995	$1,021.6	5.6 percent	$3,806
2000	$1,369.7	7.1 percent	$4,857
2005	$2,024.2	6.7 percent	$6,855
2010	$2,598.8	4.1 percent	$8,412
2015	$3,200.8	5.8 percent	$9,994
2020	$4,100.0	9.7 percent	$12,530

Source: "National Health Expenditures Summary Including Share of GDP, CY 1960-2020," Centers for Medicare and Medicaid Services. "Inflation Rate by Year," The Balance. "History of Health Spending in the United States, 1960-2013," Centers for Medicare and Medicaid Services, November 19, 2015. "U.S. Health Care Spending: Who Pays?" California Health Care Foundation, December 2015. https://www.cms.gov/data-research/statistics-trends-and-reports/national-health-expenditure-data/historical many types of cancer, mental illness such as clinical depression, anxiety, increased body pain, an overall lower quality of life, and early death.[132] According to authors David Sinclair and Matthew D. LaPlante, who wrote *Lifespan: Why We Age—and Why We Don't Have To*,[133] "These deaths do not come quickly and compassionately but in horrific ways with blindness, kidney failure, stroke, open foot wounds, and limb amputations."

- The real costs are killing us. According to the CDC, the estimated annual medical cost of obesity in the United States was nearly $173 billion in 2019 dollars.[134]

- A large 2021 study by the Centers for Disease Control and Prevention highlights the impact of obesity in a health crisis, such as the COVID-19 pandemic. It shows that, of nearly 150,000 adults at more than 200 hospitals across the United States, obesity significantly increases the risk for hospitalization, invasive mechanical ventilation, and death among those who contract COVID-19 and that the risks increased sharply as body mass index (BMI) rose.[135] In fact, the World Obesity Federation reports that COVID-19 death rates are 10 times higher in countries where more than half of the population is classified as overweight. Tim Lobstein, the report's author, said, "We now know that an overweight population is the next pandemic waiting to happen."[136]

- "The Supplemental Nutrition Assistance Program (SNAP), which the Government funds, pays for 20 million servings of sugary drinks a day, at an annual cost of $4 billion," a *New York Times* report said. "Barring recipients from using benefits to buy unhealthy beverages, researchers say, could prevent 52,000 deaths from type 2 diabetes," said the 2019 article about a call to action from the American Academy of Pediatrics and the American Heart Association.[137] Yet our Government does nothing. Philadelphia and Denver are two examples of cities that started taxing soda in 2017—at 1.5 and 2 cents an ounce,[138] respectively. A study in Philadelphia found that one year later, soda sales at major retail stores had fallen 38 percent.[139]

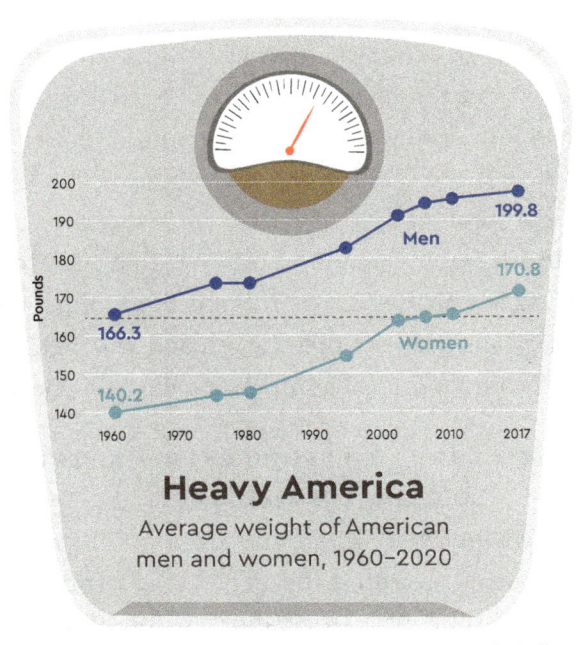

Heavy America
Average weight of American men and women, 1960–2020

- Men: 166.3 (1960) → 199.8 (2017)
- Women: 140.2 (1960) → 170.8 (2017)

Source: Source: Centers for Disease Control and Prevention. https://www.cdc.gov/nchs/fastats/body-measurements.htm

No politician wants to tell the American people that obesity is a big part of our health problem as a nation and that the citizens themselves are a big part of the solution. The next President should. Our leaders should care about your health, your family's health, and the future of our Nation. You cannot be a great nation when 42 percent of your population is obese. If you are one of the 42 percent of American people who are obese, the Government should care deeply about your health. The Government has failed you. Our Government should have a specific plan to improve your and your family's health by creating a healthier environment.

Within the first 60 days of being in office, the next President should send to Congress, the Health Improvement Act of 2025 to significantly increase the health and life expectancy of our citizens at a significantly lower cost.

....

It is my strong belief that if everyone in America took personal responsibility for their health, and if the Government provided leadership and support similar to alerting the public to the dangers of smoking or cracking down on drunk driving, our health-care costs would plummet, and the quality of life in America would skyrocket. If we want to be a great nation, we must be a healthy nation. The key points of the Health Improvement Act of 2025 that the President should deliver to Congress within the first six months of his or her administration will help all Americans improve their health and will significantly reduce the cost of health care for our Government's ballooning health-care costs:

1. PROVIDE MEDICARE 2.0 FOR EVERY AMERICAN CITIZEN CURRENTLY ON MEDICAID, ON MEDICARE, OR WHO DOES NOT HAVE HEALTH INSURANCE. There has been a debate in this country over the last 50 years regarding the Federal Government's role in the health of its citizens and its participation in the costs. For those who don't like socialized medicine or a single-payer program, the reality is that we already have one. According to the Centers for Medicare and Medicaid Services, as of October 2021, just short of 64 million people were enrolled in Medicare, the Nation's health-care program for the elderly, and more than 76 million were enrolled in Medicaid, the Nation's health-care program for the poor.[140] Added together, we now have more than 140 million Americans on a U.S. Government health program. The Health Improvement Act of 2025 would combine Medicare and Medicaid to create one national health program called Medicare 2.0. Medicare 2.0 would be our national health insurance platform to take care of those currently on Medicare and Medicaid, along with any American who needs health care. Those who currently have private health insurance programs and are happy with their coverage will be able to keep it. The President should make sure that the Department of Health and Human Resources hires an awesome team to implement Medicare 2.0.

If you are on Medicare 2.0, your cost for insurance will be the following:

Income Level	Does **NOT** Take an Annual Health Risk Assessment — Annual	Monthly	Takes an Annual Health Risk Assessment — Annual	Monthly
Under $20,000	$600	$50	$0	$0
$20,000–$30,000	$1,200	$100	$600	$50
$30,000–$50,000	$2,400	$200	$1,200	$100
$50,000–$75,000	$4,800	$400	$2,400	$200
$75,000–$100,000	$7,200	$600	$3,600	$300
$100,000–$150,000	$9,600	$800	$4,800	$400
$150,000–$250,000	$12,000	$1,000	$6,000	$500
$250,000–$500,000	$16,000	$1,333	$8,000	$667
$500,000+	$20,000	$1,667	$10,000	$833

The cost of your health care will depend on whether you have had an annual Health Risk Assessment. This is a mini-physical, free of charge, and takes less than 20 minutes. A nurse will take you through the U.S. Health Risk Assessment, and you will get a score for your overall health. I have been lucky to have Mark Timmerman, MD, as my doctor for the past 30 years, and he is the best. Dr. T. and I spent some time together and have come up with eight simple questions to score where Trek employees' level of health is today. This checklist provides a simple road map to start improving your health tomorrow. I strongly believe in the saying: "What gets measured gets done," and the U.S. Health Risk Assessment checklist has the potential to give every American on Medicare 2.0 a clear understanding of where they are, and it will give the Government and the people a clear scorecard as to the progress we are making as individuals and as a nation.

U.S. Health Assessment Checklist

Category	Your Score
Smoking No = 15; Yes = 0	
Weight BMI <25 = 20; BMI 25–30 = 10; BMI >30 = 0 (Simple BMI calculators available online.)	
Diet Fast food visits per week. none = 10; 5 or less = 5; 5+ = 0	
Alcohol Drinks less than 11 drinks per week. Yes = 10; No = 0	
Exercise 30 min daily 5 days per week. Yes = 15; No = 0	
Annual Physical or Health Risk Assessment Yes = 10; No = 0	
Mental Stimulation—reading, games, puzzles, etc. daily Yes = 10; No = 0	
Annual Dental Visit Yes = 10; No = 0	
TOTAL (out of 100 possible points)	

Medicare 2.0 accomplishes the following:

- **SIMPLICITY.** We take two programs and make them one—Medicare 2.0. No Medicare and Medicaid. No Part A, Part B, Part C, Part D, and M. A list of what is and isn't covered will be provided.

- **SIGNIFICANT COST REDUCTION BY ELIMINATING INSURANCE COMPANIES.** We spend twice as much as any other nation on health care and get the worst results. Medicare 2.0 will eliminate insurance companies from Medicare. The Government will manage the program directly with the citizens, and insurance companies will no longer be necessary. This has the potential to save taxpayers billions of dollars and provide better service.

One example of how insurance companies are crushing the American people is the story of Medicare Advantage. A *New York Times* investigation in May 2022 shows how major health insurers exploited the Medicare Advantage program to boost their profits by billions of dollars.[141] Most large insurers, including Kaiser Permanente, Anthem (now Elevance Health), and UnitedHealth Group, have been accused in court of fraud by the Justice Department. According to an estimate from a group that advises Medicare on payment policies, the additional diagnoses that insurance companies gave to patients led to $12 billion in overpayments in 2020, or even double that—more than $25 billion—according to a former top government health official. Last year, the Justice Department's civil division listed Medicare Advantage as one of its principal areas of fraud recovery.[142] "The cash monster was insatiable," said Dr. James Taylor, a former coding expert at Kaiser who is one of 10 whistleblowers

Medicare Advantage Overbilling Compared to Various Agency Budgets

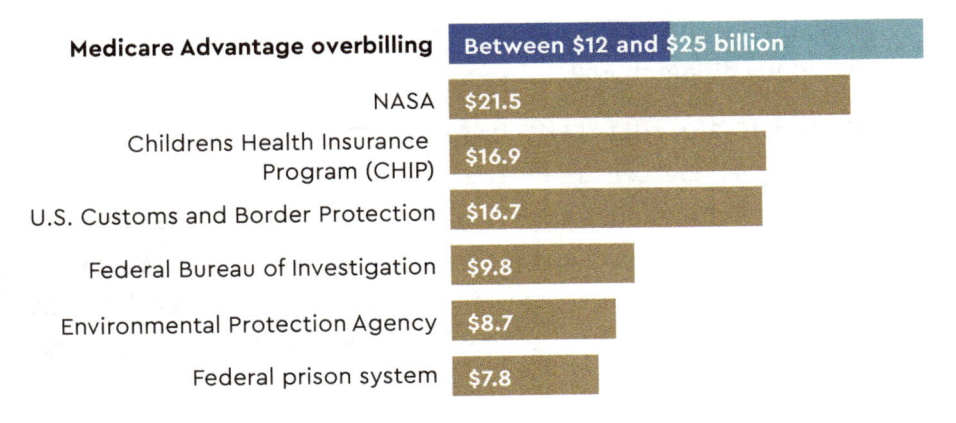

Medicare Advantage overbilling	Between $12 and $25 billion
NASA	$21.5
Childrens Health Insurance Program (CHIP)	$16.9
U.S. Customs and Border Protection	$16.7
Federal Bureau of Investigation	$9.8
Environmental Protection Agency	$8.7
Federal prison system	$7.8

Note: Figures represent outlays in the 2020 fiscal year. Sources: White House Office of Management and Budget; Medicare Payment Advisory Commission; Richard Kronick and F. Michael Chua. *New York Times*. https://www.nytimes.com/2022/10/08/upshot/medicare-advantage-fraud-allegations.html?smid=em-share to accuse the organization of fraud. "Medicare Advantage overpayments are a political third rail," said Dr. Richard Gilfillan, a former hospital and insurance executive and a former top regulator at Medicare, in an email. "The big health care plans know it's wrong, and they know how to fix it, but they're making too much money to stop."[143]

- **SIGNIFICANTLY REDUCE DRUG PRICES.** Medicare 2.0 acknowledges that the U.S. Government is the biggest customer of the health-care system in the United States. As part of the Health Improvement Act, the Government will be allowed to negotiate all prices. The President should put the best team in charge of Medicare 2.0, and make it a goal to reduce costs by 30 percent by the 2028 fiscal year. This would result in savings of more than $113.4 billion a year, based on the most recent costs of the Medicare and Medicaid programs.

- **IMPROVE CARE FOR THE PATIENTS.** Under the current system, insurance companies decide which tests and treatments they will cover for patients, often without talking to the patient or conducting a physical exam. In essence, insurance companies practice medicine without a license. By replacing insurance companies with a competent government program, we can focus on the patient, not on profits. Our Nation has the most expensive health-care system in the world, producing a rank of 55 out of 57 nations. It is time that we tried something different.

- **MEDICARE 2.0 WILL TAKE CARE OF OUR POOREST CITIZENS.** According to the Census Bureau,[144] we have 27 million Americans without health insurance. As a nation, we face a simple question: Should all American citizens be provided basic health care? My answer to this question is yes. David Sinclair and Matthew D. LaPlante, in their *New York Times* best-selling book *Lifespan: Why We Age—and Why We Don't Have To*, report the following:[145]

If you were a member of the American upper middle class in the 1970s, you weren't just enjoying a more affluent life; you had a longer one, too. Those in the top half of the economy were living an average of

1.2 more years than those in the bottom half. By the early 2000s, that number was six years. By 2018 the divide had widened, with the wealthiest 10 percent of Americans living 13 more years than the poorest 10 percent.[146]

There has been a lot of talk in our country over the past few years regarding equality but very little action by our leaders. I don't think we want to live in a country with a massive health gap between the rich and the poor. By offering all of our citizens basic health care while reducing costs at the same time, we can close the health gap so that your life expectancy is not dependent upon your income.

- **PROVIDE BETTER SERVICE.** Medicare 2.0 will put the customer first by implementing a Net Promoter Score (NPS), so that every time you go to the hospital, you will be surveyed about your level of satisfaction, and you will be able to provide any suggestions you have for improvements. Companies around the world use NPS to measure customer satisfaction. The average NPS score for a company is 32.[147] Apple's is 47, Starbucks' is 77, and Trek's is 92.[148] Part of the mission of Trek is to "provide incredible hospitality to our customers." I know what great service is, and I believe there is a great opportunity to improve the Federal Government's NPS score in health care and every other area.

In addition to the financial case for Medicare 2.0, there is also a moral case. Too many Americans have significant health problems, through no fault of their own, and have no way to pay the bills.

A friend of mine had bone cancer in the 1970s. His leg had to be amputated to stop the cancer from spreading. His family was well off, and he was fitted with a prosthetic leg. A friend of his, whom he had met during his hospital stay, also had bone cancer and lost a leg because of the disease but did not get an artificial limb. He asked his friend why not, thinking it might be because sometimes they hurt or can be difficult to use. His friend replied, "Because my parents can't afford it."

Another friend of mine recounted the fear of selling the family home to pay for her husband's care for stage 4 lung cancer treatment. They were overwhelmed with insurance claims and determining what part of the bills for treatments and hospitalizations, totaling millions of dollars, they were responsible for. The bills continued arriving even a year after her husband's death. The additional anxiety it caused the family during a health crisis is unconscionable.

In another example, detailed by Elisabeth Rosenthal, editor-in-chief of Kaiser Health News, in a March 2017 article for *The New York Times*, there's the story of Wanda Wickizer, who suffered a brain hemorrhage on Christmas Day 2013. She was flown by helicopter to the University of Virginia Medical Center in Charlottesville. After spending days in a coma, she slowly recovered. A widow who had temporarily quit working to care for her children, Wickizer, 51, had no insurance. The medical bills were $16,000 from Sentara Norfolk General Hospital (not including the scan or the emergency room doctor), $50,000 for the air ambulance, and $24,000 from the University of Virginia Physicians Group. She received a bill for $54,000 a month later from the same physicians group, which included further charges and late fees. Then the hospital bill came, amounting to nearly $357,000. When the care providers called, insisting on payment of $285,507.58—applying a 20 percent discount for uninsured patients—Wickizer explained that she didn't have that kind of money. She offered the hospital and its doctors $100,000 from her retirement account. They declined and suggested that she sign up for a payment plan of $5,000 per month to the hospital and $5,000 to the physicians. In October 2014, a sheriff affixed a summons to Wickizer's front door, saying the university was suing her for nonpayment.

"In other countries, when patients recover from a terrifying brain bleed or, for that matter, when they battle cancer, or heal from a serious accident, or face any other life-threatening health condition, they are allowed to spend their days focusing on getting better. Only in America do medical treatment and recovery coexist with a peculiar national dread: the struggle to figure out from the mounting pile of bills what portion of the fantastical charges you must pay," Rosenthal observed.[149]

Medicare 2.0 proposal would take care of someone like Wanda Wickizer. If she were enrolled in Medicare 2.0, her costs would have been covered, and she would have been able to focus on her health and her family and would not have had to worry about her mounting bills, filing for bankruptcy, and being evicted from her house.

2. BASIC NUTRITIONAL INFORMATION WILL BE REQUIRED ON EVERY FOOD ITEM FOR SALE, WHETHER IN A RESTAURANT, A GROCERY STORE, OR AT THE BALLPARK. Americans need to know what they are consuming. David Sinclair and Matthew D. LaPlante, authors of *Lifespan,* note that the number one factor in life expectancy is what you put into your mouth.[150] Let's make sure that Americans clearly understand what they are eating all the time. In addition to nutritional information, the Health Improvement Act will require labeling on all sugary drinks, candies, and high-sugar content fast foods, warning that excess sugar consumption can cause diabetes and obesity—just as labels on cigarette packages warn that tobacco causes cancer. Diabetes is killing our citizens in record numbers and costing us a fortune while our leaders do nothing because they do not have the will to take on the Health-Care Industrial complex.

3. HEALTH-CARE RELATED COMPANIES WILL BE PROHIBITED FROM MAKING CAMPAIGN DONATIONS SO THAT THE HEALTH-CARE INDUSTRIAL COMPLEX CANNOT TAKE ADVANTAGE OF THE AMERICAN PEOPLE. In the 2020 election, according to the Center for Responsive Politics, health-care executives gave $47 million to President Biden's campaign and $21 million to President Trump's campaign.[151] Until someone has the courage to fix our campaign finance laws, health-care executives can legally bribe the President of the United States and the United States Congress, and the loser is the American citizen. By reforming campaign finance laws, we would prevent the insurance companies, drug companies, and others who make up the health-care industrial complex from creating a rigged game with massive campaign contributions. We would free our representatives in Washington to vote for what is in the best interests of the American people and not for what is in the best interests of the health-care industry.

WARNING:
Drinking beverages with added sugar contributes to tooth decay, obesity, and diabetes.

A Baltimore councilman introduced legislation to require warning labels like this one on sugar-sweetened drinks in the city. But research appearing in the journal *Pediatrics* suggests that a warning label on sugary beverages might indeed deter people from buying the products.[152]

WARNING:
This product may cause mouth cancer.

WARNING:
This product may cause gum disease and tooth loss.

WARNING:
This product is not a safe alternative to cigarettes.
The Comprehensive Smokeless Tobacco Health Education Act of 1986 (Public Law 99-252) required three rotating warning labels on smokeless tobacco packaging and advertisements.

There is an amazing opportunity to improve the health of Americans, increase life expectancy, and drastically reduce the cost of our health care. As a nation, we cannot leave health care to the free market. It has not worked. The Federal Government can play a role in significantly reducing the cost of health care and improving the health of the American people. We don't leave the defense of this Nation to private companies and the market. This is especially urgent when you consider that we currently spend almost 20 percent of our Nation's GDP on health care, compared with about half that in most developed countries, and we get some of the worst results!

It is my advice that whoever is elected President should send to Congress the Health Improvement Act of 2025 within the first 60 days of their administration. Passing this legislation would improve the lives of the majority of Americans and significantly reduce our costs to help us avoid bankruptcy as a nation.

In 2006 at Trek, we had three health-related events within two months. The first involved one of our truck drivers, who had a massive heart attack while driving across Iowa. The driver was a really good guy who was overweight and smoked. The heart attack cost Trek more than $500,000 and ended the driver's career. The second event happened to the spouse of one of our employees. Her husband worked for another company, had poor health habits, and was overweight. He suffered a stroke and never fully recovered, and their family has never been the same. The third event involved a manager in one of our warehouses. He was a great guy and a great big guy. One morning, I got a phone call that he had died the night before. He was in his 40s and had two young girls. A week later, I saw the death certificate. Cause of death? Obesity. That was the final straw for me.

I met with our human resources leader and told him we could do better. I wanted to make some serious changes and boost the health of our employees. Later that week, I held an employee meeting and told the stories of what had happened over the past two months. I announced that we were going to make two specific changes to our health-care plan: (1) we would require a health risk assessment every year, and (2) employees had to reach a minimum score. If they did not meet that score, they needed to agree to take steps to improve their health by participating in company-sponsored programs, including smoking cessation programs, nutritional counseling, on-site fitness classes, and on-site medical services, including weight, blood pressure, and cholesterol counseling. Failure to meet the minimum score or to participate in programs intended to address their health concerns would mean they would pay a significantly higher share of their insurance up to the maximum allowed by the law.

My message was simple: We will give you one year to get on the program. We will provide seminars, individual coaching, smoking cessation assistance, and a fitness center. We will revamp our café to make sure that we have healthy options. But in the end, it is up to you.

> We care about your health.
> If you do not care about your health,
> we are not going to pay for all of it.

What were the results? Let's take smoking. At the time, the national average of Americans who used tobacco products was more than 20 percent; at Trek, the number was 22 percent. Today, less than 2 percent of Trek employees use tobacco. When we started the health risk assessment program at Trek, our average score out of 1,000 points was a mediocre 772. Today, our average score is 901. We have significantly increased the health of employees at Trek because we were both compassionate and demanding. **The biggest winners were the employees. Trek has not had a health plan cost increase in the past eight years.**

I know the same type of program can work in every company, every school, and other organizations across the country. I also know that our Government, which is paying the bill and setting the rules for health care in this country, could provide better leadership. Whoever is elected President should do everything in their power to pass the Health Improvement Act of 2025, and when that happens, the results will be amazing. **If you are tired of being a citizen in the country with the highest health-care costs in the world and close to the worst results, then be more demanding of your candidates and your current representatives. No candidate in presidential history has ever had a plan to significantly improve the health of the American people. It is about time that someone did, and we, the American citizens, should demand from our candidates that someone come forward with a plan to make the dream of longer life expectancy at a significantly lower cost a reality.**

5

Rebuild America

"President Eisenhower ... gave the nation its biggest construction project, the huge interstate-highway program that changed the shape of American society and made possible the expansion of the suburban middle class."

—James M. Perry, *The Wall Street Journal*, Oct. 27, 1995[153]

President Eisenhower challenged America to do something great by establishing the interstate highway system. Mostly built in the 1950s and 1960s, our transportation system was the envy of the world. It connected Americans from all over the country and drove commerce by making goods available and allowing them to flow freely and efficiently. Unfortunately, what was once the world's greatest transportation system is in steep decline. Over the past 20-plus years, our generation of political leaders has decided that it is more important to hold taxes down than maintain a world-class transportation system. The good news is that for the first time in a very long time, President Biden has passed a sweeping infrastructure bill.[154] The bill will spend $550 billion in new investments over the next five years to address the decline in America's infrastructure. The bill includes $110 billion to improve roads and bridges, $66 billion for freight and passenger rail investments, $39 billion for public transportation, $65 billion for broadband, and $55 billion to upgrade water systems and remove lead pipes.[155] Unfortunately, there are three pieces of bad news for America. First, President Biden asked for twice the amount of spending and was denied by Congress, once again showing that our leadership does not understand that America is falling apart and falling behind the other leading economies of the world. Second, the $550 billion Biden bill covers 21.3 percent of the $2.59 trillion gap between where our transportation system is and where we need it to be by 2029. Third, the bill just spends money; nothing was done to generate revenue to pay for the President's spending. We are more than $34 trillion in debt, and we just passed a bill that only takes care of 21 percent of the problem, and once again, we have passed the check on to our children and grandchildren.

What facts describe our current transportation system?

1. OUR NATION'S INFRASTRUCTURE IS RATED A CUMULATIVE C- BY THE AMERICAN SOCIETY OF CIVIL ENGINEERS (ASCE), WITH 11 CATEGORIES FALLING IN THE D RANGE.[156] This is an embarrassing grade for the largest economy in the world. Our roads, bridges, water pipes, airports, and railways are in sad shape. You can drive around the country and see it everywhere—congestion, potholes, and roads in terrible shape. The infrastructures in Europe, China, and Japan are all superior to what we have in the United States. The following are key points from the American Society of Civil Engineers' 2021 Infrastructure Report Card:

- As a result of years of inadequate funding, the Nation's roads and bridges have a backlog of $836 billion worth of repairs, expansion, and enhancements needed.
- Roads merited a D grade. The report says of the more than four million miles of roads across the Nation, one of every five miles of highway

2021 Infrastructure Grades

✈ AVIATION	D+	⚓ PORTS	B-		America's Cumulative Infrastructure Grade
🌉 BRIDGES	C	🚂 RAIL	B		
🏞 DAMS	D	🛣 ROADS	D		**C-**
💧 DRINKING WATER	C-	🏫 SCHOOLS	D+		
⚡ ENERGY	C-	🗑 SOLID WASTE	C+		
☢ HAZARDOUS WASTE	D+	🌧 STORM WATER	D	A	EXCEPTIONAL
🌊 INLAND WATERWAYS	D+	🚌 TRANSIT	D-	B	GOOD
🚧 LEVEES	D	🚽 WASTEWATER	D+	C	MEDIOCRE
🌳 PARKS AND RECREATION	D+			D	POOR
				F	FAILING

Source: The first infrastructure grades were given by the National Council on Public Works Improvements in its report Fragile Foundations: A Report on America's Public Works, released in February 1988. ASCE's first Report Card for America's Infrastructure was issued a decade later.
The 2021 Report Card's investment needs are over 10 years. The 2013 Report is over eight years. In the 2001, 2005, and 2009 Report Cards, the time period was five years. https://infrastructurereportcard.org/wp-content/uploads/2020/12/2021-Grades-Chart.jpg

is in poor shape, and the battered pavement cost motorists an extra $130 billion in additional vehicle repairs and operating costs in 2019.

- Of 16 types of infrastructure assessed, all but six—rail, bridges, ports, drinking water, energy, and solid waste—netted a D or D+.

- Bridges earned a C, down from 2017's C+, but of more than 617,000 bridges nationwide, 46,154 or 7.5 percent, were structurally deficient in 2020, and vehicles made 178 million trips across them every day. Nearly four out of every 10 bridges are at least 50 years old.[157]

- Drinking water, carried through one million miles of pipes, got a C grade. Many of the pipes were installed in the early to mid-20th century, with an expected lifespan of 75 to 100 years. There is a water main break every two minutes, and an estimated six billion gallons of treated water is lost each day in the U.S.—enough to fill more than 9,000 swimming pools! A recent example of our Nation's water infrastructure failure is in Jackson, Mississippi, where in 2022, an aged, trouble-plagued water treatment plant was overwhelmed yet again. This time it meant 180,000 residents had no water coming from the tap to drink, brush their teeth, or flush toilets for nearly two months.[158]

2. OUR ROADS ARE NOT AS SAFE AS THEY SHOULD BE. In 2020, it was estimated that there were more than 42,000 deaths and 4.8 million serious injuries on our roads.[159] Apart from the tragic loss of life, these car accidents cost the economy approximately $474 billion in 2020, according to the National Safety Council.[160] American motorists, pedestrians, and cyclists should be outraged when comparing death rates to other countries. For example, the American motor vehicle crash death rate per 100,000 population is about two times that of Canada and three times that of Denmark and Holland.[161]

3. GOOD INFRASTRUCTURE DRIVES THE ECONOMY. The transportation system does not just matter when you are going from point A to point B in your car. The transportation system provides services that support economic growth by increasing the productivity of workers and capital. The better our transportation system, the better our economy will be.

The ASCE says it would take $5.9 trillion to fix the entire U.S. infrastructure system by 2029. The infrastructure bill that just passed through Congress comes up with $550 billion in new funds in addition to the $650 billion already appropriated. We are short $4.7 trillion.[162]

We have the engineers, the workers, and a list of all the projects. We just don't have the money. The gas tax is a simple solution to come up with the money. The gas tax has funded transportation projects since 1932 and, at one point, created the greatest transportation system in the world.[163] For some reason, our leaders decided it was more important to keep the gas tax down than it was to maintain a world-class transportation system.

The new President, in his or her first month in office, should send to Congress the Eisenhower Two Transportation Act of 2025. The proposed legislation will provide the resources to significantly upgrade our current transportation system and pay for it.

To have the best transportation system in the world, we need to pay for it. As the saying goes, "You get what you pay for." Other than Mexico, which has no gasoline tax, we have the lowest gas tax by far in the Western world, and the condition of our transportation system is the worst. We are getting what we pay for.

The gas tax has not been raised since 1993,[164] while inflation has increased by 113 percent.[165] Since 1993, the U.S. population has grown by 184.55 million people, or 219 percent,[166] and the number of registered vehicles has grown to nearly 300 million, or 39 percent.[167] With more people driving more cars, and more bridges and roads to maintain, we are spending 76.4 percent less due to inflation. And we wonder why our transportation system is a mess. Our leaders in Washington, D.C., do not have the political courage to fund great infrastructure. They are more interested in staying in power by not increasing taxes than in making decisions in the best long-term interest of the country. The Eisenhower Two Transportation Act of 2025 will propose increasing the gas tax from 18.4 cents to either .50 cents or $1 per gallon to rebuild America. The updated gas tax is below:

Gas Price	Tax Per Gallon	Eisenhower Two
Less than $3.00	.184	1.00
More than $3.00	.184	.50

According to the Congressional Budget Office, the current tax on gasoline and diesel fuel was expected to generate $43 billion for our transportation needs in 2022 (prior to the Federal tax holiday).[168] Using the maximum $1 per gallon gas tax I propose would generate approximately $190 billion annually and provide the funding necessary to transform our transportation system over the next decade.

Boosting the gas tax up to $1 per gallon is a simple and bold plan that would create the revenue necessary to rebuild our crumbling transportation system, improve our economy by speeding the flow of goods, put millions of Americans to work in high-paying construction jobs, and save thousands of lives every year. A $1 per gallon gas tax would still leave our combined Federal and average state gas tax at less than 50 percent of the rates in Germany, the U.K., and most other Western nations.[169]

....

We cannot be the greatest nation in the world or have the best economy if we have the worst transportation system of any major industrialized nation. The Eisenhower Two Transportation Act of 2025 will provide the resources necessary to rebuild our transportation system over the next 20 years. No presidential candidate has campaigned on increasing the gas tax. There should be a candidate with the vision and the will to be candid with the American people and let them know that our reluctance to raise the gas tax is crippling our Nation's transportation system. We need leaders who can tackle difficult issues and have adult conversations with the American people. If we want a world-class transportation system that will help deliver a globally competitive economy over the next 50 years, we need to pay for it.

6

Save Social Security and Expand It!

> "How can we love our country and not love our countrymen, and loving them, reach out a hand when they fall, heal them when they are sick, and provide opportunities to make them self-sufficient so they will be equal in fact and not just in theory?"
>
> —Ronald Reagan[170]

On August 14, 1935, President Franklin Roosevelt signed the Social Security Act.[171] What followed over the next eight decades has been one of our Nation's most successful and effective programs. Frank Bane, executive director of the first Social Security Board, said, "The Social Security Act, our first organized and nation-wide security program, is designed to meet no less than five problems. It is designed to protect childhood, to provide for the handicapped, to safeguard the public health, to break the impact of unemployment, and to establish a systematic defense against dependency in old age."[172]

The Social Security program, despite its critics, has accomplished most of the goals that President Roosevelt set almost 90 years ago.

While most Americans are aware that Social Security provides a retirement benefit, most people do not understand all of the benefits of Social Security:

- There are nearly 13 million American children who live in poverty.[173] More than 6.5 million of those children come from homes that receive Social Security benefits, and in which 1.1 million children were able to be lifted out of poverty in 2020.[174]

- Elderly Americans depend on Social Security. Almost half of the elderly would be poor without Social Security. Currently, the program keeps nearly 16 million elderly Americans out of poverty.[175] Among Social Security beneficiaries age 65 and older, 37 percent of men and 42 percent of women receive 50 percent or more of their income from Social Security.[176]

- With fewer American workers having pension plans available to them, Social Security will be a bigger part of the financial future for people who are retiring.

- Social Security provides disability, medical, and dependent coverage for workers, their spouses, parents, and children. Nearly 90 percent of people ages 21 to 64 who worked in 2018 were insured through Social Security in case of disability.[177]

Most Americans have paid into the Social Security system and depend on its future availability. When so many are counting on this program in the future, why is it on the brink of bankruptcy?

1. THE SOCIAL SECURITY SYSTEM IS RUNNING OUT OF MONEY. In 2020, for the first time, Social Security expenses exceeded revenues. It is projected that in 2035, the trust funds will be depleted, and Social Security will then be able to pay only about 75 cents on the dollar.[178]

2. DEMOGRAPHICS ARE NOT OUR FRIEND WHEN IT COMES TO SOCIAL SECURITY. The baby boomer generation is retiring, and its effect on Social Security will be massive. According to the Social Security Administration, by 2035, more than 78 million Americans will be 65 or older, up from 56 million today. The number of people paying into the system to fund the Social Security payments will fall to 2.3 workers per retiree compared with 2.8 workers per beneficiary today.[179] When Social Security was passed in 1935, giving benefits to those at age 65, the average life expectancy was barely over age 60.[180] Today, the age at which you can receive your full benefits is 67, but life expectancy for men and women is near 76.[181] When the program was put into place in 1935, the math made sense. The math makes no sense today, and we keep kicking the can of responsibility down the road to the next generation.

3. WE HAVE A HIGHER PERCENTAGE OF HIGH-WAGE EARNERS WHO DO NOT PAY ANY SOCIAL SECURITY TAXES FOR EARNINGS OVER $147,000. In 1937, 92 percent of all U.S. earnings were subject to Social Security taxes. Years later, in 1983, it dropped to 90 percent. Today, only 83 percent of earnings fall within the Social Security tax requirement.[182]

4. THE BIRTH RATE IS WORKING AGAINST US. Since the 1960s, the birth rate has been in decline.[183] We have fewer young people working to pay for people entitled to Social Security. This trend is not going away.

Given the above problems that plague our Social Security system as it is currently administered, how do we fix it? How can we change a system that has done so much for so many and remains a program that most Americans depend on to be there in the future?

Unfortunately, Social Security is the perfect example of how incompetent our current Presidential candidates are. Of all the people running for President, no one has a real plan to deal with one of the most important programs in our Nation. Since the candidates won't tell you what needs to be done, I will. I think we should have some creative thinking from those seeking the highest office in the land, and I believe that they should propose the Franklin Roosevelt Social Security Act of 2025.

....

The next President, in the first 30 days of their administration, should propose the Franklin Roosevelt Social Security Act of 2025:

1. SCRAP THE CAP. According to my estimates, if Congress made one simple change and eliminated Social Security's cap on taxable income, the Trust Fund would remain in a surplus until 2067. An additional $190 billion would flow into Social Security every year. This amount of money would secure the future of this amazing program and would allow the program to be expanded to help more people who cannot help themselves.[184]

Why scrap the cap? The cap favors the wealthy. Removing the cap will make sure that all Americans pay their fair share. Americans pay 6.2 percent of their income into Social Security on their first $147,000 of income. If

Scrap the Cap
Social Security employee tax as percentage (%) of income

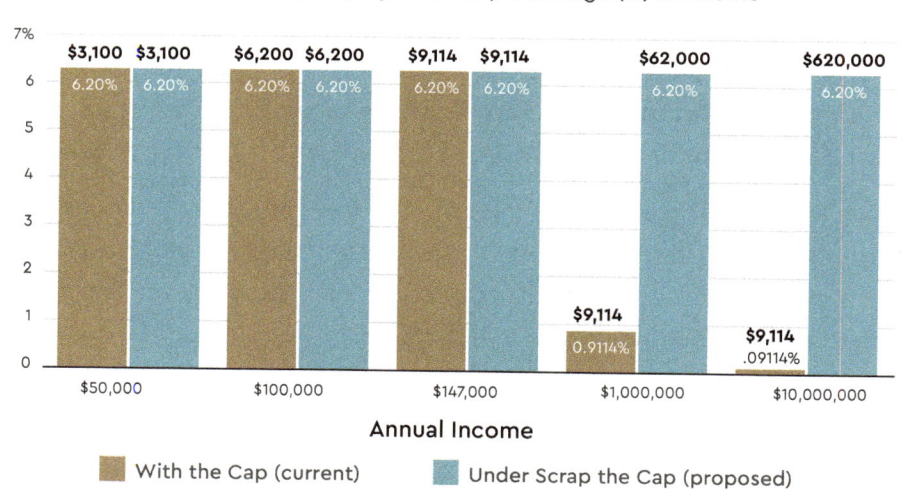

Annual Income	With the Cap (current)	Under Scrap the Cap (proposed)
$50,000	$3,100 (6.20%)	$3,100 (6.20%)
$100,000	$6,200 (6.20%)	$6,200 (6.20%)
$147,000	$9,114 (6.20%)	$9,114 (6.20%)
$1,000,000	$9,114 (0.9114%)	$62,000 (6.20%)
$10,000,000	$9,114 (.09114%)	$620,000 (6.20%)

Source: Social Security Works, Washington | ssworkswa.org

they earn more than this cap, there is no additional tax. Scrapping the cap is supported by 81 percent of Americans,[185] and it would make a huge difference in the program's viability. Warren Buffett, one of the richest men in the world, is a supporter of scrapping the cap, having stated: "If anything, taxes for the lower and middle class and maybe even the upper-middle class should even probably be cut further. But I think that people at the high end—people like myself—should be paying a lot more in taxes. We have it better than we've ever had it."[186] Scrapping the cap will ensure the future viability of the Social Security Program, and it will take a large step in solving the income inequality gap that exists in America today by requiring the wealthiest Americans to pay more in taxes and investing those funds in the people at the lower end of the economic ladder, which will help build the middle class of the future.

2. RAISE THE FULL RETIREMENT AGE. Americans are living longer, yet Social Security rules have not changed to reflect that. When the Social Security program began in 1935, the average American was expected to live to age 61. Today, on average, Americans can expect to live to be 76.1 years old.

I propose adopting the following option developed by the Congressional Budget Office and supported by 75 percent of respondents in a recent CNBC survey: Raise the full retirement age from age 67 by two months per birth year, beginning with workers who turn 62 in 2023, until it reaches age 70 for workers born in 1978 or later (who will turn 62 beginning in 2040).[187]

This option would shrink Federal Government payouts by $28 billion through 2028. By 2048, the plan would decrease Social Security outlays under current law by 8 percent or approximately $92 billion per year, by my estimate, and put Social Security on firm financial footing for the rest of the century.

3. REFORM THE SOCIAL SECURITY DISABILITY PROGRAM. The disability program offered through Social Security should be reformed by requiring those eligible for disability payments to reapply for the program

Current Disability Program Reviews vs My Proposal

CURRENT DISABILITY PROGRAM REVIEWS	MY PROPOSAL
At 6-8 months for conditions expected to improve	at 6 months
3 years for conditions possible to improve	at 2 years
7 years for conditions to improve	at 5 years

Source: https://www.ssa.gov/pubs/EN-05-10053.pdf

every six months for conditions that are expected to improve, every two years for conditions that are possible to improve, and every five years for conditions not expected to improve. Calls for reform have described this program as a "secret welfare system" with its own "disability-industrial complex" ravaged by waste and fraud.

The late Senator Tom Coburn, a physician who was the ranking Republican on the Senate Subcommittee on Investigations, conducted a study in 2013 and concluded that 25 percent of people on disability should never have been approved, while another 20 percent were highly questionable.[188] The 2023 budget for Social Security is $1.37 trillion with over $147 billion being spent on the disability program that former Senator Coburn calls "highly questionable."[189] Putting people on disability who should not be on disability is costing our country billions of dollars. Even worse, in 2015, "the Social Security Administration paid a billion dollars to claimants' lawyers out of its ... disability trust fund." Seventy million dollars "went to ... the largest disability law firm in the country." Yes, you, the taxpayer, paid $70 million to one law firm to get people onto disability.

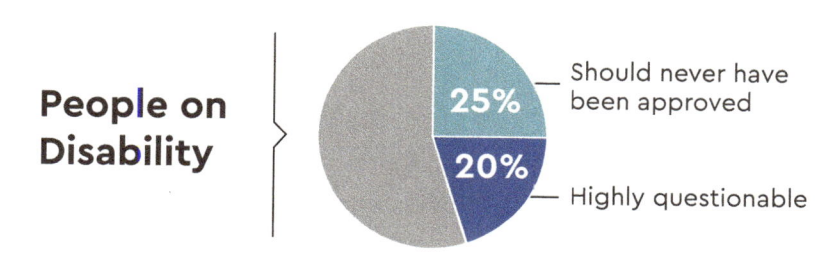

People on Disability

- 25% — Should never have been approved
- 20% — Highly questionable

4. CREATE THE EVERY KID HAS A CHANCE PROGRAM WITH THE GOAL OF REDUCING CHILDHOOD POVERTY BY 50 PERCENT IN THE NEXT 10 YEARS AND BY 90 PERCENT OVER THE NEXT 25 YEARS.

How can our Federal Government plan to spend $1.2 trillion over the next 30 years modernizing our nuclear weapons program, but we tolerate 18.8 percent of our children living in poverty?

Charles M. Blow, in a 2015 column in *The New York Times,* called America's child poverty level "unconscionable:"[190]

> People may disagree about the choices parents make, including premarital sex and out-of-wedlock births. People may disagree about access to family planning methods, including contraception and abortion. People may disagree about the size and role of government, including the role of safety-net programs.
>
> But surely we can all agree that no child, once born, should suffer through poverty. Surely we can all agree that working to end child poverty—or at least severely reduce it—is a moral obligation of a civilized society.

Share of Adults by class—1971 v. 2021

Percentage (%) of adults in each income tier

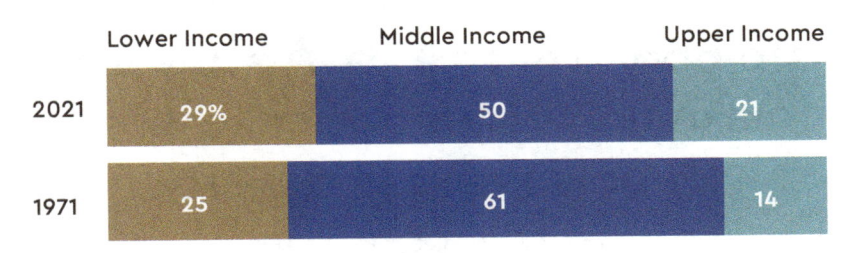

Year	Lower Income	Middle Income	Upper Income
2021	29%	50	21
1971	25	61	14

Note: Adults are assigned to income tiers based on their size-adjusted household incomes in the calendar year prior to the survey year. Shares may not add to 100 percent due to rounding.

Source: Pew Research Center analysis of the Current Population Survey.
Annual Social and Economic Supplement (IPUMS). PEW RESEARCH CENTER

Source: https://www.pewresearch.org/short-reads/2022/04/20/how-the-american-middle-class-has-changed-in-the-past-five-decades/#:~:text=In percent20this percent20analysis percent2C percent20 percentE2 percent80 percent9Cmiddle percent2D,for percent20a percent20household percent20of percent20three

Within the Franklin Roosevelt Social Security Act of 2025, the next President should recommend legislation to create the Every Kid Has a Chance Program. For those kids whose families are below 50 percent of the poverty level, Social Security will provide the following:

- Free basic Medicare.

- Head Start for all American children who qualify. The current Head Start program covers more than one million American children. It currently covers only 36 percent of eligible three- and four-year-olds and 11 percent of eligible infants and toddlers. An investment of $50 billion a year would allow Head Start to cover all American children who qualify.

- Free education from preschool until the age of 22.

The Every Kid Has a Chance Program would take a giant step forward in giving the poorest children in our society a chance in life and by producing more taxpaying citizens for the future. This program would also give kids and their families at the bottom of the socioeconomic ladder hope for the future. An old saying states, "Show me the boy at seven, and I will show you the man."

Nearly 11 million children are poor. That's **1 in 7 kids** who make up almost one-third of all people living in poverty in this country.

Source: https://www.americanprogress.org/article/basic-facts-children-poverty/

Two years ago I met Naya Persaud, a grade school principal who ran a school in a low-income area of Arizona, and asked if she agreed with the saying. Naya responded, "I can tell you at the end of third grade which kids are going to be successful and which kids are going to have challenges." I agree with Naya, and the business part of me says invest money in children between birth and third grade to make sure we as a society do everything possible to make kids successful by the end of third grade. If we make this early investment in kids, there is a high probability that they will lead successful lives.

Proportion of children living in poverty in these countries in 2020

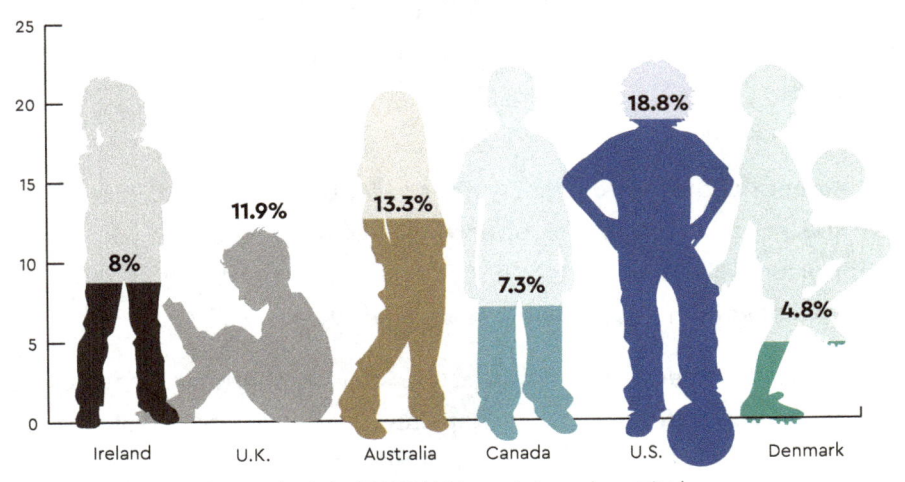

Country	Percentage
Ireland	8%
U.K.	11.9%
Australia	13.3%
Canada	7.3%
U.S.	18.8%
Denmark	4.8%

Source: https://www.statista.com/statistics/264424/child-poverty-in-oecd-countries/

Imagine the long-term cost difference for a kid born in poverty who stays in poverty, ends up in jail, goes through the legal system, and winds up on welfare compared to the kid who is born into poverty through no fault of their own and has guaranteed health care and a free education starting in preschool and all the way through college. Over the long haul, which program makes more sense for our country in terms of dealing with childhood poverty? Our current system? Or the Every Kid Has a Chance Program? Which program holds the higher moral ground? Which program costs less over the long term? This is an opportunity for the Government to help people who cannot help themselves and save money by helping to create more taxpaying citizens for the future. It is my belief that our highly partisan, poor performing government is not very creative. The Every Kid has a Chance Program is the kind of creativity that we should expect from our leaders.

5. HAVE THE DEPARTMENT OF EDUCATION OFFER TO TAKE OVER THE COUNTRY'S POOREST PERFORMING 1 PERCENT OF PUBLIC SCHOOLS.

Education matters. American children hold the key to our future, whether rich or poor. In our country, rich kids are cared for by better schools and parents who have the resources to raise productive citizens. I know this. I was born with two amazing parents and have lived a great life. I have mentored kids born poor with tough family situations through no fault of their own and have watched the cycle of poverty destroy hope, futures, and lives. Chief Justice Earl Warren wrote in the 1954 *Brown v. Board of Education* ruling:

> It is doubtful that any child may reasonably be expected to succeed in life if he is denied the opportunity of an education. Such an opportunity, where the state has undertaken to provide it, is a right which must be made available to all on equal terms.[191]

The reality in America today is that our children born into poverty do not have the equal opportunity that Chief Justice Warren wrote about. The vast majority of kids born into the cycle of poverty can't get out. As *The Atlantic* reported, students in higher-income towns in Connecticut, such as Greenwich and Darien, have easy access to guidance counselors, school psychologists, personal laptops, and up-to-date textbooks, and those in high-poverty areas, like Bridgeport and New Britain, do not. Such districts tend to have more students in need of extra help, and yet they have fewer guidance counselors, tutors, and psychologists. According to a lawsuit, they have lower-paid teachers, more dilapidated facilities, and bigger class sizes than wealthier districts. Greenwich spends $6,000 more per pupil per year than Bridgeport, according to the state's Department of Education. *The Atlantic* article notes a landmark 2013 report from a group convened by the former Education Secretary Arne Duncan, the Equity and Excellence Commission, which concluded, "Our system does not distribute opportunity equitably."[192]

For the most part, children below 50 percent of the poverty line come from disadvantaged or single-parent households with limited or no financial resources and attend the Nation's worst schools. Within the Every Kid Has a Chance Program, the President should propose to Congress that states are given the opportunity to cede control of any of their schools in the poorest performing 1 percent to the Department of Education. The states would give the Department of Education the money they are spending on these schools. With a high sense of urgency, the Department of Education will put together a special division and invest money beyond the state money, funded through Social Security, to take control of these schools and turn them around fast so the poorest children in our country can have a realistic chance of becoming productive, taxpaying citizens of the future. These schools will be named after Horace Mann, the first great American advocate of public education who believed that education should be free and universal and reliant on well-trained professional teachers.[193] The Horace Mann Schools will have the full power of the Department of Education and the Presidency behind them. If we can transform these schools from poorly financed and significantly underperforming to the best public schools in America, we can transform America so that every child, no matter what circumstance they are born into, has an equal chance of life, liberty, and the pursuit of happiness.

Current Poorest Performing 1 Percent	Horace Mann Schools
Below-average funding	Same funding as the top 10 percent of schools
Local school boards	No school boards
Teachers' unions	No teachers' unions
Below-average pay for staff	Top pay for staff equal to the challenge
Average principals	Exceptional principals
Federal support	Full Federal support

If this test succeeds, the President should recommend to Congress that the program be expanded. If this program fails, the President should recommend that the program be shut down. I believe in looking at problems, trying new things, keeping what works, and getting rid of what doesn't.

Social Security is an amazing program. It provides a retirement program for the vast majority of American seniors and disability coverage for most American workers and their families. I am proposing five specific changes to Social Security to make sure that this important program will not only last for the next 50 years but will also be upgraded to help solve the problems of income inequality and childhood poverty. Rebuilding Social Security can be a key part of rebuilding the American middle class.

7

Reform Congress

"I wish there was a way I could wave a magic wand and put back when people were respectful of each other, and the Congress was working for the good of the country and not just along party lines. Someday there will be great people, great elected representatives who will say, 'enough of this nonsense, let's be the kind of legislature the United States should have.' I hope that day will come when I'm still alive."

—Ruth Bader Ginsburg, Supreme Court Justice[194]

Ask anyone which of our three branches of Government has been the least effective over the past 20 years, and the likely answer is Congress. Congress has had an average approval rating of around 18.5 percent over the past 10 years.[195]

Why does the performance of Congress matter? Because Congress is in charge of a lot of important tasks. Congress is in charge of making laws, declaring war, raising revenue, overseeing all Government spending, approving presidential appointments, approving international treaties, and oversight of the Government. In addition to all of these tasks, Congress is in charge of representing the people. As a citizen, I see two major problems with Congress today:

1. CONGRESS IS IN CHARGE OF OUR NATION'S FINANCES. Not a dime can be spent without the approval of Congress, other than through an executive order by the President. We have a national debt now exceeding $34 trillion, which translates to more than $99,962 for every American.[196] Congress has primary responsibility for this—not the President. Congress has completed appropriations before the start of the fiscal year only four times in the past 40 years.

2. MONEY HAS BECOME THE MAJOR INFLUENCE IN CONGRESS. CONGRESS DOES NOT MAKE DECISIONS IN THE LONG-TERM BEST INTEREST OF THE UNITED STATES. CONGRESS MAKES DECISIONS THAT WILL GET THEIR MEMBERS REELECTED. IN 2020 $7 BILLION WAS SPENT ON CONGRESSIONAL CAMPAIGNS IN THE UNITED STATES according to projections by the Center for Responsive Politics.[197] In 2020, close to 90 percent of candidates running for a seat in the House of Representatives and 72 percent of Senate contenders who outspent their opponents during their campaigns won their respective elections.[198] One of the major problems with Congress is that it is awash with money, yet Congress has done basically nothing to address campaign finance reform. And it doesn't stop when members leave Congress. A recent study by Public Citizen found that in 2019 nearly 66 percent of former members of Congress had moved into jobs working for lobby firms, consulting firms, trade groups, or targeted business groups; in 1974, that number was just 3 percent.[199] Why are so many members of Congress turning into lobbyists? Because corporations are willing to pay them to lobby their former colleagues to influence legislation that might be worth hundreds of millions or billions of dollars.

One example is former Representative Billy Tauzin (R-LA), who made almost $20 million as a lobbyist for the pharmaceutical industry between 2006 and 2010, according to the *New York Daily News*.[200] During Tauzin's time in Congress, where he served from 1980 to 2005, he helped pass President Bush's prescription drug expansion.[201] As a well-paid lobbyist, his association helped block a proposal allowing Medicare to negotiate drug prices. That proposal, had it passed, would have saved American taxpayers billions of dollars.

The Open Secrets database identifies 40 former members of the 115th Congress who left their offices in January 2019 and subsequently joined the ranks of 460 former congressional members who are now lobbyists who spend their days attempting to influence the Federal Government in which they used to serve.[202] The high salaries that lobbying firms are paying former members of Congress are cheap compared to what value former members of Congress can deliver to special interest groups once they leave Congress. Our democracy is for sale, and there is no better example of our Government being for sale than Congress.

Without an effective Congress we cannot have a great country. If we can fix Congress, the impact will be massive throughout the country. The President should propose the Congressional Reform Act of 2025, as well as two constitutional amendments:

1. ELIMINATE THE FILIBUSTER. A filibuster is a political procedure where one or more members of Congress stage a long debate over a proposed piece of legislation to delay or entirely prevent a decision from being made on the proposal. It is sometimes referred to as "talking a bill to death." The filibuster can force any controversial proposal in the Senate to require 60 of the 100 senators' votes, meaning that not even a simple majority can carry the day and that a group of 41 senators can block any legislation.[203]

The impact of the filibuster has been massive. Our inability to confront major issues like gun violence and climate change is partially due to the

Number of Senator Cloture Votes 1940–2020

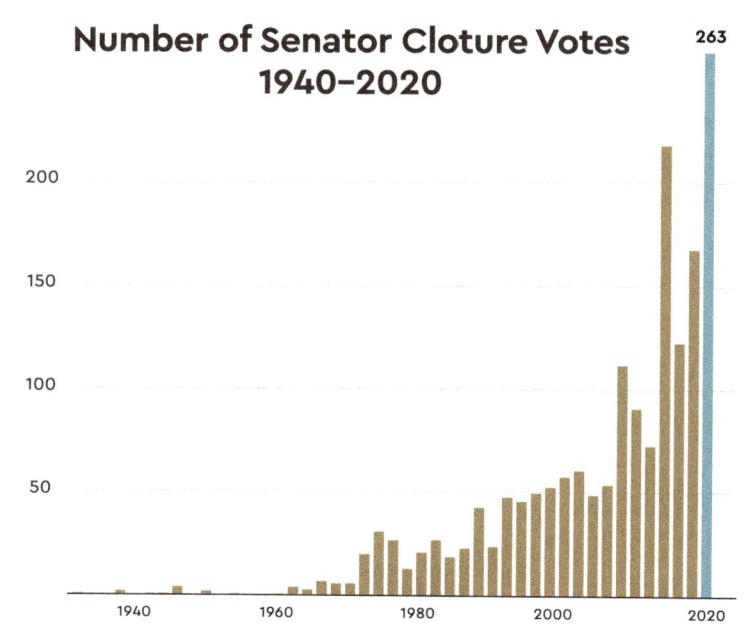

263

Source: https://www.vox.com/21424582/filibuster-joe-biden-2020-senate-democrats-abolish-trump

filibuster. As a nation, we have big problems that need to be solved, and the Senate should abolish the filibuster and allow the majority to carry the day.

2. END GERRYMANDERING. As part of the Congressional Reform Act of 2025, the President should ask Congress to eliminate gerrymandering—the practice of redrawing congressional districts to benefit one political party—and have nonpartisan, independent commissions put in charge of drawing districts. By putting an end to gerrymandering, less extreme candidates will have a better chance of success, and so will compromise. For examples of how politicians have rigged the game by changing the borders of their districts to increase their odds of reelection, look no further than Maryland and Pennsylvania. A Federal judge said Maryland's Third District map looked like "a broken-winged pterodactyl,"[204] while David Daley, publisher of *The Connecticut Mirror*, described Pennsylvania's Seventh District as Goofy kicking Donald Duck.[205] Both states were ordered to redraw the district borders.

The Gerrymandering of Maryland's Third District

83rd Congress
1953–1955

113th
2013–2015

The Gerrymandering of Pennsylvania's Seventh District

83rd Congress
1953–1955

113th
2013–2015

Source: Source: Shapefiles maintained by Jeffrey B. Lewis, Brandon DeVine, Lincoln Pritcher, and Kenneth C. Martis, UCLA. Drawn to scale.

3. ELIMINATE PENSIONS FOR MEMBERS OF CONGRESS. The President should propose that the pension program for Congress be terminated for all members. Under the current system, senators and representatives can pull in a pension at age 62 if they have held office for at least five years or at age 50 if they have served in Congress for 20 years,[206] and at ANY age after completing 25 years of service. As of October 2022, there were 619 retired members of Congress getting pensions,[207] according to the Congressional

Research Service. We are spending $36.3 million a year on congressional pensions when we are $34 trillion in debt. Congress survived without a pension program until the 1940s, and the Nation cannot afford it today. All current balances should be paid out.

Additionally, in order to improve Congress's performance for the people, the President should propose the following constitutional amendments:

1. INSTALL TERM LIMITS. The 22nd Amendment states that the President can serve two four-year terms. Let's take an idea that is already working and send it down Pennsylvania Avenue to Congress. Members of the Senate and the House of Representatives should be able to hold office for 12 years maximum. Two six-year terms if you are a senator and six two-year terms if you are a member of the House.

Here are the potential benefits:

- The idea of the "career politician" would cease if the maximum time that anyone could serve in Congress was 12 years.

- Members of Congress would have more time to spend on solving the Nation's problems instead of raising money and running for reelection.

- The quality of political candidates would improve. By imposing term limits, we are more likely to attract political candidates interested in serving their country, not creating a career. **Washington, Jefferson, Adams, and Franklin served their country, not their careers.**

2. GIVE THE PRESIDENT THE LINE-ITEM VETO. Congress is in charge of the Nation's checkbook. We are more than $34 trillion in debt, and the current system is clearly not working. Congress rarely passes clean bills to be signed. When the President signs a bill, it usually comes with numerous unrelated, unnecessary, political back-scratching add-ons. As a check and balance, the President should be able to protect the American taxpayer. Currently, 44 state governors have a line-item veto.[208] It is time that we give this power to the President, whether they are a Democrat, Republican, or an independent. President Clinton had the line-item veto from April 1996 to June 1998, when it was declared unconstitutional by the U.S. Supreme Court. In the time President Clinton had the line-item veto, he cut 82 items from 11 spending bills saving taxpayers more than $2 billion.[209] It was not just the $2 billion that President Clinton saved taxpayers; it was the fact that Congress knew President Clinton had the ability to veto any out-of-line spending. The line-item veto provided necessary financial discipline to Congress. Unfortunately, in 1998 the United States Supreme Court ruled that the line-item veto was unconstitutional in a 6-3 decision in *Clinton v. City of New York*.[210] In the first 100 days of his or her Presidency, the new President should propose a constitutional amendment to give the President the line-item veto. This will not be easy and will take time, but it needs to be done if we want to run a better government.

By proposing the Congressional Reform Act of 2025 along with two constitutional amendments, the new President can make a massive difference in improving the performance of our Government. Over the years there have been plenty of candidates running for President who have talked about reform in Washington in broad generalities, and nothing ever gets done. We need a President who has the will to propose legislation that will improve Congress for the benefit of the American people.

8

Right-Size Defense Spending

> "Every gun that is made, every warship launched, every rocket fired signifies, in the final sense, a theft from those who hunger and are not fed, those who are cold and are not clothed."
>
> —Dwight D. Eisenhower[211]

Throughout our history, the American military has kept our Nation safe and preserved our way of life. Millions have served, and many of our fellow countrymen have paid the ultimate price. Along with our allies, our military succeeded in saving Europe in World War I and virtually the entire world in World War II. Our military oversaw the end of the Cold War, and most recently, our military personnel and our allies have been laying their lives on the line for the Global War on Terror in the Middle East.

Every American owes a debt of gratitude to the men and women who have served in our armed forces. As with anything, times change, and as a nation, we must realize that we spend more money on defense than we can afford. This opinion has nothing to do with questioning the men and women who have served in the military; it has everything to do with the recognition that we have a $34 trillion debt, and to solve it, we need to put every expense on the table, including how much money we spend in the Department of Defense.

In order to get our financial house in order, the President should work with the military leadership team to develop a plan to reduce total defense-related expenditures from the current $857.9 billion[212] to $657.9 billion by 2028, while at the same time improving our national security. This would be an overall reduction of $200 billion. Admiral Mike Mullen, the former chairman of the Joint Chiefs of Staff, has said, "The greatest threat to our national security is our debt."[213] Below are some facts that illustrate just how big of an opportunity we have to reduce our expenditures within the Department of Defense without compromising our national security:

1. IN 2021, THE UNITED STATES MADE UP APPROXIMATELY 4.3 PERCENT OF THE WORLD'S POPULATION,[214] YET WE WERE RESPONSIBLE FOR 38 PERCENT OF THE PUBLICIZED GLOBAL MILITARY EXPENDITURES.[215] We spend more money on defense than the next 10 countries combined.[216]

2. WE HAVE MORE MILITARY BASES AROUND THE WORLD THAN WE NEED, BUT WE DO NOT HAVE THE POLITICAL COURAGE TO RIGHT-SIZE OUR BASES. In addition to all the military bases inside the United States, the Defense Department operates approximately 750 bases overseas in at least 80 nations.[217] Russia has 25 current and planned overseas bases,[218] and China has five.[219] We cannot afford 750 overseas bases.

The United States spends more on defense than the next 10 countries combined

Defense Spending (Billions of Dollars)

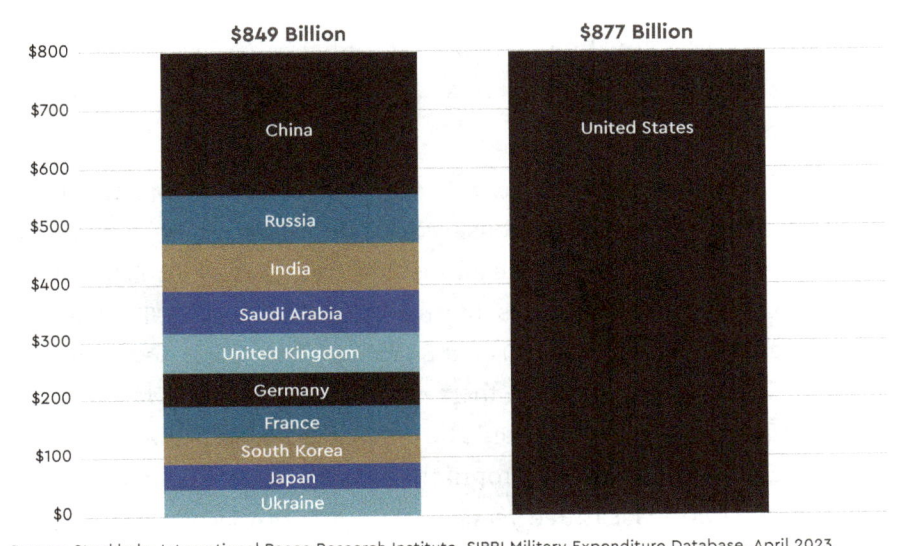

$849 Billion — China, Russia, India, Saudi Arabia, United Kingdom, Germany, France, South Korea, Japan, Ukraine

$877 Billion — United States

Source: Stockholm International Peace Research Institute, SIPRI Military Expenditure Database, April 2023.

Notes: Figures are in U.S. dollars converted from local currencies using market exchange rates. Data for the United States are for fiscal year 2022, which ran from October 1, 2021 through September 30, 2022. Data for the other countries are for calendar year 2022.

The source for this chart uses a definition of defense spending that is more broad than budget function 050 and defense discretionary spending. ©2023 Peter G. Peterson Foundation.

https://www.pgpf.org/chart-archive/0053_defense-comparison

3. THE UNITED STATES DEFENSE DEPARTMENT'S WEAPONS PROGRAM IS INEFFICIENT. The current poster child for costly and inefficient weapons is the F-35 combat aircraft. The Pentagon is set to purchase more than 2,400 F-35s for $1.7 trillion,[220] making the F-35 the most expensive weapons project of all time. In 2016, as the project was running seven years behind schedule and already had run up a cost of more than $400 billion—almost twice the initial estimate—Senator John McCain called the overruns "disgraceful," "outrageous," and "a tragedy."[221]

Why are we spending $1.7 trillion on the F-35 program? Lockheed Martin, who makes the plane, spends a lot of money influencing Government officials. According to Open Secrets for 2022, number one on their list is Chuck Schumer, the democratic leader of the Senate, having received approximately $108,000 between 2017 and 2022 in campaign contributions. They also gave just under $42,000 to Defense Appropriations ranking member Kay Granger, they spent $116,000 on the Democratic Congressional Campaign and just over $74,000 on the Republican Congressional Campaign. **Our highest-ranking Government officials, who make trillion-dollar decisions, are influenced by those profiting from their decisions.**[222]

Defense contractors spending money for votes goes beyond the F-35. According to Open Secrets, defense contractors gave members of the House Armed Services Committee almost $3.4 million in the 2022 election cycle.[223] From 2019 to 2020, Representative Mac Thornberry (R-TX) alone, a ranking member of the House Armed Services Committee, netted nearly $428,819—the most money from the sector of any member of Congress, for a cumulative $2.1 million since 2001. Senator Richard Shelby (R-AL), who chaired the powerful Appropriations Committee and its defense subcommittee for the last three years, outraised Thornberry, cumulatively raking in more than $3.5 million since 2001.[224]

Wasting taxpayer dollars goes beyond paying off campaign contributors. In an effort to benefit their districts, a number of members of Congress have pushed to spend money on military projects the Pentagon does not want. One example is the production of M-1 tanks. In March 2012, the late U.S. Army Chief of Staff General Raymond Odierno told the House Appropriations Committee that the Army did not need new tanks and that the tanks it had did not need to be upgraded until 2017. The Army and Marine Corps had 6,000 tanks in inventory at that time. Only 1,000 were used in the Iraq War. The Army and the Marines were trying to make a decision in the best long-term interest of the country. Unfortunately, by canceling the M-1 tanks, a large factory in Lima, Ohio, would have been idled, and subcontractors in Pennsylvania, Michigan, and other key states would have also been affected. General Dynamics, a defense supplier that has donated millions of dollars to congressional elections over the past decade, mobilized its supporters and saved the M-1 tank. **The American taxpayer is paying for tanks that the military does not want.**[225]

It gets worse. Last year the Pentagon announced that nine of the 11 Freedom-class combat ships would be retired after averaging only four years in service instead of the planned 25 years due to numerous problems with the ship. The Navy estimated that this decision would save $4.3 billion over the next five years. The Navy stated that this decision would free up resources that would be of greater benefit to the country. Unfortunately, military contractors building the ships and making money off the ships called in the lobbyists to pressure Congress to keep the ships that the Navy did not want. Congress reacted quickly and offered amendments to the 2023 Pentagon budget prohibiting the Pentagon from retiring five of the nine ships.[226]

Another example is the development of the Zumwalt, a new class of Navy destroyer stealth ship approved by Congress in 2006. The project, named after the late Chief of Naval Operations, Admiral Elmo Zumwalt, originally called for building 32 vessels at the cost of $9.6 billion. As costs

Zumwalt-Class Destroyer

Initial Plan: **32 vessels for $9.6 billion**
= **$300 million per vessel**

Outcome: **3 vessels for $22.5 billion**
= **$7.5 billion per vessel**

Budget overspent:
25 times

overran estimates, the quantity was reduced to 24, then to seven, and finally to three. In April 2016, the program's total cost was $22.5 billion, and the American taxpayer got three ships. We overspent the budget by 234 percent and got three ships instead of 32.[227]

....

The President should challenge the Defense Department's leadership team to develop a simplification plan to hit the financial targets we need as a country and to increase our security at the same time. I am confident that this can be done. In the first six months of his or her Presidency, the President should send the Defense Simplicity Act of 2025 to Congress.

What follows are six examples of opportunities to reduce spending that should be at the top of the President's list when he or she sits down with the leadership group of the Defense Department:

1. CREATE A SIMPLIFICATION PLAN. The President should ask the leadership team at the Defense. Department to come up with a plan to simplify the Defense Department, significantly reduce costs without reducing the real defense capabilities of the country, and present this plan within the first six months of his or her administration. I firmly believe that it is possible to reduce complexity and cost and, at the same time, improve the defense capabilities of the country. It is the story of Apple when Steve Jobs came back to Apple, reduced the product line by 70 percent, reduced the number of suppliers by 75 percent, and created the most valuable company in the world. It happened at Ford when Alan Mulally spun off secondary brands like Jaguar, Volvo, and Mercury. Mulally simplified the product line from 27 platforms down to nine.[228] Home Depot, Lego, and hundreds of other organizations have used simplicity to significantly improve performance.

The Air Force currently has more than 5,000 jets.[229] In addition, the Army has over 4,000 aircraft, the Navy has around 2,500, the Marine Corps has over 1,300, and the Coast Guard has 200.[230] Add it all up, and we have 179 types of jets and helicopters in our arsenal of more than 13,000 aircraft.[231]

Aircraft is just an example of all the opportunities within the Defense Department's budget to reduce our spending by hundreds of billions of dollars without reducing our national security.

2. REDUCE THE SIZE OF THE U.S. MARINE CORPS. As a nation, we have not conducted an amphibious landing since the Korean War in the early 1950s. The Marine Corps currently has more planes, ships, armored vehicles, and personnel in uniform—181,200 active duty Marines and 36,200 reservists[232]—more than double the entire British Army.[233]

3. REDUCE OVERSEAS DEPLOYMENT OF TROOPS AND BASES. We have roughly 750 overseas military bases spread across 80 nations.[234] We have 119 bases in Germany alone. The U.K. is second to the U.S. with 145 overseas bases, Russia has 25, and China has five.[235] We have a major opportunity to reduce our defense spending by closing a large number of overseas bases.

Overseas Military Bases

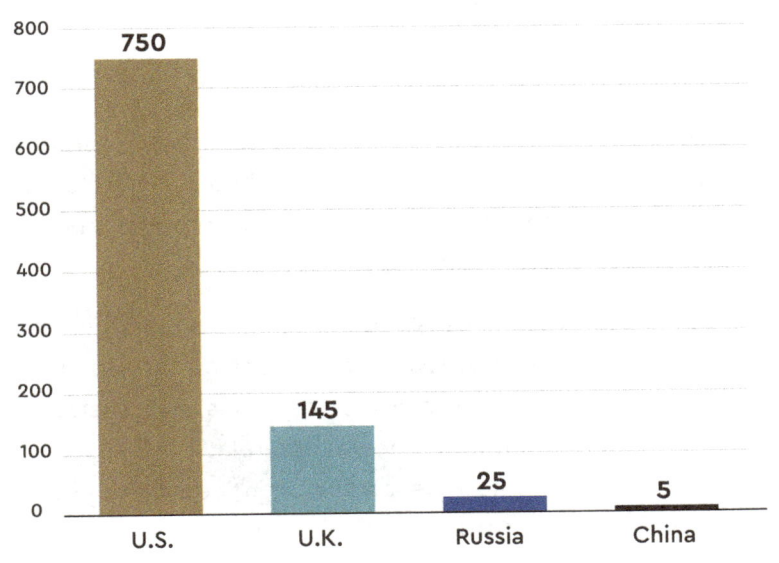

U.S.	750
U.K.	145
Russia	25
China	5

Source: https://www.cato.org/commentary/750-bases-80-countries-too-many-any-nation-time-us-bring-its-troops-home

4. REDUCE THE SIZE OF THE ARMY. We could save billions of dollars by cutting back the Army from around 485,000 active duty service members[236] to a force of 360,000. As warfare becomes more technologically oriented, we can make the tough decision to have fewer forces on the ground.

5. REDUCE THE SIZE OF OUR NUCLEAR ARSENAL. The cost of maintaining the U.S. nuclear arsenal over the next 10 years has been estimated at $494 billion.[237] We currently have an arsenal of more than 5,244 nuclear weapons.[238] Do we want to spend $494 billion over the next 10 years when we have so many other needs in our country?

6. BAN MEMBERS OF CONGRESS FROM ACCEPTING CAMPAIGN DONATIONS FROM DEFENSE CONTRACTORS. Over the past 20 years, defense contractors have spent $285 million in campaign contributions and over $2.5 billion in lobbying to influence members of Congress. Just so you have this right, defense companies are spending millions of dollars to elect congressional members.[239] Then, they spend hundreds of millions of dollars influencing the members they help elect to make decisions that benefit their companies. This is legalized corruption at the highest level. There are over 800 reported defense lobbyists[240]—more than one for every member of Congress.

In 1961, President Eisenhower gave one of the most historic of all presidential farewell addresses. What did Eisenhower, a lifelong military man, talk about? The growing military-industrial complex and what he feared could happen in the future. He stated this:

> A vital element in keeping the peace is our military establishment. Our arms must be mighty, ready for instant action, so that no potential aggressor may be tempted to risk his own destruction. Our military organization today bears little relation to that known by any of my predecessors in peacetime or, indeed, by the fighting men of World War II or Korea.
>
> Until the latest of our world conflicts, the United States had no armaments industry. American makers of plowshares could, with

time and as required, make swords as well. But we can no longer risk emergency improvisation of national defense; we have been compelled to create a permanent armaments industry of vast proportions. Added to this, three and a half million men and women are directly engaged in the defense establishment. We annually spend on military security more than the net income of all United States corporations.

This conjunction of an immense military establishment and a large arms industry is new in the American experience. The total influence—economic, political, and even spiritual—is felt in every city, every state, every office of the federal government. We recognize the imperative need for this development. Yet, we must not fail to comprehend its grave implications. Our toil, resources, and livelihood are all involved; so is the very structure of our society.

In the councils of government, we must guard against the acquisition of unwarranted influence, whether sought or unsought, by the military-industrial complex. The potential for the disastrous rise of misplaced power exists and will persist.

We must never let the weight of this combination endanger our liberties or democratic processes. We should take nothing for granted. Only an alert and knowledgeable citizenry can compel the proper meshing of the huge industrial and military machinery of defense with our peaceful methods and goals, so that security and liberty may prosper together.[241]

In retrospect, everything that Eisenhower feared has come to fruition. We have a vast military-industrial establishment that spends more than $1 trillion annually. The military-industrial complex spends roughly $100 million a year to lobby Congress to keep spending hundreds of billions of dollars more on the military than we need.[242] We must start making decisions that are in the best interests of the citizens of the United States, not in the best interests of the military-industrial complex. Just like every business or any individual family, we need to make choices, and we need to continuously evaluate our spending. I am confident that as a nation, we can save $200 billion in th defense budget without sacrificing any of our defense capabilities. In fact, I am guessing as we eliminate unneeded bases, simplify weapons programs, and improve processes, we will take the best military in the world and make it even better. At the same time, the $200 billion saved could go toward paying down our debt or funding other programs that the country desperately needs.

9

Administer a Responsible Foreign Policy

"Words can destroy. What we call each other ultimately becomes what we think of each other, and it matters."

—Jeane Kirkpatrick, the first woman to serve as
U.S. ambassador to the United Nations, 1981–1985[243]

At the start of the 21st century, the mission statement of the State Department read: "To advance freedom for the benefit of the American people and the international community by helping to build and sustain a more democratic, secure, and prosperous world composed of well-governed states that respond to the needs of their people, reduce widespread poverty, and act responsibly within the international system."[244]

Why Should Foreign Policy Matter to You?

1. THE WORLD IS GETTING SMALLER. Seventy years ago, it took 30 days to travel from New York City to Germany. Today, it takes eight hours. The computer, the internet, and the smartphone have revolutionized how the world communicates and conducts global business. As the world gets smaller, our neighbors have a greater impact on us. We either become closer friends or more bitter enemies. Friendship has benefits—trade partners are formed, new markets are opened, and peace can be expanded. An effective foreign policy in an age where the world is getting smaller can make a big difference to every American. A good foreign policy can make the difference between war and peace.

2. THE GLOBAL ECONOMY. As the world becomes smaller, trade between nations increases. In 1960, the share of exports in the world gross domestic product was 10 percent. By 2000, it had climbed to 20 percent.[245]

Exports of Goods and Services

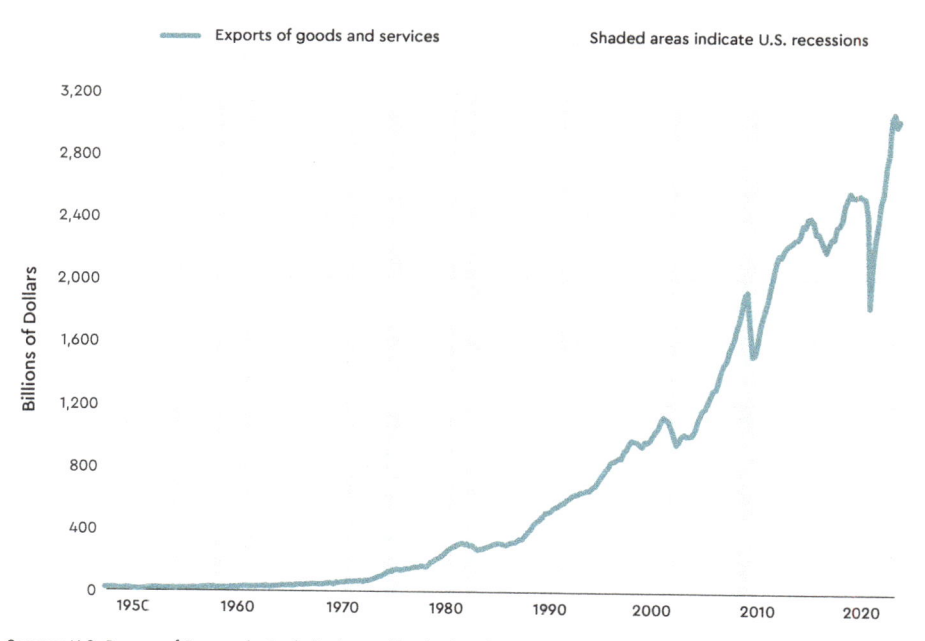

Source: U.S. Bureau of Economic Analysis. https://fred.stlouisfed.org/series/EXPGS

In 1960, U.S. companies reported $25.9 billion in global trade.[246] In 2022, that number reached $3.1 trillion,[247] 100 times the 1960 level. The bottom line is that our economy and job growth depend on doing business with other countries. The better relationships we have worldwide, the more markets we can open, and the more people will be interested in investing in the United States.

Increased global trade leads to greater opportunities for American workers and American companies. Increased trade and mutually beneficial commerce lead to stronger relationships that keep the peace.

3. SECURITY. It is said that in the history of the world, 90 percent of wars have been started because of miscommunication. Foreign policy helps to keep the world at peace. David Brooks wrote the following about foreign policy in an editorial in *The New York Times*:

> Most of human history has been marked by war. Between 1500 and 1945, scarcely a year went by without some great power fighting another great power. Then, in 1945 that stopped. The number of battlefield deaths has plummeted to the lowest levels in history. The world has experienced the greatest reduction in poverty in history, as well as the greatest spread of democracy and freedom. Why did this happen? Mostly it was because the United States decided to lead a community of nations to create a democratic world order: That order consisted of institutions like NATO, the U.N., and the World Bank. But it was also enforced by the pervasive presence of American power—military, economic and cultural power as well as the magnetic power of the democratic idea, which inspired dissidents worldwide.... But the U.S. having been dragged into two world wars, leaders from Truman through Obama felt they had no choice but to widen America's circle of concern across the whole world. This was abnormal. As Robert Kagan writes in *The Jungle Grows Back*, "Very few nations in history have ever felt a responsibility for anything but themselves."[248]

An effective American foreign policy significantly impacts every American citizen and every person around the globe. We should take great pride in the stability our foreign policy has brought to the world since the end of World War II.

4. WE CAN CHANGE THE WORLD. We have a long, proud tradition of playing a leadership role in keeping the peace around the globe. In his final letter to America, the late Senator John McCain, a retired U.S. Navy captain and war hero, summed up America's role in the world: "We are citizens of the world's greatest republic, a nation of ideals, not blood and soil. We are blessed and are a blessing to humanity when we uphold and advance those ideals at home and in the world. We have helped liberate more people from tyranny and poverty than ever before in history. We have acquired great wealth and power in the process."[249]

5. WE HAVE ONLY BEEN ABLE TO PLAY A LEADERSHIP ROLE AND GET THINGS DONE IN THE WORLD BECAUSE WE HAVE FRIENDS. Friends allow us to multiply our influence and make a bigger difference in the world. One of the greatest challenges of our time is climate change. The best way to solve the global environmental crisis is to work with other like-minded countries. An effective foreign policy can help the United States work with like-minded countries to win the battle against climate change and save the only planet we have.

6. FOREIGN POLICY FAILURES ARE COSTLY. The U.S. wars in Iraq and Afghanistan have cost the American taxpayers more than $8 trillion since the September 11, 2001, attacks on the World Trade Center.[250] Although foreign policy will not prevent all military action, great cooperation among like-minded nations over the years has prevented many wars. Foreign policy prevented the 1962 Cuban Missile Crisis from becoming a global disaster.

As the world gets smaller and smaller, foreign policy becomes more important to every American citizen. Here are four pieces of advice for the next President:

1. GLOBAL LEADERSHIP MATTERS. The next President should work with like-minded leaders around the world to create a more secure, prosperous, and democratic world, in order to expand peace and freedom and hold bad actors accountable for poor behavior. Two good examples of American-led foreign policy in the past few decades are George H. W. Bush's handling of the 1990–1991 Gulf War (the first Iraq War) and President Biden's handling of Russia's invasion of Ukraine. In the Gulf War, President Bush worked with the international community, built a group of allies, and gave Iraq clear demands and consequences. The free world acted together. The same can be said of the current situation in Ukraine. When Russia invaded Ukraine in early 2022, violating its territorial integrity and international rights, President Biden did an exceptional job of bringing together like-minded allies to hold Russia's President Putin and Russia accountable for their barbaric behavior. We do our finest work when we collaborate with other nations and hold bad actors accountable.

James Mattis, a well-regarded retired Marine Corps four-star general and President Donald Trump's first Secretary of Defense, said in his new book: "To preserve our leadership role, we needed to get our own country's act together first, especially if we were to help others…. An oft-spoken admonition in the Marines is this: 'When you're going to a gunfight, bring all your friends with guns.' Having fought many times in coalitions, I believe we need every ally we can bring to the fight. From imaginative military solutions to their country's vote in the U.N., the more allies, the better. I have never been on a crowded battlefield, and there is always room for those who want to be there alongside us."[251]

I completely agree with Secretary Mattis. Having friends around the world is a good thing, and the next President should work to foster great relationships across the globe.

2. EXPAND THE PEACE CORPS BUDGET FROM $410.5 MILLION TO $10.4 BILLION.[252]

Congress should take $10 billion of the $200 billion that we will save in the Defense Department and create an expanded Peace Corps 2.0. In one of his columns, *New York Times* columnist Thomas Friedman explained, "If the Army, Navy, Air Force, Coast Guard, and Marine Corps constitute our 'defense,' the Peace Corps would be our 'offense.' Its primary task would be to work at the village and neighborhood levels to help create economic opportunity and improve governance, helping more people to live decently in their home countries and not feel forced to move to other nations."[253] As an example, Friedman wrote about the Arab awakening in May 2012: "During that time, the United States made two financial commitments to the Arab world that each began with the numbers 1 and 3. It gave Egypt's military $1.3 billion worth of tanks and fighter jets, and it gave Lebanese public school students a $13.5 million merit-based college scholarship program that is currently putting 117 Lebanese kids through local American-style colleges that promote tolerance, gender, and social equality…. The $13.5 million in full scholarships has already bought America so much more friendship and stability than the $1.3 billion in tanks and fighter jets ever will…. Jumana Jbar, an English teacher in a public school in Amman, Jordan summed it up better than I ever could: One is 'for making people,' she said, 'and the other is for killing people.'"[254]

We must try different things as a nation if we want different results. Elevating the Peace Corps and spending part of our defense savings on building hope around the world would be a new approach and a worthy investment. If the Peace Corps 2.0 approach works, it could significantly impact United States foreign policy for the next 50 years. If it fails, it could be shut down after a two-year trial period.

3. AMERICAN TROOPS ON THE GROUND AS A LAST RESORT.

The President should commit to putting troops on the ground as a last resort to solve any international problem. We learned in Vietnam, Iraq, and Afghanistan that we could not use our massive military might to solve all problems. At the same time, if we cannot solve a crisis through diplomacy, and if force is necessary, I strongly believe in the "Powell

Doctrine" of overwhelming force. We have massive military power, and if, as a last resort, it needs to be used, the President should have a clear objective, make sure that we have as many friends on the team as possible, and use overwhelming force to accomplish that objective.

4. WORK HARD TO BE AN EXAMPLE FOR THE REST OF THE WORLD.
The most powerful tool we have in our foreign policy toolbox is to be a positive example for the rest of the world. President Ronald Reagan described America as a shining city upon a hill. **I firmly believe our best days are ahead of us if we do the hard work and if we make the difficult decisions that need to be made. The best thing we can do to improve our foreign policy is to become a more perfect nation at home.** From the outside, people see a good America and a bad America:

THE GOOD AMERICA:

- The American Revolution was led by an incredible group of Founding Fathers who put the country's success ahead of their own and who founded a democracy that has been the envy of the world.
- America has had a long history of welcoming immigrants.
- America was one of the first nations to make public education available to all.
- America helped save large parts of the world from tyranny in World War I and World War II. After the wars, we helped to rebuild. We have a rich tradition of helping other nations who need help.
- Our Government put the first man on the moon and helped to create many of the leading technologies that have helped change the world and make our economy prosper, including the internet.
- America stared down the Soviet Union and communism for more than 40 years.

THE BAD AMERICA:

- America has 5 percent of the world's population and produces nearly 30 percent of the carbon dioxide in the atmosphere.[255]

- The United States has the largest prison population per capita in the industrialized world.[256] We have six times the amount of our citizens locked up in jails per capita compared to Canada and nine times compared to Germany.

- Our health-care costs are two times that of any other wealthy nation, and for that, we have one of the worst life expectancies in the modern world, and our children's health ranks 47th out of 50 countries.[257]

- The Organization for Economic Co-operation and Development (OECD) indicates that the United States has "substantially higher and more extreme" poverty and inequality compared to other high-income countries.[258]

- Our homicide rate is among the worst in the world when compared to other higher-income nations. Some people are scared to visit our country.[259]

In the 248 years that we have existed as a country, we have made some mistakes, but during our history, we have done more to liberate people from tyranny and poverty than any country in history. We can take great pride that America has made the world a better place. As our world becomes smaller, as technology increases the speed of our world, and as we face big issues like climate change and nuclear sanity, the future of the world depends on American leadership. The world is not a zero-sum game. For every winner, there does not need to be a loser. For every growing economy, there does not need to be a shrinking one.

Our security and prosperity have the best chance when other countries are also successful.

We should use the foreign policy of the United States to build positive relationships around the globe to make our world more secure and prosperous. When America helps to create a global environment where countries are more secure and prosperous, hundreds of millions of lives can be positively impacted. That impact, in turn, can have a positive effect on America.

10

Reduce Gun Deaths in America

> "At the end of the day, the students at my school felt one shared experience—our politicians abandoned us by failing to keep guns out of schools."
>
> —Cameron Kasky, a 17-year-old student who survived the mass shooting at Marjory Stoneman Douglas High School in Parkland, Florida, in 2018[260]

We have a problem with gun violence in America. In 2020, 45,222 people died from gunshot wounds in the United States.[261] This number translates into 14.6 gun deaths per 100,000 people, including suicides and murders, according to a Pew Research Center report in April 2023.[262] By comparison, Australia reported one gun death per 100,000 population.[263] That means you are more than 14 times more likely to be shot and killed in the United States than in Australia. In Japan in 2017, only

0.04 of every 100,000 people were gun death victims, according to the Institute for Health Metrics and Evaluation.[264] **Your chances of being shot and killed in the United States are 300 times more likely than in Japan. Firearms recently became the number one cause of death for children in the United States, surpassing motor vehicle deaths. The leaders of our country have done nothing to address a problem that will most likely kill another 45,000 people in the coming year. Just think about it. In the next 365 days, more than 45,000 people in the United States will die of gunshot wounds. We know this, and our leaders are doing nothing about it. In Australia that number will be 3,478, and in Japan that number will be 150, and our leaders have done nothing to solve the problem.**[265]

Why is the United States so much more violent than any other wealthy nation? Why are your chances of being shot so much higher in the United States than in any other wealthy nation? The answer is that, unlike any other civilized country in the world, we lack simple gun control laws. **Our leaders have failed to protect us. If we really care about the 45,000 people dying every year, if we really care about the 85,000 people being injured every year,**[266] **if we really truly want our children to be safe at school, if we truly want people to be able to go to concerts or sporting events or high school graduations and feel safe, then we have to change our gun laws.** My belief that we need to change our gun laws is based on the following facts:

1. WE ARE THE MOST VIOLENT HIGH-INCOME COUNTRY IN THE WORLD. NO OTHER COUNTRY IS EVEN CLOSE.

Why are gun deaths in Australia so low? I will give you two guesses: (A) They have the same gun laws as the United States, but they have really nice people, or (B) They had a big gun problem in Australia, and the Government changed the laws in 1996 to ban all automatic and semi-automatic weapons.[267] If you picked B, you are the winner! The sad truth is that the United States is one of the most violent countries in the world, and our leaders have done nothing to solve the problem.

Rates of Firearm Homicides Per 100,000 Population

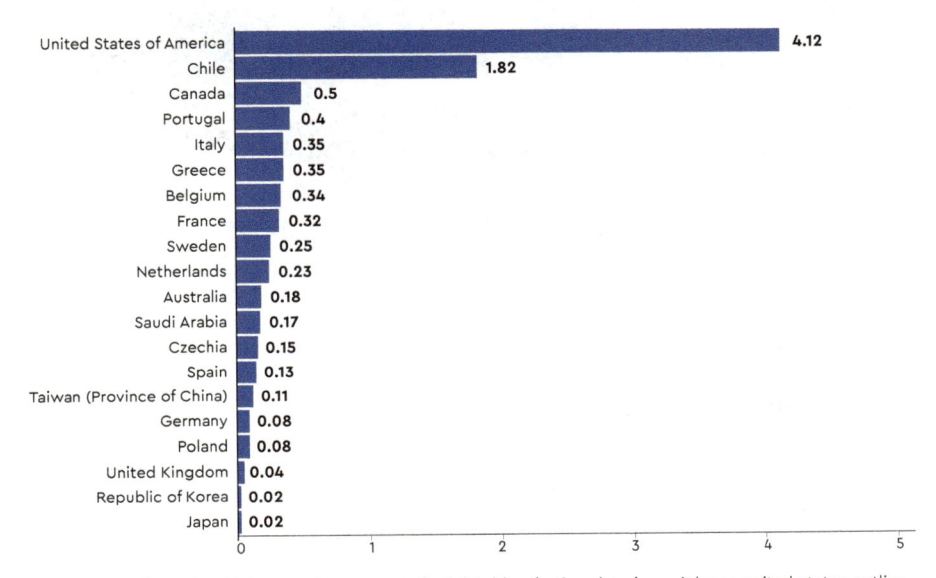

Country	Rate
United States of America	4.12
Chile	1.82
Canada	0.5
Portugal	0.4
Italy	0.35
Greece	0.35
Belgium	0.34
France	0.32
Sweden	0.25
Netherlands	0.23
Australia	0.18
Saudi Arabia	0.17
Czechia	0.15
Spain	0.13
Taiwan (Province of China)	0.11
Germany	0.08
Poland	0.08
United Kingdom	0.04
Republic of Korea	0.02
Japan	0.02

Source: https://www.healthdata.org/news-events/insights-blog/acting-data/gun-violence-united-states-outlier
Among World Bank high-income countries with a population greater than 10 million. Age-standardized rates.

2. GUN VIOLENCE COSTS THE U.S. ECONOMY MORE THAN $557 BILLION ANNUALLY.[268] Just think about the health-care costs of taking care of the more than 85,000 people who are shot every year but survive—productivity lost from those who cannot work, jail costs for those who ruin lives by using firearms, police costs, etc. Just ask any mayor of "Big City, U.S.A.," what would happen to their police budgets if the gun control laws in this country were the same as in any other civilized country and the amount of gun violence decreased by 90 percent. They would tell you their budgets could be significantly less than they currently are. I went to a high school graduation a few years ago, and lurking in the background were two sheriff's cars and an ambulance. At a high school graduation? Who is paying the cost to have these resources at a high school graduation in case of a shooting? In another example, last month I took a friend to the emergency room in Santa Barbara on a beautiful Friday afternoon. Before we could get into the emergency room we were greeted by three security officers,

Cause of Death for U.S. Children and Teens in 2020

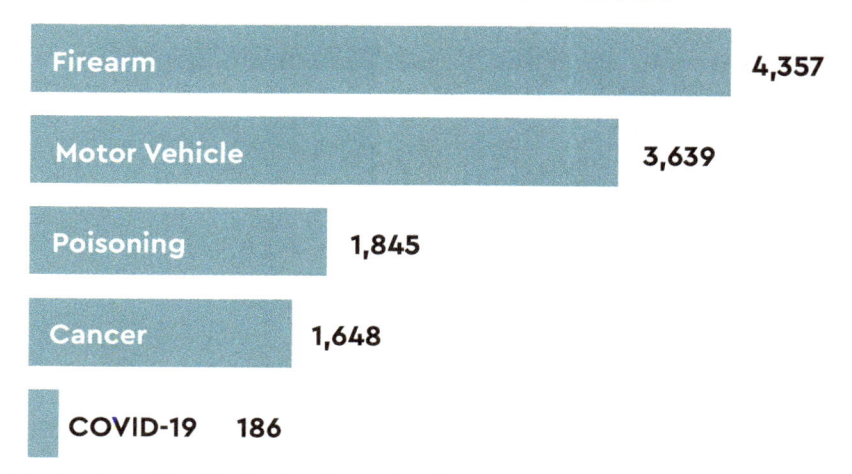

Cause	Count
Firearm	4,357
Motor Vehicle	3,639
Poisoning	1,845
Cancer	1,648
COVID-19	186

Sources: https://www.kff.org/health-reform/press-release/firearms-are-the-leading-cause-of-death-for-children-in-the-united-states-but-rank-no-higher-than-fifth-in-other-industrialized-nations/

As of 2020, https://everytownresearch.org/graph/firearms-are-the-leading-cause-of-death-for-american-children-and-teens/

passed through a metal detector and hand wanded. In what other country do you think you need to go through security to enter an emergency room? **As a nation with $34 trillion in debt and spending almost twice as much on health care as any other Western country, we cannot afford the cost of having more than 130,000 of our fellow citizens killed or injured by firearms every year.**

Costs incurred directly as a result of gun violence in the U.S. top $557 billion.[269] In addition, there are costs that people and organizations incur to try to protect themselves against gun violence. The industry to make your school safe from guns is booming—high-tech security systems, resource officers, $2.1 million panic-alert systems, classroom lockdown kits, weapons training for educators, and more. In 2021, this industry (not including sales of bulletproof doors or backpacks) was worth an estimated $3.1 billion and is expected to grow at least 8 percent annually.[270] Schools are spending hundreds of millions of dollars to prepare for gun violence at taxpayer expense. Our friends in the U.K., Germany, and Japan pay for none of this. They have common sense gun control laws that we lack.

A friend of mine was a teacher in Colorado for more than 20 years. Because of the significant increase in gun violence in schools, she was given a classroom lockdown kit that included six sanitation bags, two pairs of vinyl gloves, 30 moist towelettes, one 5-by-7-foot vinyl privacy tarp, duct tape, one toilet paper roll, and a toilet seat lid so that the bucket, which contains all of the materials, can double as a toilet. (For the elementary students, they also threw in a bag of lollipops "to keep the kids calm.") **How embarrassing is it that our teachers need a lockdown kit because we lack simple gun control laws? If you want to have the best teachers in the world, do you think they are motivated by lockdown kit training?**

3. THE TREND IS NOT OUR FRIEND. IT KEEPS GETTING WORSE.

In 2022, we witnessed a year of gun violence in America that is hard to believe. The start of 2023 was even worse. In late January, over a period of 44 hours, three mass shootings in California left 19 dead and dozens of others injured. According to the Gun Violence Archive and reported on by *Forbes* magazine, the first half of 2023 saw more than 300 mass shootings across the U.S.[271]

On May 6, 2023, in Allen, Texas, a gunman opened fire at a crowded mall outside Dallas, killing at least eight people and injuring at least seven before a police officer killed him. On May 29, 2023, in Hollywood, Florida, at least nine people were wounded on Memorial Day when gunfire erupted between two groups near a beach. And on July 2, 2023, two people died and at least 28 others were injured in a shooting at a block party in Baltimore.[272]

I was watching *60 Minutes*, and there was a segment on Olena Zelenska, the First Lady of Ukraine. She was talking about the war's violence and its impact on students, and she said, "Around 3,500 schools will operate online only because schools cannot receive students and because their parents are afraid to send their children to school. Ukraine's children went to school this year, and the first thing they learned is where the bomb shelter is, how to get there, and what to do in case a missile strikes. We will fight. We will not give our children up."[273]

Deaths in U.S. Mass Shootings

September 29, 2019–May 24, 2022

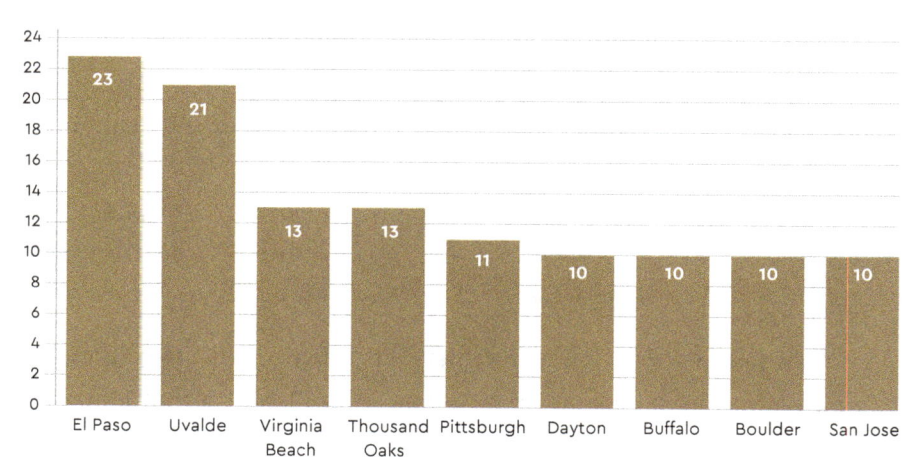

Location	Deaths
El Paso	23
Uvalde	21
Virginia Beach	13
Thousand Oaks	13
Pittsburgh	11
Dayton	10
Buffalo	10
Boulder	10
San Jose	10

Source: https://www.cbsnews.com/chicago/news/mass-shootings-in-america-by-the-numbers/

When I saw this on *60 Minutes,* and when I see all the mass shootings in schools across America, I ask myself, *Have we given up on our children? Have we failed our children by not taking on gun violence and turning it from a political tug-of-war to instead an objective discussion based on the facts?* **It doesn't make sense to me that after Columbine, Sandy Hook, Marjory Stoneman Douglas, Uvalde, and many other mass shootings, we send our children off to school in the morning and wonder if they will come home in the afternoon.**

What have we done as a nation to fix this problem? Nothing. Ezra Klein, writing for *The Washington Post,* put it best:

> If roads were collapsing all across the United States, killing dozens of drivers, we would surely see that as a moment to talk about what we could do to keep the roads from collapsing. If terrorists were detonating bombs in port after port, you can be sure Congress would be working to upgrade the nation's security measures. If a plague were ripping through communities, public health officials would be working feverishly to contain it.

Only with gun violence do we respond to repeated tragedies by saying that mourning is acceptable but discussing how to prevent more tragedies is not.... Talking about how to stop mass shootings in the aftermath of a string of mass shootings isn't "too soon." It's much too late.[274]

4. THE WORLD HAS CHANGED SINCE THE SECOND AMENDMENT OF THE CONSTITUTION WAS RATIFIED IN 1791. The Second Amendment of our Nation's Constitution does not guarantee the right of citizens to walk around our streets with assault rifles.

The Second Amendment states: **"A well-regulated militia, being necessary to the security of a free state, the right of the people to keep and bear arms, shall not be infringed."**[275] Do we really think our Founding Fathers would support semi-automatic rifles that disperse 20 bullets in as many seconds? Their intent was the protection of the Nation at a time when there were relatively few people in the military, and citizens had to be prepared to fight for their country. Think of Paul Revere riding his horse to warn his fellow colonists that "The British are coming!" At that point in time, our emerging Nation needed citizens like Paul Revere to be armed to protect itself.

Today, we have the Army, the Air Force, the Navy, the Marines, and the Coast Guard to protect our Nation. In addition, we have police in every city across our country. Do we need citizens armed with semi-automatic assault rifles to protect our country?

1 million

Nearly one million women alive today have been shot or shot at by an intimate partner.

Source: Sorenson S. B., Schut R. A. Nonfatal gun use in intimate partner violence: A systematic review of the literature. "Trauma Violence Abuse," 2016. https://pubmed.ncbi.nlm.nih.gov/27630138/

Second Amendment supporters frequently quote the Constitution stating that "the right of the people to keep and bear arms shall not be infringed." They forget to mention the words that precede that phrase in the same sentence: 'A well-regulated militia, being necessary to the security of a free state ... the right of the people to keep and bear arms shall not be infringed." The late Chief Justice Warren Burger, a conservative appointed by a Republican president, said in a 1991 PBS interview that the Second Amendment "has been the subject of one of the greatest pieces of fraud, I repeat the word fraud, on the American public by special interest groups that I have ever seen in my lifetime."[276]

5. OUR CHILDREN ARE NOT SAFE AT SCHOOL. Do you think the statement is true or false? I believe it is true. I do not think our children are safe when they go off to school, and here are just some of the reasons why:

1. Columbine High School: April 1999, 13 killed, 24 injured
2. Santana High School: March 2001, 2 killed, 13 injured
3. Virginia Tech: April 2007, 32 killed, dozens injured
4. Sandy Hook Elementary School: December 2012, 26 killed, 1 injured
5. Marjory Stoneman Douglas High School: February 2018, 17 killed, 17 injured
6. Marshall County High School: January 2018, 2 killed, 20 injured
7. Santa Fe High School: May 2018, 10 killed, 14 injured
8. STEM School Highlands Ranch: May 2019, 1 killed, 8 injured
9. Robb Elementary School: May 2022, 21 killed, 17 injured
10. St. Louis Performing Arts High School: October 2022, 2 killed, 7 injured
11. Michigan State University: February 2023, 3 killed, 5 injured[277]

School shootings almost never happen in any other country in the world. The only thing worse than the tragic loss of our children's lives is the complete inability of the adults in the room to solve the problem. It is so bad that after the Uvalde, Texas, elementary school shootings—when 19 students were shot dead along with two adults and another 17 were injured—the response from the state of Texas was to pass a law where school districts are distributing DNA kits to parents according to the *Houston Chronicle* in October 2022. The kits are being made available so that parents can identify their children's bodies in the event of another school mass shooting. One parent likened the DNA kits he received from the Clear Creek Independent School District to those used prior to soldiers deploying to Iraq or Afghanistan. "Some families have found the [DNA test kits] program chilling, considering that police asked parents waiting to find out if their children were slaughtered at Robb Elementary on May 24 to provide DNA samples to help identify the dead," the *Houston Chronicle* reports.[278] The fact is that if your child goes off to school, you cannot be 100 percent certain that they will be coming home. I don't think that is acceptable in the United States of America. We should not only be embarrassed, but we should also take immediate action.

6. THE MAJORITY OF AMERICANS SUPPORT COMMON-SENSE MEASURES TO PREVENT GUN VIOLENCE. Polls in 2021 showed that 84 percent of Americans support expanding background checks on gun purchases.[279] Yet the gun lobby protects the views of the 16 percent who disagree. Is our Government elected to represent the 84 percent majority or the 16 percent minority? The National Rifle Association has convinced its members that any kind of gun control is the same as having all of your guns taken away.

....

As citizens, we are paying a price for poor leadership. In this case, poor leadership is costing 45,000 people a year their lives, another 85,000 people are being shot but are not dying, and the cost, both emotional and financial, is crippling our country. Yet, a small well-financed group is getting in the way of the people's government from solving the problem. The United States needs a President who can level with the American people, share the facts, and propose the Gabby Giffords Violence Reduction Act of 2025. The simple solutions in this proposed legislation are as follows:

1. BAN ALL ASSAULT WEAPONS AND EXTENDED MAGAZINES. The Glock 19 semi-automatic pistol that was used in the 2011 shooting of U.S. Representative Gabby Giffords emptied 33 rounds in less than 30 seconds.[280]

These were the guns used in some of the recent 2022 mass shootings:

- Buffalo, NY: 10 dead in a supermarket with an AR-15 style rifle[281]
- Uvalde, TX: 21 dead in an elementary school with an AR-15 style rifle[282]
- Highland Park, IL: 7 dead at a 4th of July parade with an AR-15 style rifle[283]
- Greenwood, IN: 4 dead in a mall food court with a Sig Sauer M400 semi-automatic rifle, an AR-15 semi-automatic style rifle, and a Glock 33 semi-automatic pistol[284]
- Brooklyn, NY: 10 shot on a subway with a Glock semi-automatic pistol[285]
- Colorado Springs, CO: 5 dead at a nightclub with a .223 Remington AR-15 style rifle[286]
- Chesapeake, VA: 6 dead at a Walmart with a 9mm semi-automatic pistol[287]

The gun that was used in Congresswoman Gabby Giffords' shooting

emptied 33 rounds
in less than 30 seconds

2. ASSAULT WEAPON BUY-BACK PROGRAM. In addition to banning civilian ownership of all assault weapons, the Gabby Giffords Violence Reduction Act of 2025 will get all assault weapons off the streets by launching a program to buy back all of these weapons. People who own assault weapons will be paid the current value or the price that they paid to purchase the gun, whichever is higher. In 1996, Australia banned assault rifles and extended magazines, and the homicide rate plummeted 59 percent over the next decade.[288]

3. IMPOSE A UNIVERSAL BACKGROUND CHECK ON 100 PERCENT OF GUNS PURCHASED AND SET UP A NATIONWIDE DATABASE OF GUN OWNERS. An estimated 22 percent of guns are acquired without a background check.[289] Recent polls show 92 percent of Americans think background checks should also be required for people who buy guns in private transactions or at gun shows.[290] Let's give the people what they want and require that all gun owners have a background check.

Here's an example of why all gun sales should require a background check. The shooter in the 2019 Odessa, Texas, mass shooting, who killed eight people and wounded 25 others, had been determined in court to be mentally unfit to own a gun, was stopped from purchasing a weapon from a licensed gun dealer in 2014. But thanks to a loophole in the law, he bought his rifle through a private sale, not covered by Federal background check requirements.[291]

Currently in America, any time a police officer wants to connect a gun to its owner, the request ends up at the National Tracing Center in Martinsburg, West Virginia. On any given day, agents are running about 1,500 traces on a shoestring budget, sorting through boxes of paper records, thanks to a law the NRA worked to get Congress to pass in 1986, preventing a simple, searchable database of gun owners from being established.[292]

4. REQUIRE MANDATORY GUN LICENSES FOR GUN OWNERS. Guns should be treated the same as cars. Why do you need to get a license to drive and get a car registered? Because driving a car is a big responsibility,

About 22 percent of purchased guns require no background check.

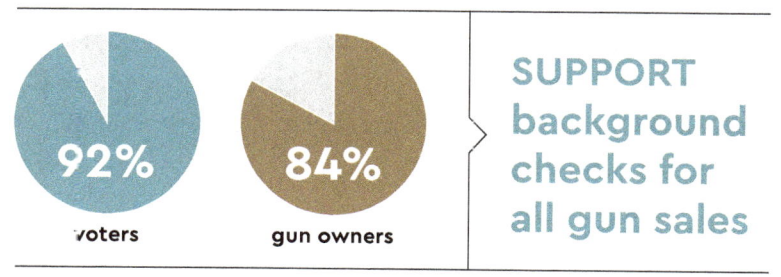

92% voters   **84%** gun owners   > **SUPPORT background checks for all gun sales**

Source: https://news.gallup.com/poll/1645/guns.aspx; https://www.npr.org/2022/07/08/1110239487/most-gun-owners-favor-modest-restrictions-but-deeply-distrust-government-poll-fi

and if you misuse the car, you can cause serious damage to yourself and others. Operating a gun is as dangerous as operating a car, if not more so. People should have to get a license to have a gun. It is in everyone's interest to make sure that everyone who has a gun is capable of safe gun ownership. Right now, you can go to a gun show and buy a gun and never have to get it registered. That would be like having to get a registration for a new car but not for a used one. The NRA has convinced Congress that it is a bad thing to require guns to be registered. It is not a bad thing; it is a common-sense practice that would benefit all Americans, whether you own a gun or not.

5. REPEAL THE PROTECTION OF LAWFUL COMMERCE IN ARMS ACT.

This law bans lawsuits against gun manufacturers and sellers for the harm they cause and immunizes the gun industry from responsibility for the thousands of U.S. gun deaths every year. In the 2017 Las Vegas shooting, in which nearly 60 people were massacred and hundreds more injured,[293] the hotel and the concert organizers are being sued. Still, the 2005 Protection of Lawful Commerce in Arms Act, supported by the NRA, has shielded the gun industry from lawsuits.[294]

The NRA only represents about five million of the 105 million Americans who own guns. Ninety-two percent of Americans favor requiring background checks for all gun sales, 81 percent support red flag laws, and 77 percent support a waiting period for purchasing a gun.[295] The American public wants the issue of gun violence addressed. American citizens should not live in fear when they go out in public, and they should not have to worry when they send their kids off to school in the morning if they will see them at the end of the day.

In a TV interview, Susan Orfanos, whose son was killed in the Thousand Oaks, California, shooting after surviving the Las Vegas massacre, said she doesn't want prayers. "I don't want thoughts. I want gun control, and I hope to God nobody sends me any more prayers."[296]

The Gabby Giffords Violence Reduction Act of 2025 is the kind of legislation that we should expect from our leaders. No prayers, no thoughts—just simple, clear, bold legislation so we can regulate guns the same way we regulate cars and end the madness.

We can save tens of thousands of lives, we can prevent more than 100,000 people from being shot every year, we can help prevent further misery for the hundreds of thousands of American families who have lost loved ones to gun violence, and we can save the Nation billions of dollars in health-care costs by showing some leadership and changing our gun laws.

11

Fix the Legal System

"Equal justice under the law is not merely a caption on the facade of the Supreme Court building. It is perhaps the most inspiring ideal in our society."

—Former U.S. Supreme Court Justice Lewis F. Powell Jr.[297]

A large number of lawyers in America are feasting on a flawed system, and because they make a significant amount of money and because they donate substantial sums of money to political candidates, they keep the system intact. In fact, as time goes on, the legal system gets worse. The worse the system is, the more the legal profession benefits. Our legal system is broken in two major ways: (1) it allows anyone to sue anyone for anything without consequences, and (2) we lock up more human beings in cages than any other wealthy nation by a long shot. The combination of our legal system and corrupt political system has given us the prison-industrial complex, where the United States currently has less than 5 percent of the world's population but nearly 25 percent of the world's prison population. We have 2.2 million people locked up, 9 million people who move in and out of our jails, and more than 70 million American citizens with conviction histories.[298]

What facts exist to prove that our legal system needs an overhaul?

1. WE HAVE TOO MANY LAWYERS. The late Warren Burger, U.S. Supreme Court chief justice, predicted 40 years ago that America was turning into "a society overrun by hordes of lawyers, hungry as locusts." According to *The Boston Globe*, May 9, 2014, "With 1.3 million lawyers ... the United States is choking on litigation, regulation, and disputation."[299] How do we fare compared to other countries in the number of lawyers per capita?

The U.S. has one lawyer for every 248 inhabitants while Germany has one lawyer for every 516 people.[300]

2. WE HAVE MORE PRISONERS PER CAPITA THAN ANY COUNTRY IN THE WORLD. The United States has 2.2 million people locked behind bars—a 500 percent increase over the past 40 years. This equates to 629 people in jail or prison for every 100,000.[301] Meanwhile, Russia has 326 per 100,000; the U.K. has 131 prisoners per 100,000; China has 119 per 100,000; Canada has 104 per 100,000; and Germany has 70 per 100,000.[302] Either these countries are doing something right that we are missing, or there are a lot of people roaming their streets who should be locked up.

3. WE ARE SPENDING A LOT OF MONEY LOCKING PEOPLE UP. According to a publication by the Prison Policy Initiative, the total cost of America's public prison system is approaching $81 billion every year.[303] If the total number of inmates in the United States is approximately 2.2 million, that means the average cost of locking someone up in the United States is roughly $37,000 per year. Just imagine, if we had half the prison population, we would free up more than $40 billion a year that we could put into public schools, our transportation system, finding a solution to climate change, debt reduction, tax relief, or the national parks.

4. OUR LEGAL SYSTEM ALLOWS ANYONE TO SUE ANYONE ELSE WITH NO CONSEQUENCES. In a small Southern California community, a neighborhood group put in speed bumps to slow down traffic and improve safety. A teenager riding a motorized scooter over the speed limit hit a speed bump and crashed. The parents sued the neighborhood association for more than $1 million, and the neighbors settled for $250,000 on the advice of their lawyers.

Trek was sued for patent infringement on a bicycle design. We actually had a real example of the prototype we had independently developed before the patent in question was filed and a mountain of other evidence that we did not infringe. We won the case only after spending $3 million in legal fees. Or how about the Trek retailer who held a special event for women? A male consumer sued him for discrimination because he was not invited to the event. The retailer settled the case for $17,000 because his lawyer told him that if he fought it, he could lose more than $100,000. These are just three stories out of hundreds of thousands more about how our legal system lacks common sense, is overly bureaucratic, and never gets updated or improved. It just gets worse with time. The winners in this game are lawyers, and the losers are citizens who pay higher and higher prices for products to cover the cost of a flawed legal system that lawyers take advantage of.

....

The next President should put partisan politics aside and make two modifications to our judicial system that would be in the best long-term interest of the United States:

1. REQUIRE LOSERS OF LITIGATION TO PAY ATTORNEY FEES AND LITIGATION COSTS OF THE WINNER. In the United States, we have a massive number of lawsuits because people can sue anyone for anything with no personal risk. Why so many lawsuits? Because lawyers encourage people to file lawsuits by not charging them any money unless they win. And if they win, they take a percentage of the winnings. Neither the person filing the lawsuit nor the lawyer taking the case has any real risk. By making one simple change and adopting the "English rule," where the losing party could be required to pay the legal fees and the prevailing party's costs, we would reduce lawsuits in this country by 50 to 75 percent.

Every other Western democracy uses some variation of the English rule for a reason. Many countries around the world have copied parts of our Government. Yet, no country has followed our process for suing people. None. If we adopt the English rule in the United States, lawyers would not want to take on frivolous cases they did not think they could win because they would have some financial risk. The result would be a significant reduction in the number of court cases in our system, the cases would be dealt with much faster, and Americans would be less likely to be subject to baseless or weak lawsuits. Also, consumers would not be affected by increased prices from businesses that need to cover their costs in fighting frivolous lawsuits.

2. SET THE GOAL OF REDUCING THE PRISON POPULATION IN THE UNITED STATES BY 50 PERCENT BY THE END OF 2028. We cannot spend $81 billion a year locking up 629 people per 100,000 while the rest of the Western world averages fewer than 150 people per 100,000 in prison, according to the World Prison Brief, an online database that uses United Nations statistics.[304]

The next President could accomplish this by making the following changes:

- **REDUCE SENTENCES FOR NONVIOLENT CRIMES, ESPECIALLY DRUG USERS.** There are 353,000 people currently incarcerated because of drug-related offenses.[305] I believe there is a major opportunity to review all nonviolent Americans in prison and work with the legislative and judicial branches to figure out how we can reduce the nonviolent prison population. Let me be clear: I believe there is a significant opportunity to reduce our overall prison population. I am also a firm believer that no one is above the law. The recent crime wave in cities is unacceptable, and everyone in our society should be held accountable to the rule of the law.

Nonviolent Drug Users in Prison

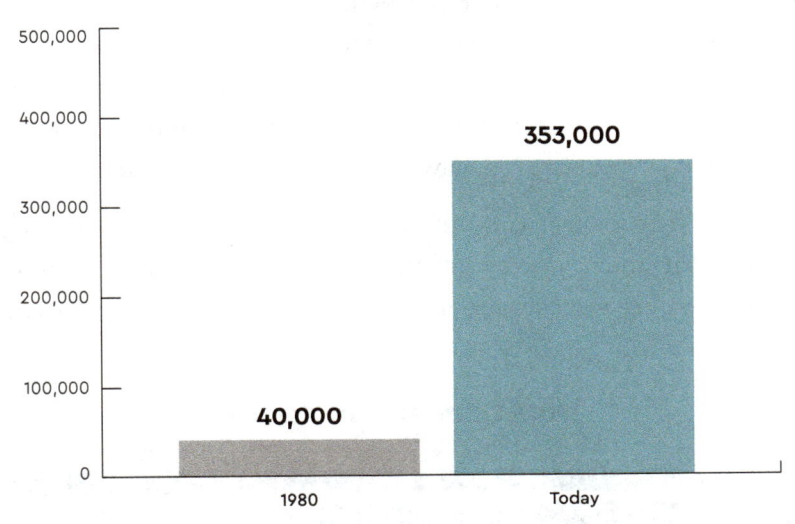

1980	40,000
Today	353,000

Sources: https://www.prisonpolicy.org/graphs/pie2023_drugs.html; https://www.fedbar.org/wp-content/uploads/2015/09/Sidebar-pdf-1.pdf

- **CHANGE THE BAIL SYSTEM IN THE UNITED STATES.** Many of our citizens can't pay bail, so they sit in jail. For example, two people are accused of the same crime. One has money and the other doesn't. The one with money hires a good lawyer and gets out on bail the same day. The second one sits in jail for up to six months—or longer—and gets a court-appointed attorney. Adding insult to injury, the bail business is extremely lucrative and produces over $2 billion in profits per year.[306] I had dinner with a friend recently who told me the story of his son who was addicted to opioids. His son got into a bunch of trouble, and each time my friend was able to have his attorney get his son out of jail. The story ends well, and his son has been clean for the past 10 years, has a job, is married, and has a great family. What if my friend's son did not come from a family of wealth? Where would he be today? Odds are in prison. The next President should propose that we overhaul the bail system so everyone receives the same treatment regardless of economic status.

- **ALLOW FEDERAL AND STATE JUDGES TO USE THEIR DISCRETION DURING THE SENTENCING PROCESS.** Judges are professionals, and they know their business better than legislators. Two Supreme Court justices have expressed disapproval of mandatory sentences. The late Chief Justice William Rehnquist said mandatory sentences are "a good example of the law of unintended consequences."[307]

Former Chief Justice Anthony Kennedy said, "I think I'm in agreement with most judges in the federal system that mandatory minimums are an imprudent, unwise, and often unjust mechanism for sentencing."[308]

Incarceration Rates

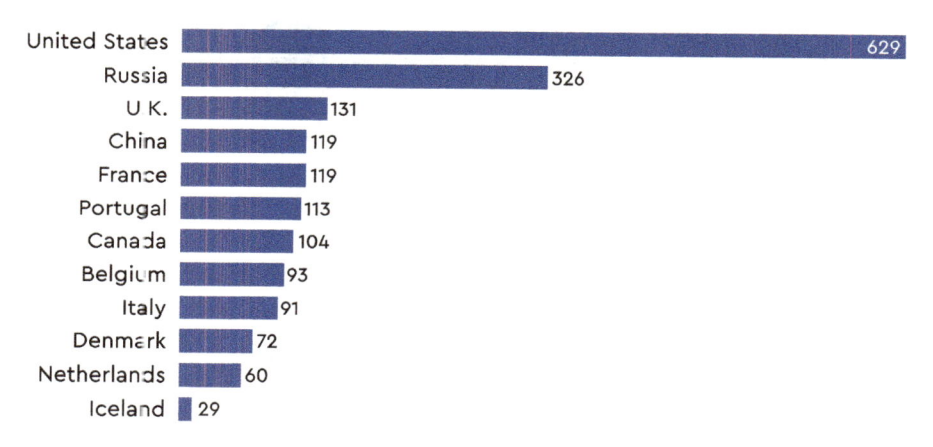

United States	629
Russia	326
U.K.	131
China	119
France	119
Portugal	113
Canada	104
Belgium	93
Italy	91
Denmark	72
Netherlands	60
Iceland	29

Incarceration rates per 100,000 population

Source: https://www.prisonstudies.org/sites/default/files/resources/downloads/world_prison_population_list_13th_edition.pdf

A great essay was written by retired Denver District Court Judge Morris Hoffman, who in 1995 sentenced a teenage armed robber to 146 years in prison. In an article published in *The Wall Street Journal*, February 17, 2019, he wrote about the injustice of extreme sentences.[309]

I think that Judge Hoffman's story is a very important one for Americans to understand:

In 1995, I sentenced a teenage armed robber to 146 years in prison. Believe it or not, that was just a little over the mandatory minimum sentence. With good time and "early" release on parole, he could be out as soon as 2065, having served a little less than 70 years. He'll be almost 90. The teenager's crime was horrible. He robbed a small restaurant at gunpoint, ordered the patrons onto the floor and ended up having a shootout with one customer who happened to have a gun. Miraculously, the only person injured was the robber, who was shot in the foot....

Today, we lead the Western world in average length of prison sentences, at 63 months. According to the Justice Policy Institute, Canada's average is four months, Finland's 10, Germany's 12, and rugged, individualistic Australia's average prison term is 36 months.

These numbers are even more striking considering that the modern prison is an American invention and the average sentence started out at a few months, not years. The Quakers invented prisons in the late 1700s as a more humane alternative to death or banishment, then the punishment for all serious crimes. But the penitentiary wasn't intended to be a criminal warehouse. Criminals were expected to work, pray and think about their crimes—to be penitent about them in a kind of moral rehabilitation.... A 1785 New York statute was typical: It limited all non-homicide prison sentences to six months. French diplomat and historian Alexis de Tocqueville, whose visits to America began with a tour of U.S. prisons in 1831, wrote, "In no country is criminal justice administered with more mildness than in the United States." But over the next 150 years, America went from mildest punisher to harshest...

We have a duty to punish wrongdoers, but that duty comes with the obligation not to punish criminals more than they deserve. Much of our criminal justice system has lost that moral grounding, and our use of prisons has become extreme.... It won't be easy. No one gets elected by calling for shorter prison sentences. But as a policy matter, there is simply no evidence that, say, a 70-year sentence for aggravated robbery does more than a 30-year sentence to deter other potential robbers. Moreover, violent crime rates decrease rapidly as criminals age out of their 20s. Releasing a middle-aged prisoner earlier does pose more risk, of course, than keeping him behind bars, but that marginal danger will be very small indeed when we are comparing 30-year and 70-year sentences.[310]

I agree with Judge Hoffman that "no one gets elected by calling for shorter prison sentences." And yet, I believe that if we want change in our country, we need to be open to new ideas. We need to focus on the facts and make decisions in the best long-term interest of the people. Shorter prison sentences is an issue that should be discussed in the campaign, and voters should look at the facts and respect leaders who have the courage to challenge conventional thinking. From 1983 to 2013, according to a report from The Pew Charitable Trusts, the United States became more punitive by 165 percent.[311]

Enacting these proposals would save taxpayers more than $40 billion a year in prison costs and would trigger a significant increase in the economy because businesses would not have to worry about defending themselves against frivolous lawsuits.

12

Embrace the Immigration Advantage

"I am a beneficiary of the American people's generosity, and I hope we can have comprehensive immigration legislation that allows this country to continue to be enriched by those who were not born here."

—Madeleine Albright, the first woman to serve as U.S. Secretary of State, 1997–2001[312]

The Statue of Liberty is one of the great monuments in our Nation. It depicts a robed woman representing Libertas (Roman goddess of freedom). Libertas holds a torch above her head with her right hand, and with her left, she carries a tablet with the date July 4, 1776. At her feet lay a broken chain as she walks forward. Over the years, the Statue of Liberty has become an icon of the United States and a welcoming sight to immigrants arriving from around the world.

Here are some key facts you should know when forming an opinion on the issue of immigration:

1. AS A NATION, WE USED TO BE MORE WELCOMING TO IMMIGRANTS THAN WE ARE TODAY. In 1981, as President Reagan came into office, he faced a refugee crisis with suffering families from Cuba, Vietnam, and Cambodia. Filled with his vintage optimism, Reagan responded to the crisis with these words: "We shall seek new ways to integrate refugees into our society," and he delivered on that promise.[313]

2. A LOW-GROWTH POPULATION TREND IN THE UNITED STATES WILL MAKE LONG-TERM GROWTH DIFFICULT. Studies show that immigration boosts productivity and economic growth; restricting it has the opposite effect. Economic output is simply determined by how much each worker produces multiplied by the size of the workforce. The labor force in the United States is not growing as fast as baby boomers are retiring. The U.S. birth rate fell from 2.12 in 2007 to 1.64 in 2020.[314] It is now well below 2.1, the value considered "replacement fertility," which is the rate needed for the population to replace itself without immigration.[315] In June 2022, the U.S. Bureau of Labor Statistics reported that there were 10.7 million job openings in the United States.[316] We need help filling them.

According to the U.S. Chamber of Commerce, 2023 data showed the U.S. had close to 9 million job openings,[317] but only around six million unemployed workers.[318] If every unemployed person in the country found a job, we would still have three million open jobs. Fewer immigrants coming to the U.S. means that crucial sources of talent for American businesses are drying up, contributing to the significant workforce problems companies are currently facing.

3. IMMIGRANTS ARE ADDING VALUE TO THE AMERICAN ECONOMY. If you analyzed immigration as an investment, experts would tell you that the American people are making an excellent return on their immigration investment. Medical offices, farms, restaurants, hotels, manufacturers, and retail businesses—all sectors of the economy—benefit directly or indirectly from immigrant labor.

Occupations of Immigrants

30% of physicians

15% of nurses

17% of grocery store workers

18% of food delivery drivers

19% of truck drivers

Source: https://www.bushcenter.org/publications/resources-reports/reports/immigration-white-papers/citizenship-matters-encouraging-immigrants-to-become-americans.html

According to a fact sheet published in 2020 by Forward US (FWD.us), a centrist organization:

> Immigrants added $2 trillion to the U.S. GDP in 2016 and $458.7 billion to state, local, and federal taxes in 2018. In 2018, after immigrants spent billions of dollars on state, local, and federal taxes, they were left with $1.2 trillion in spending power, which they used to purchase goods and services, stimulating local business activity. Immigrants make significant contributions to our economy on virtually every front, including on tax revenue, where they contributed $458.7 billion to state, local, and federal taxes in 2018. This includes undocumented immigrants, who contribute roughly $11.74 billion a year in state and local taxes, including more than $7 billion in sales and excise taxes, $3.6 billion in property taxes, and $1.1 billion in personal income taxes.[319]

International Students Who Became Entrepreneurs of Billion-Dollar Companies

Name	University/Degree	Company Co-Founded/Founded	Employees	Value of Company
Ash Ashutosh	Penn State, MS Computer Science	Actifio	350	$1.1 B
Mohit Aron	Rice, PhD Computer Science	Nutanix	864	$2.0 B
Alexander Asseily	Stanford, BS/MS Electrical Engineering	Jawbone	395	$3.3 B
Noubar Afeyan	MIT, PhD Biochemical Engineering Therapeutics	Moderna	326	$3.0 B
Amr Awadallah	Stanford, PhD Electrical Engineering	Cloudera	1,100	$4.1 B
Jay Chaudhry	Univ. of Cincinnati, MBA and MS Computer Engineering, Industrial Engineering	Zscaler	600	$1.1 B
John Collison	Harvard	Stripe	380	$5.0 B
Patrick Collison*	MIT	Stripe	(380)	($5.0 B)
Nicolas Desmarais	Amherst, BA Economics & Political Science	AppDirect	400	$1.0 B
Borge Hald	Stanford, MBA, Ross School of Business (U. of Michigan), BBA	Medallia	850	$1.3 B
David Hindawi	UC–Berkeley, PhD Operations Research	Tanium	300+	$3.5 B
Tomer London	Stanford, MS Electrical Engineering Physics, Wharton School (UPENN), BS Business	Gusto	300	$1.1 B
Elon Musk	Univ. of Penn., BA, Economics & Physics	SpaceX	4,000	$12 B
Dheeraj Pandey*	Univ. of Texas, Austin, MS Computer Science	Nutanix	864	$2.0 B
Adam Neumann	CUNY Baruch College	WeWork	1,200	$10 B
Dhiraj Rajaram	Wayne State, MS Computer Engineering, Univ. of Chicago, MBA	Mu Sigma	3,500	$1.5 B
Daniel Saks*	Harvard, MA Finance & Accounting	AppDirect	(400)	($1.0 B)

Name	University/Degree	Company Co-Founded/ Founded	Employees	Value of Company
Mario Schlosser	Harvard, MBA Insurance Health	Oscar	415	$1.7 B
Eric Setton	Stanford, PhD and MS Electrical Engineering	Tango	260	$1.0 B
K.R. Sridhar	University of Illinois at Urbana–Champaign, MS Nuclear Energy Engineering, PhD Mechanical Engineering	Bloom	1,200	$2.9 B
Ragy Thomas	NYU, MBA	Sprinklr	325	$1.2 B
Renaud Visage	Cornell, MS Engineering	Eventbrite	500	$1.0 B
Michelle Zatlyn	Harvard, MBA	Cloudflare	225	$1.0 B

Source: National Foundation for American Policy, company information, CrunchBase. https://nfap.com/wp-content/uploads/2016/03/Immigrants-and-Billion-Dollar-Startups.NFAP-Policy-Brief.March-2016.pdf

*Denotes second international student from same company. Values as of January 1, 2016.

4. IMMIGRANTS START NEW COMPANIES AT TWICE THE RATE OF NON-IMMIGRANTS. According to a 2020 fact sheet published by FWD.us, 43 percent of legal immigrants had earned at least a bachelor's degree—compared to 29 percent of U.S.-born residents.[320] And one study from the National Foundation for American Policy finds that "55 percent, or 50 of 91 of the country's $1 billion startup companies, had at least one immigrant founder."[321] Other facts that further highlight this point are that immigrants represent 30 percent of new entrepreneurs while making up only 13 percent of the population and that immigrants and their children founded 45 percent of Fortune 500 companies.[322]

....

Immigration has been a major issue in America for more than 20 years, and our leaders have failed to make any progress. After reviewing the facts, I believe that the next President should implement the Statue of Liberty Immigration Act of 2025 with the understanding that immigration has been a key to our Nation's success in the past and can be an important part of our future. Here are key parts of the act:

1. TIGHTEN SECURITY ALONG THE MEXICAN BORDER. As President George W. Bush said in his May 15, 2006, address on immigration: "Our border should be open to trade and lawful immigration, shut to illegal immigrants, as well as criminals, drug dealers, and terrorists."[323] The next President, within the first 10 days of their Presidency, should travel to the U.S.-Mexico border and meet with those in charge of protecting the border and listen carefully and make sure that those in charge of securing the border have all the tools needed to get the job done. If local resources are not enough, I believe that our next President should use the military to help protect the border. We cannot have porous borders.

2. REMOVE ALL LIMITS ON H-1B VISAS TO ATTRACT HIGHLY-SKILLED FOREIGN WORKERS. The United States is an amazing country, and many people around the world want to live here. The H-1B visa program lets companies obtain visas for people with specialized knowledge in biotechnology, computing, engineering, etc. Most H-1B visa applicants must have a bachelor's degree. The next President should ask Congress to remove all quotas on H-1B visas. I believe it is in the best interest of the United States to recruit talented people from around the world and encourage them to live here. By removing limits on H-1B visas, we can attract the best and the brightest from all over the world to help build our country for the future.

As a nation, we are missing a very easy lever to build our country and economy. Caleb Watney, a co-founder of the Institute for Progress, said it well:

> Want to supercharge science? Immigrants bring breakthroughs, patents, and Nobel Prizes in droves. Want to stay ahead of China? Immigrants drive progress in semiconductors, AI, and quantum computing. Want to make America more dynamic? Immigrants launch nearly 50 percent of U.S. billion-dollar start-ups. The rest of the world is begging international talent to come to their shores while we are slamming the door in their face.[324]

The Statue of Liberty Immigration Act of 2025 will open the door to qualified immigrants and is a no-cost way of improving our economy and increasing the amount of taxes collected at zero cost. We are crazy to open our university system to immigrants and then send them home once they have their degrees.

3. STREAMLINE THE PROCESS OF BECOMING AN AMERICAN CITIZEN. As part of the Statue of Liberty Immigration Act of 2025, The President should ask Congress to streamline the process of citizenship. We currently have a great process to become an American citizen; it just takes way too long—averaging 7.2 years.[325]

The current process is as follows:

1. Get a green card. The qualifications to get a green card are (1) be at least 18 years old; (2) speak, read, and write English; and (3) be a person of good moral character. This means you are an upstanding member of society who has a job, pays taxes, and doesn't break the law.

2. Satisfy the residency requirements, which include (1) being lawfully admitted to the United States, (2) being a resident for five years, and (3) being present in the U.S. for 30 months during those five years.

3. Meet the personal requirements. These are the same as those for getting a green card.

4. Submit your naturalization papers, pay $640 for an application.

5. Pay $85 for a biometrics (fingerprint) appointment, and pass a civics test by answering six out of 10 questions in English.[326]

This is a great process. The only problem is that once you get a green card, you must wait five years to become an American citizen. Five years ago, there was a backlog of 200,000 cases for citizenship. Today the backlog is approaching two million cases.[327] We have 11 million open jobs and two million people who would love to become American citizens and help fuel our economy for the future. Let us look at immigration as an opportunity. The Statue of Liberty Immigration Act of 2025 will propose that we reduce the time that someone must hold a green card before applying for citizenship from the current five years to three years, while keeping the requirement that you reside in the United States for 30 months. The new President should commit to review the process and the funding to reduce the backlog from two million applicants to the historic level of 200,000 by the end of their second year in office.

4. CREATE A SOLUTION FOR UNDOCUMENTED IMMIGRANTS. There are currently 11.047 million illegal immigrants in the United States.[328] A 2020 Statista survey found that 75 percent of American respondents believed there should be a way for the undocumented to stay legally in this country.[329] The next President should propose passage of the Statue of Liberty Immigration Act of 2025 that would allow and encourage a path to citizenship for illegal immigrants if they meet the following criteria:

- Physically present in the United States for five years
- A person of good moral character for those five years, which means an upstanding member of society who has a job, pays taxes, and doesn't break the law
- Has not committed a crime
- Can speak, read, and write English

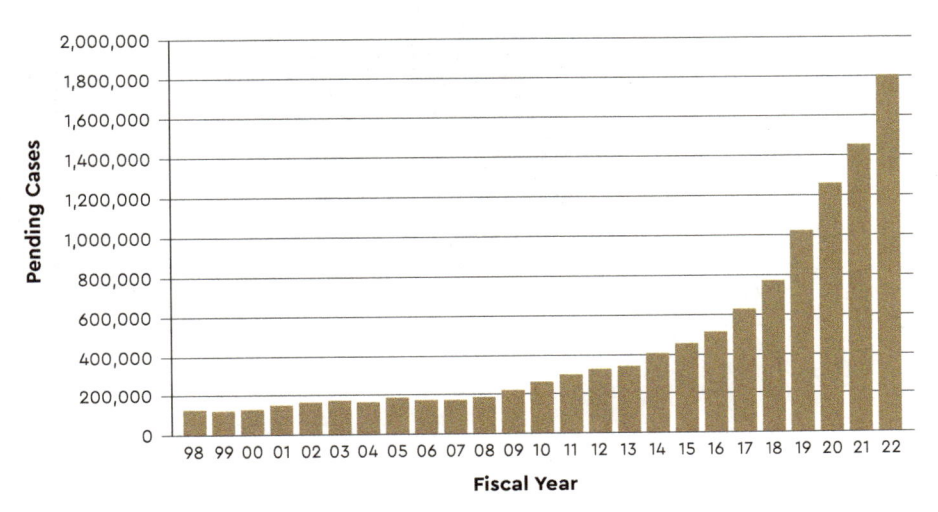

Backlog in U.S. Immigration Courts
United States

Steeply upward: The growing case backlog in U.S. immigration courts.
Transactional Records Access Clearinghouse.
Source: https://www.gao.gov/blog/u.s.-immigration-courts-see-significant-and-growing-backlog

The new President should propose in the Statue of Liberty Immigration Act of 2025 a simple, straightforward, low-cost solution to a complex problem. We are a nation of immigrants, and this immigration plan seeks to improve the ability of competent and committed immigrants to become productive, tax-paying U.S. citizens. Once again, our leaders have failed us when it comes to immigration. They have turned immigration into a wedge issue to divide the American people and to increase the level of hate in our society when they know better. It is my hope that the new President will step back, look at all of the facts, and then make a decision in the best long-term interest of the United States. The time has come to move the country forward.

13

Reform Campaign Finance

"If the need for comprehensive campaign finance reform was not already clear, the Supreme Court ruling in Citizens United permitting unlimited corporate and union spending in campaigns certainly made it so in 2010."

—Alan K. Simpson, former Republican Senator from Wyoming[330]

A simple tenet of a true democracy is one person, one vote. No one's vote should count more than anyone else's. The Pew Research Center reports that 77 percent of Americans believe that major donors should not have more influence than regular citizens.[331] If the opposite happens and major donors hold more power in elections than the average voter, then the game is rigged, and over time, people will stop playing. And over time, the democracy we have built over 248 years will fall apart. This will not happen all at once; it will happen over time, and as a nation, we are traveling down that very slippery slope.

Money has infiltrated our political process to the point that the determining factor in who wins a campaign in the United States is not who is the most competent candidate or who has the best ideas; it is who has been able to raise the largest amount of money. People do not give massive amounts of money to politicians for the good of the country. They give massive amounts of money to politicians to obtain influence, and they expect favors in return for campaign donations.

What facts support the theory that money in politics is out of control and that the core principle of our democracy is in danger? Consider the following:

1. ELECTIONS ARE WON BY THE HIGHEST BIDDER. In House elections, 90 percent of the candidates who spend more money than their opponents win their elections. For Senate contenders, more than 70 percent were the winners in every election since 2000.[332]

A friend of mine ran for public office. While he was contemplating the race, he met with an expert and asked me to join the meeting. I asked the political expert what my friend needed to do to win. "Well, he needs to be really good at raising money, and he needs to be a good liar." This is the system that we live in today.

2. THE RISING COST OF ELECTIONS IS GETTING WORSE WITH TIME. The amount of money spent in the 2022 midterm elections once again shattered records. The total amount of money spent on state and Federal elections was $16.7 billion.[333] The Georgia Senate race between Herschel Walker and Raphael Warnock set the all-time record at $425 million,[334] while the Pennsylvania Senate race, between Democrat John Fetterman and Republican Mehmet Oz, spent $312 million.[335] To put this into perspective, in the 2000 presidential race between George W. Bush and Al Gore, the total spent was $343 million.[336]

3. WEALTHY PEOPLE ARE SPENDING LARGE SUMS OF MONEY TO INFLUENCE ELECTIONS. Directly following the Supreme Court's Citizens United ruling, billionaires contributed just $31 million to elections in 2010. By 2016, billionaires contributed at least $684 million, according to the Americans for Tax Fairness report.[337] It also does not measure contributions to "dark money" nonprofit organizations that are allowed to fund super PACs and make their own electioneering expenditures but are not legally required to disclose their donors publicly. Such vehicles are preferred by mega-donors such as Democrat-backing George Soros and Republican-backing Charles Koch, who don't prominently factor into the report. It is believed these dark money contributions are significant. A *New York Times* analysis found that "15 of the most politically active nonprofit organizations that generally align with the Democratic Party spent more than $1.5 billion in 2020—compared to roughly $900 million spent by a comparable sample of 15 of the most politically active groups aligned with the GOP."[338]

4. "TODAY'S POLITICIANS SPEND AS MUCH AS 50 PERCENT OF THEIR TIME RAISING MONEY FOR THE NEXT ELECTION, up from 10 to 15 percent in the 1980s and 1990s," said Nick Penniman, CEO of Issue One, which describes itself as a "cross-partisan" political reform group.[339] Would you rather have your public servants representing the people and attending to the Nation's business or raising money?

....

One of my favorite books is called *The Power of Habit* by Charles Duhigg. One of the key lessons in the book is that you don't need to solve every problem in your organization, but if you focus on solving one key issue, it can have a positive impact on many other areas of the organization. In his book, Duhigg used the example of the late Paul O'Neill when he took over Alcoa Aluminum. In his first few months on the job, O'Neill studied the company and came to the conclusion that the key to success was worker safety. When he explained this to Wall Street analysts, they all ran to the phone banks (pre-cell phones), called the office, and said ... SELL. Despite the pushback, O'Neill spent his time fixing worker safety. He solved worker safety, cleaned up the plants, increased employee morale, forced the factories to evaluate processes, and the list goes on and on. In the spirit of worker safety, the company was transformed, and over the next 10 years Alcoa grew sales by five times and profits by 10 times. It is my belief that if we could fix one simple thing in our democracy, it would be to limit the influence of money. Money has corrupted our public officials by forcing them to raise money to win reelection and then repay their sponsors by making decisions in the best interest of their sponsors and their party instead of the best long-term interest of the United States. If we can reform campaign financing, we will see a significant improvement in the performance of our Government. It is my belief that the next President should seek constitutional amendment with these two basic principles:

1. ELIMINATE CAMPAIGN CONTRIBUTIONS TO CANDIDATES FROM BUSINESSES, UNIONS, OR OTHER ORGANIZATIONS, INCLUDING POLITICAL ACTION COMMITTEES. The only contributions allowed will be from people eligible to vote. **We don't let businesses, PACs, or unions vote, so why do we let them donate money and influence elections?**

2. PROHIBIT OUT-OF-STATE MONEY IN STATE ELECTIONS. I don't think that it is in the best interest of our democracy that someone from California can donate to a candidate running for governor in Nebraska. In 2020, out-of-state donors accounted for 68 percent of individual contributions, up from 31 percent in 2012.[340] Do you want someone from outside of your state influencing the outcome of an election in your state?

The benefits of passing this constitutional amendment:

- **Presidents, governors, and members of Congress, along with their staff, would be able to spend significantly more time doing their jobs instead of raising money for the next election.** The productivity of our highest-ranking officials would increase significantly.

- **Government officials would not owe favors to big-money contributors.** More decisions would be made in the best interests of the United States and its citizens and less in paying off the big contributors. Our leaders in Washington are making significant decisions every day in the best interest of their campaign supporters versus the citizens they were elected to represent in Washington. Major campaign contributions from health-care companies influence health-care policy. Major contributions from defense companies influence our Nation's national-defense strategy. Major contributions from wealthy individuals and corporations influence our tax system, which has significantly impacted the income gap in our country.

I was recently invited to a political fundraiser. The invitation stated that I could attend the event with a $10,000 contribution and have my picture taken with the elected official for $50,000. Why would someone offer a photo for $50,000? Because they were selling influence. One of the reasons we have such a large income gap in the United States is that the very wealthy in this country make significant campaign contributions and, in return, ask for and receive favorable tax laws. The favorable tax laws significantly increase their wealth at the expense of those who cannot afford to play the political money game. I don't think we truly understand the impact campaign spending has had on our democracy.

In "The Federalist Papers" #52, James Madison wrote: "The door of this part of the Federal Government is open to merit of every description; whether native or adoptive, whether young or old, and without regard for poverty or wealth, or to any particular profession of religious faith." Madison would cringe if he were alive today. The door of the Federal Government is hundreds of times more open to politically active people with a lot of money than it is to the average American.

The new President should ask Congress to pass a constitutional amendment that will eliminate campaign contributions from organizations that cannot vote and put an end to people influencing elections in states where they do not reside. These two simple solutions will take a massive amount of cash out of politics which will result in better decision-making that will be in the best interests of the American people and strengthen our democracy.

14

Simplify the Tax Code and Balance the Budget

"The hardest thing in the world to understand is the income tax."

—Albert Einstein, Nobel Prize-winning physicist[341]

People don't like to pay taxes—they never have and never will. Unfortunately, reducing taxes has become an American political sport. We love to reduce taxes without reducing spending. This is how you get elected in America: "I will cut your taxes, and I will cut ridiculous Government spending." Taxes are cut, and no one ever cuts the ridiculous spending. The result of this behavior by both parties is that we, the American citizens, have now amassed a debt of over $34 trillion.

The Tax Cuts and Jobs Act of 2017[342] promised to achieve three things—to be revenue neutral, meaning it would not add to the deficit; to be simple; and to be fair. What actually happened—the 2017 tax program is expected

Deficit by President
United States budget deficits under each president

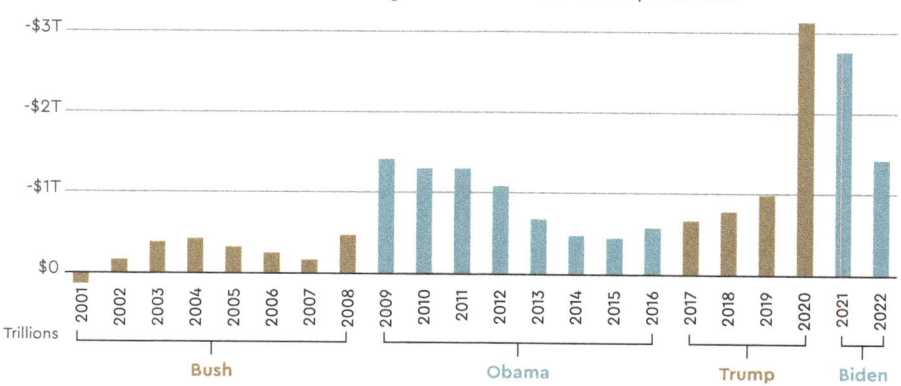

[Bar chart showing U.S. budget deficits from 2001 to 2022, grouped by presidential administration: Bush (2001-2008), Obama (2009-2016), Trump (2017-2020), and Biden (2021-2022). Deficits reach approximately -$3T in 2020 and nearly that in 2021.]

Source: https://fiscaldata.treasury.gov/americas-finance-guide/national-deficit/

to add $1.8 to $1.9 trillion to the deficit over the next 10 years.[343] The bill is almost 200 pages long,[344] and more than 60 percent of the benefits go to the top 20 percent of taxpayers.[345] Mayor John Hamilton of Bloomington, Indiana, wrote, in an editorial for *The Washington Post* in opposition to the 2017 tax cuts: "If I asked the city council to approve tripling our local debt to give hundreds of thousands of dollars per year to a few hundred of our most prosperous residents, they would ask me what I was smoking. 'Preposterous,' they would say."[346] That's exactly what we did at the Federal level.

A study by University of California, Berkeley economists Emmanuel Saez and Gabriel Zucman shows that in 2018—for the first time in history—the 400 wealthiest American families paid an average effective tax rate of 23 percent, while the bottom half of U.S. households paid an average effective rate of 24.2 percent.[347] That included Federal, state, local, and corporate taxes, as well as what the economists called "indirect taxes," such as vehicle and business licenses. By comparison, in 1980, the richest households had an effective tax rate of 47 percent. In 1960, they paid as much as 56 percent, while a *Washington Post* story said that the effective tax rate for lower earners has held steady over the years.[348] The wealthiest people in this country are paying a significantly lower share of the taxes than they paid 50 years ago. As a society, we must ask a simple question: Are we happy with that change?

Although everyone hates to pay taxes, I think we have lost sight of the fact that the money we pay in taxes provides us with significant benefits. Part of our responsibility as citizens is to pay our fair share of taxes. Even though there are massive opportunities to reduce Federal spending and significantly improve our Government's performance, we get real value for our tax dollars. Here are my top 20 things, among many others, that the Government provides for citizens:

1. A military that protects our citizenry from outside threats.
2. A Supplemental Nutrition Assistance Program (SNAP), which is the old food stamps program that feeds people who cannot afford to feed themselves. There are 42 million Americans who benefit from this program, and your tax dollars help feed the poor.[349]
3. Social Security, Medicare, and Medicaid benefits that keep nearly 16 million elderly Americans out of poverty and provide health care to 148 million seniors, disabled, and low-income citizens.[350]
4. Free and universal public education to nearly 50 million K–12 students across nearly 100,000 public schools.[351]
5. The Food and Drug Administration, the Environmental Protection Agency, and thousands of Federal, state, and local agencies keep us safer and healthier than we'd be in their absence.
6. Public dollars for the basic research that private companies turn into life-saving drugs, allowing the U.S. Food and Drug Administration to approve new medicines each year. The success of the U.S. COVID-19 vaccine effort didn't happen on its own; decades of long-term investments by the Federal Government enabled it.

7. Monitoring of the 39 billion tons of cargo transported annually by passenger and freight carriers by the Transportation Security Administration. Every major mode of transportation—from canals to airports—has received critical financial support from the Government.[352]

8. An air traffic control system for more than 29.4 million square miles of airspace that is among the safest in the world, thanks to the Federal Aviation Administration.[353]

9. The legal and social framework within which the economy operates.

10. Processing and delivery of 167.3 million pieces of first-class mail each day through the U.S. Postal Service.[354]

11. Protecting our national parks and 21,000 miles of trails through the Department of the Interior and the National Park Service.[355]

12. Protecting bank accounts through the Federal Deposit Insurance Corporation.

13. Providing information on storms and hurricanes by way of the National Weather Service.

14. Prohibiting employment discrimination through Federal laws.

15. Helping U.S. citizens traveling abroad through our network of 163 embassies and 93 consulates spread all over the world.[356]

16. Supporting victims of natural disasters through the Federal Emergency Management Agency (FEMA).

17. Maintaining the Nation's ports, harbors, and navigation channels by the U.S. Army Corps of Engineers.

18. Helping Americans start, grow, and build businesses through the Small Business Administration.

19. Treating the medical needs of approximately nine million American veterans each year and supporting close to 900,000 veterans and their dependents with education benefits.[357]

20. Printing, minting, and circulating U.S. currency and coins.

I recently read a book entitled *Loonshots: How to Nurture the Crazy Ideas That Win Wars, Cure Diseases, and Transform Industries*. In the book, the author Safi Bahcall writes about the story of Vannevar Bush, a professor of engineering at Massachusetts Institute of Technology (MIT). Bush traveled to Germany in the 1930s and was alarmed at how the Germans were bringing technology to their military. When he returned to the United States and confronted the military with the brutal facts, he was told we needed more men and guns. Bush didn't give up and went to Washington to see President Franklin Delano Roosevelt's close adviser Harry Hopkins.

On June 12, 1940, Bush and Hopkins met with FDR in the Oval Office. They made a case for an urgent need for technology to be included in the war effort and advocated the creation of the Office of Scientific Research and Development within the Federal Government. After 10 minutes, FDR approved the plan. Under Bush's leadership, the new agency reported directly to FDR and invested in hundreds of new technologies. Many of these investments, including sonar radar, helped to win World War II.

Bahcall recounts that "Since the end of World War II, hundreds of industry-changing or industry-creating discoveries including the Global Positioning System (GPS), personal computers, the biotechnology industry, the internet, pacemakers, artificial hearts, magnetic resonance imaging, the chemotherapy cure of childhood leukemia, and even the original Google search algorithm," came from the wise use of tax dollars by the Federal Government.[358] **Good government won World War II. Good government has spawned hundreds of game-changing industries. Tax dollars fund good government. Our problem in this country is not the Government; it is bad government. We have too much bad government in this country, and politicians have figured out that an easy way to get elected is to criticize the Government. The solution is not to eliminate the Government and tear down our institutions. The solution is that we should fix the Government, support it, create the best government in the world, and be proud of it!**

Our Federal Government does a horrible job marketing itself. The Government is not helped by the fact that many Government leaders complain about the cost and performance of the Government without ever doing anything about it. We rarely hear about the essential programs the Government runs that help our families every day. Taxes are dues that we pay to be members of the club. In our case, the club is to be a citizen of the United States, the greatest nation in the history of the world. Former U.S. Supreme Court Justice Oliver Wendell Holmes Jr. said, "I like to pay taxes. With them, I buy civilization."[359] You might not like to pay taxes, but we need to understand that our country does not function without them.

Here are the reasons why our current tax code is not working:

1. THE CURRENT TAX CODE IS TOO COMPLICATED. Our tax code is 6,871 pages long.[360] In 1913, it was 400 pages.[361] In the 2021 filing season, more than 10 million returns were not processed by the end of the year,[362] and phone calls to the Internal Revenue Service (IRS) skyrocketed from 39 million in 2019 to 195 million.[363] What is our Government's response to the complexity? Instead of simplifying the tax code, in the Inflation Reduction Act, Congress has agreed to spend an additional $80 billion over the next decade to modernize the IRS's systems and add agents.[364] We are $34 trillion in debt and will spend an additional $80 billion on the IRS instead of simplifying the tax code for free! The question of the day is whether you would vote to spend $80 billion on (1) systems and people to be more effective in collecting taxes based on a 6,871-page tax code or (2) modify the tax code to 10 pages or less and save the $80 billion. I vote for number two.

2. CORPORATIONS CAN GAME THE SYSTEM. General Electric, one of the largest corporations in America, filed a 57,000-page Federal tax return for 2011 and ended up paying zero in taxes on $14 billion in profit.[365] General Electric has done nothing legally wrong. It just has the right accountants and lawyers who can figure out how to pay zero while making $14 billion.

Apple held $246 billion offshore—more than any other company—to avoid paying $76.7 billion in U.S. taxes, according to 2017 studies by the U.S. Public Interest Research Group and the Institute on Taxation and Economic Policy. Citigroup reported $47 billion held in other countries on which it would owe $13.1 billion in U.S. taxes, and Goldman Sachs held $31.2 billion offshore.[366]

The late Republican Senator Tom Coburn described our current system well when he said, "The biggest breaks go to corporations and individuals who can afford the best lobbyists, lawyers, and accountants, leaving everyday Americans to fill the gap."[367]

3. THE TAX CODE CHANGES ALL THE TIME. From 2001 through 2012, there were nearly 5,000 alterations, or an average of one change per day.[368] How can you keep up with a game whose rules switch once a day? Imagine if the NFL changed its rules once a day.

4. THE CURRENT TAX CODE IS EXPENSIVE AND EATS UP THE RESOURCES OF THE U.S. GOVERNMENT AND ITS PEOPLE. It is so complicated that Americans spend $168 billion a year to hire a professional to do their taxes or use software to calculate their returns on their own.[369]

5. THERE ARE TOO MANY LOOPHOLES IN THE CURRENT TAX CODE. For example, Exxon paid $1.1 billion to settle its disastrous oil spill in Alaska in 1989.[370] Because of the tax code, Exxon could deduct about half the cost. Owners of corporate jets receive faster depreciation rates than commercial airlines do for their jets because of a tax loophole. NASCAR can depreciate race tracks over seven years when the Government actually estimates that tracks depreciate over 39 years.[371]

According to *Forbes* magazine, people and organizations take advantage of the nonprofit tax deduction using names like Find the Children, The Veteran Fund, and Cancer Fund of America. According to the *Forbes* article, the Cancer Fund of America spent less than 1 percent of its donations on charitable giving, and over 10 years, it paid its founders more than $5 million. "Despite millions in profits, the NHL and the PGA Tour are classified as nonprofit organizations, exempting their earnings from Federal income tax," the *Forbes* article said. The new rules in college football allow players to be compensated by booster clubs. Donations made to the booster clubs are, you guessed it, tax deductible. There is no difference between a government handout and a tax break. The list goes on and on. The tax system makes no strategic sense.[372] It has been cobbled together by politicians influenced by big money over the past 50 years. It is the opposite of "good wine." It keeps getting worse with time. For example, in 2018, according to the Institute on Taxation and Economic Policy, 60 of the Fortune 500 companies paid zero taxes on $79 billion in profits.[373] The tax code doesn't change because the few who benefit from its complexity have so much more money and power than the average American.

6. TAX BREAKS ARE REALLY GOVERNMENT EXPENDITURES.

The reality of the current system is that top earners received an average tax cut of $66,384 in 2011, while the bottom 20 percent saw a tax break of $107.[374] With the Trump administration's Tax Cuts and Jobs Act of 2017, Americans on the lowest end of the pay scale received a benefit of about $60 in 2018, while middle-class households saw an average tax break of $930.[375] Meanwhile, the top 0.1 percent—those with an average annual adjusted gross income of $7.3 million or more—had an average gain of $193,380, according to an analysis by the Tax Policy Center.[376]

Most people see tax deductions as taxes they don't have to pay. Although that is true, tax breaks should be considered Government spending. There is no difference between the $100 that the Government spends on a program and the $100 that the Government gives as a tax break.

....

The facts would say the our current tax system is not working. The question that should be asked of our leaders is this: "Can you please provide the citizens with a tax plan that is simple, clear, and fair?" It is not that hard!

The new President should propose a tax code that the American people can understand and that works for the people, not the special interest groups. The new President should propose a 10-page tax code that is simple and straightforward so that all Americans know the rules of the game. The new President should implement the Tax Simplification Act of 2025 within 30 days. Here are the plan's objectives:

1. SIMPLIFY THE TAX CODE FROM 6,871 PAGES DOWN TO 10 PAGES. The next President should give the American people a tax code they can understand and one that works for the people, not the special interest groups—a straightforward 10-page code that all Americans will understand.

2. SIGNIFICANTLY REDUCE THE NUMBER OF TAX BREAKS BY ADOPTING THE BOWLES-SIMPSON TAX RECOMMENDATION.[377] The proposal will eliminate all tax breaks except the child credit, earned income tax credit for very low-income earners, foreign tax credits for taxes paid abroad, employer-sponsored health insurance reduced rates, charitable-giving deductions, retirement savings reduced rates, and mortgage interest reduced rates. Everything else goes, and this is how we get down to a simple, understandable tax code that levels the playing field for all Americans.

3. TAX CAPITAL GAINS AND DIVIDENDS AT NORMAL TAX RATES. Both capital gains and dividends are income, just like a salary or an hourly wage. Simplify the tax code, and call all income "earned income."

Tax it all the same. I estimate this simple change would raise $40 billion in revenue annually.

4. ELIMINATE ALL CORPORATE TAX BREAKS AND LEAVE THE RATE AT 21 PERCENT. The Trump 2017 tax plan reduced the corporate rate to 21 percent so U.S. companies could be globally competitive.[378] In the Tax Simplification Act of 2025, the new President should ask Congress to eliminate all corporate tax breaks. The Government should not be in the business of picking winners and losers in the marketplace through tax policy. Why should oil companies get big tax breaks while running shoe companies do not? Why should certain farmers get big tax subsidies while others get nothing? Our tax system is overly complicated, and we should simplify it by getting out of the business of letting members of Congress pick winners and losers with the tax code.

If the U.S. Government wants to help a specific industry because it is in the best interests of the people of the United States, then that industry should get a subsidy. Then it should be put in a budget so that everyone can see what the subsidy is, how much it costs the people of the United States, and that the subsidy has a time limit. We need to get out of the business of letting politicians and lawyers bury hundreds of billions of dollars worth of benefits for special interests that last forever in our 6,871-page document called the tax code.

When the 2017 Tax Cuts and Jobs Act was passed, and the published corporate tax rate was reduced to 21 percent, the average Fortune 500 company actually paid 11 percent after deductions in 2018.[379] The Tax Simplification Act of 2025 would have every company in America paying 21 percent. This would level the playing field and raise $96 billion a year, by my estimates, and significantly reduce our annual deficit.

5. HAVE THE IRS SEND YOU A PRE-FILLED TAX RETURN WITH ALL THE RELEVANT INFORMATION. As described by Harvard Law School professor Cass R. Sunstein, this approach is called the simple return. It has been proposed by Austan Goolsbee, former chairman of the Council of Economic Advisers. All you would need to do is review the information and sign it. The entire process would take five minutes to complete. Many countries, including Denmark, Sweden, Germany, Japan, and the United Kingdom, offer some form of return-free tax filing.[380] Within 12 months, the President could have a simple return option. The Government exists to serve the people, and eliminating the estimated 10 hours the average person spends on calculating tax returns is something simple that the Government can do for its citizens.

Under the Tax Simplification Act of 2025, the American people will realize the following benefits:

- I estimate this plan would generate more than $150 billion in additional revenue annually. This tax plan would do what Congress has been unable to—simplify the tax code and significantly increase revenues.

- We would bring some sense of fairness and logic to the tax code. We could take the 6,871-page tax code and reduce it to 10 pages. Americans would actually understand the rules of the game.

This would simplify people's lives. I estimate that the time to fill out a tax form would be reduced by 98 percent.

Specific Plan to Balance the Budget

When it comes to our Nation's finances, we have one problem that is bigger than the tax code, and that is our debt. Politicians will come and go, but we own the debt. Due to poor leadership, our current debt is $34 trillion. We are on the way to bankruptcy, and yet none of the candidates running for the highest office in the land have a plan to deal with it. As citizens and the owners of the country, we should demand that our leaders come up with a plan to bring fiscal discipline to our country. It is not that hard! Here is an accounting of the proposals that I have recommended that the new President introduce when he or she takes office:

Specific Spending Reductions

- **HEALTH-CARE COSTS REDUCTION OF $284 BILLION PER YEAR.** (Chapter 4) We spend more than $4.3 trillion per year on health care. This number is 18.3 percent of our GDP. The Federal Government spends 34 percent of this number, or $1.46 trillion. State and local governments spend $645 billion.[381] The health-care proposal will save at least $284 billion on our health-care bill by 2028. My proposals in Chapter 4 would not only reduce the Federal Government's cost on health care, but these same policies would also reduce the state and local governments' out-of-pocket costs. I believe that we actually have an even bigger opportunity to save money on health care. The second highest spending country in the world on health care is Germany, at 12.8 percent of GDP.[382] If we hit German levels, we could save more than $1 trillion per year throughout the health-care system.

- **DEPARTMENT OF DEFENSE BUDGET REDUCTION OF $200 BILLION.** (Chapter 8)

- **CONGRESSIONAL PENSION SAVINGS OF $36 MILLION PER YEAR.** (Chapter 7) A small number but many small numbers all over the Government add up to one big number.

- **CHANGE THE GUN LAWS.** (Chapter 10) Every year, 130,000 people are shot in America. Change the gun laws, and the vast majority of those people are not shot, will not need medical care, will not need to go on disability, etc. The estimated cost of each nonfatal shooting in America is $25,150 × 85,000 = to save $2.13 billion annually.[383] Lost productivity, medical bills in year two and beyond, security costs, and I estimate that the annual savings introducing similar gun control laws to the rest of the world would be a minimum of $25 billion per year.

- **PRISON POPULATION.** (Chapter 11) We have almost two times the prison population that Russia has, five times the prison population of the U.K., and nine times the prison population of Germany. We spend $80 billion a year on prisons.[384] By 2028, we can reduce the prison population by 50 percent and save $40 billion per year.

- **SOCIAL SECURITY DISABILITY.** (Chapter 6) We spend $144 billion a year on Social Security Disability.[385] It is estimated that 20–25 percent of this number is fraud. I believe we could save 10 percent or $14 billion annually.

- **MISCELLANEOUS BUDGET CUTS THROUGHOUT THE FEDERAL GOVERNMENT OF $44 BILLION.** The new President should challenge every agency within the Federal Government to reduce spending. It is my belief that we will be able to find $44 billion per year.

Total cost annual savings: $607 billion per year

Revenue Increases

- **INCREASE THE GAS TAX.** (Chapter 5) Increase the gas tax by $190 billion annually to improve our infrastructure, leading to a better economy, better-paying jobs, and more tax revenue.

- **SCRAP THE CAP ON SOCIAL SECURITY.** (Chapter 6) Have all income taxed at the same 6.2 percent rate. This results in $190 billion of increased revenue for Social Security.

- **TAX ALL INCOME THE SAME, WHETHER IT IS NORMAL INCOME OR DIVIDEND INCOME.** (Chapter 14) This would increase revenue by $40 billion per year.

- **ELIMINATE ALL CORPORATE TAX BREAKS.** (Chapter 14) Everyone pays 21 percent. If you want Government support, go and ask for it and have it included in a budget so that everyone can see it. Increased revenue equals $96 billion.

- **ENACT THE BOWLES-SIMPSON TAX PLAN FOR INDIVIDUALS.** (Chapter 14) By my estimate, the revenue increase equals $100 billion.

Total revenue increase: $616 billion

New Programs that the new President Should Spend Money On

- **EVERY KID HAS A CHANCE.** (Chapter 6) For those children at 50 percent of the poverty level or worse, free medical, Head Start, and a free education until age 22. I estimate that this program costs $70 billion per year.

- **INCREASE PEACE CORPS SPENDING BY $10 BILLION PER YEAR.** (Chapter 9) We are the richest nation in the world, and we can do a lot of good around the world for $10 billion.

- **HORACE MANN SCHOOLS.** (Chapter 6) The Federal Government takes over the worst public schools if the state wants to give them up—$30 billion per year.

- **TRANSPORTATION SPENDING INCREASES BY $190 BILLION PER YEAR.** (Chapter 5) The same as the gas tax revenue.

Total spending increase: $300 billion

In addition to the hard costs, many of the proposals outlined in this book will positively impact the foundation of our economy for decades to come and will have a positive effect on America's finances. Many of these positive economic impacts are hard to quantify:

- The long-term benefit of the Every Kid Has a Chance Program. More of our at-risk children end up as productive tax-paying citizens versus ending up in the legal system and jail.

- The productivity of the 130,000 victims per year of gun violence. What if they had never been shot? Tax revenue increase, disability savings, etc.

- Healthy Americans. Our obesity rate is 42 percent.[386] What if the obesity rate was 32 percent? What if it was 21 percent? The productivity increase would be massive, and the health-care bill would be significantly less.

- The immigration bill. The size of our economy is the number of people multiplied by productivity. There are hundreds of thousands of super-smart job creators who would love to live in our country. We can let them in and watch them work, start businesses, and pay taxes at no cost to the taxpayer!

- Excellent public schools for ALL Americans. Ninety-two percent of our kids go to public schools. The impact on our economy would be huge if we had the best public schools in the world.

- What would the benefit be if we had a Congress not beholden to PACs and corporations and wealthy individuals so that they would make decisions in the country's best interest, not in the best interest of their donors?

- Fixing our legal system would result in 50 percent fewer lawsuits, the business climate would significantly improve, and hundreds of thousands of jobs would be created.

Have you ever seen a list of specific expense reductions from a presidential candidate? Have you ever heard from a presidential candidate who explains the need to increase taxes? If you are interested in having a straightforward tax code, saving you significant time preparing your tax return and believe that the wealthiest Americans and corporations should not use a complicated tax code to avoid paying taxes, then you should demand more of your candidate. This plan will deliver a simple, fair, and honest tax code for the American people. This plan will also bring financial discipline to our Nation and stop kicking the "deficit can" to our children. We are $34 trillion in debt, and we need national leaders to lead. We need leaders to put the long-term best interest of the country first and propose a plan to cut expenses, raise taxes, and create a better environment for the economy to grow over the long term. Cleaning up our financial mess will set up our country for long-term success.

Conclusion

"There's a moment where you have to choose whether to be silent or to stand up."

—Malala Yousafzai, education activist and youngest Nobel Prize laureate[387]

We have a lot of problems in our country. We also have an incredible amount of potential. The solution in my mind is two-fold. First, we need leaders who care more about the country than they do about themselves or their party. We need leaders who can make decisions in the best long-term interest of the United States.

Second, we need better citizens. People fail in their jobs for two reasons. The first is they were never told what the job is and second, they were never trained to do it. I think as a country we have done a lousy job of developing and publicizing expectations for being a good citizen.

If we have great leaders and great citizens, this is what you could see in your lifetime:

An America that has the best government in the world. Where every unit of our Government is the best in the world at what they do. The best public schools, the best health-care system, the best transportation system, the best national parks, the best defense, etc. We set high expectations, and we get after it!

An America that leads the world in turning the tide on climate change. We all breathe the same air, we all drink the same water, and we all live or die by the same weather conditions. The U.N. Secretary-General said in November 2022, "We are on a highway to climate hell with a foot on the accelerator." May the U.N. Secretary-General someday say, "The tide has turned in regard to climate change, and I am pleased to say that the leadership of the United States has made a big difference." Wouldn't it be amazing if we felt as proud of our contribution to solving climate change as we did when we put a man on the moon?

An America that not only brings the world back from the brink of nuclear war but takes a leadership role to rid the world of the nuclear threat and frees up the financial resources in the U.S. and other countries to build up mankind rather than destroy it.

An America that focuses its health-care system on improving the overall health of the American people. Imagine the impact on America if our obesity rate went from 42 percent to 20 percent over the next five years—improved mental health, significantly lower health-care costs, and a massive productivity increase.

An America that improves its transportation system from a C- to an A over the next 10 years by (1) making the investment necessary and (2) paying for that investment through an increase in the gas tax. The result would be the creation of hundreds of thousands of high-paying jobs and the infrastructure to power our economy for the 21st century.

An America that secures the future of Social Security by scrapping the cap and having the richest Americans pay more to help those who cannot help themselves and to lift up the forgotten children of this country by creating the Every Kid Has a Chance Program so all Americans have access to the American dream.

An effective Congress that represents the people and the long-term interest of the United States and is not influenced by special interests but is committed to doing what is right for the people. A productive Congress is key to a successful America.

A military that does a better job protecting the United States at a significantly lower cost, freeing that money up so that we are more fiscally responsible and stop kicking the deficit can to our kids and grandkids.

A foreign policy that continues in the best traditions of the United States where we advance freedom for the benefit of the American people and the international community.

An America where we eliminate more than 90 percent of the gun deaths and 90 percent of gun-related injuries that also shatter lives. Envision an America that is safe enough to send your kids to school without worry and where our hospitals, schools, and public places don't have armed guards.

An America where we clean up the legal system by cutting the number of lawsuits in half and where we continue to dispense justice but cut our nonviolent prison population in half and save $40 billion a year.

An America where we finally embrace the fact that the majority of us are immigrants and that controlled immigration is key to the future growth of our country. We can both protect our borders and allow people who can make a contribution into the United States.

An America where one person equals one vote, where the rich cannot buy elections with massive contributions, and our elected public servants serve the public and not their campaign contributors.

An America where we scrap our 6,871 page tax-code and replace it with a 10-page tax code that citizens understand.

An America that balances its budget and starts to pay down its massive debt.

There is work to be done, and there is a choice to be made. As a nation, we stand at a fork in the road.

One road is entitled "More of the Same." We can keep electing the same kind of candidates, and we can continue to be citizens who don't know the most important facts about the issues in our country, don't vote very often, and focus our disdain on the other side.

The other road is called "Humility." The journey down this road is a humble journey where we acknowledge our problems, focus on the facts, and have the iron will to fix the problems. We hold our leaders and ourselves to higher standards.

The National Leadership Scorecard and the Citizen of the United States Scorecard are simple places to start. We should have higher expectations of our leaders, and we need to reimagine and reinvigorate the responsibilities of citizenship. Americans must educate themselves on key issues, and we all need to vote in both Presidential and mid-term elections.

The humility road is the one that George Washington traveled at the founding of our Nation. Lincoln traveled this road when he saved the Nation. Roosevelt traveled it when he rallied the Nation through the Great Depression and World War II. It is also the road that Eisenhower traveled when he warned the Nation in his farewell address of the growing military-industrial complex.

Now it is our turn. It is the time for all good people to stand up and be heard, to do something for our country, and be worthy of the title, Citizen of the United States.

About the Author

John Burke began working at Trek Bicycle in 1984 and has been president of the company since 1997. In 2021, Trek was named one of *Time* magazine's most influential companies. And in 2023, Trek was named a Top 100 place to work by *Fortune* magazine. In addition to leading Trek, John served as chairman of President George W. Bush's President's Council on Physical Fitness and Sports.

John is an avid cyclist, sustainability advocate, runner, and published author. His first book, *One Last Great Thing*, chronicles the life and lessons of John's late father and Trek Bicycle founder, Richard Burke. His second book, *12 Simple Solutions to Save America*, and third book, *Presidential Playbook 2020: 16 Nonpartisan Solutions to Save America*, strip partisan spin from the pressing issues facing the United States, exposing the facts and potential nonpartisan solutions to each. John and his wife, Tania, live in Madison, Wisconsin.

Acknowledgments

I loved writing this book. It took many twists and turns along the way. I have had some incredible help from many people. I want to thank Cindy Wagner, my assistant and "CEO" (Chief Empathy Officer). I have worked with Cindy for the past 29 years, and she provided amazing advice on this book and was always there to get this over the line. I also want to thank Marina Lopez Del Carril, who was my first assistant back in the day, who moved out to Colorado and was a schoolteacher for 20 years. Marina helped with the research and with the editing of the book. She was amazing. While writing the book, I asked for a lot of help from some very smart people who truly love their country. I received some great feedback from Mark Joslyn, Mark Murphy, Tim Blumenthal, Pat Sullivan, Bob Burns, Dr. Mark Timmerman, Mike Douglas, Pat Cunnane, Jim Hendley, and Dan Titus, along with many others. Many thanks to Kristin Mitchell from Little Creek Press. Kristin brought the book to life with an excellent layout. Thank you to my son, Richie Burke, and his team at Story Mark Studios for their excellent multimedia work in getting my message out. A big thank you goes to my wife and life partner, Tania, who gives me amazing feedback every day, and this book was no exception.

Endnotes

Introduction

1   U.S. Debt Clock, accessed January 18, 2024, https://www.usdebtclock.org.

2   "Nuclear Weapons Worldwide," Union of Concerned Scientists, accessed on February 8, 2023, https://www.ucsusa.org/nuclear-weapons/worldwide.

3   Niccolo Conte, "Ranked: Top 10 Countries by Military Spending," Visual Capitalist, August 18, 2022, accessed February 10, 2023, https://www.visualcapitalist.com/rankedtop-10-countries-by-military-spending/.

4   Lee J. Miller and Wei Lu, "Asia Trounces U.S. in Health-Efficiency Index Amid Pandemic," Bloomberg, December 17, 2020, https://www.bloomberg.com/news/articles/2020-12-18/asia-trounces-u-s-in-health-efficiency-index-amid-pandemic.

5   Angel Adegbesan, "Caring for U.S. Victims of Gun Violence Costs $2.5 Billion in the Year After Shooting," Bloomberg, April 2, 2022, https://www.bloomberg.com/news/articles/2022-04-04/u-s-gun-victims-care-costs-2-5-billion-in-year-after-shooting?embedded-checkout=true.

6   Helen Fair and Roy Walmsley, "World Prison Population List," World Prison Brief, accessed February 11, 2023, https://www.prisonstudies.org/sites/default/files/resources/downloads/world_prison_population_list_13th_edition.pdf.

7   Kate Davidson, "Social Security Costs to Exceed Income in 2020, Trustees Say: The Trust Fund to be Depleted by 2035, They Add," *The Wall Street Journal*, April 22, 2019, accessed February 9, 2023, https://www.wsj.com/articles/social-security-trust-fund-to-be-depleted-in-2035-trustees-say-11555946113.

8   Adam Kazda, "The More Complex the Tax Code, the More the Wealthy Benefit," The Hill, July 25, 2017, accessed February 12, 2023, https://thehill.com/blogs/pundits-blog/economy-budget/343645-the-more-complex-the-tax-code-the-more-the-rich-benefit/.

9   "Andrew Young," Life Stories, https://www.lifestories.org/interviewees/andrew-young.

10   "Remarks in Nashville at the 90th Anniversary Convocation of Vanderbilt University, May 18, 1963," John F. Kennedy Presidential Library and Museum, https://www.jfklibrary.org/archives/other-resources/john-f-kennedy-speeches/vanderbilt-university-19630518#:~:text=He%20percent20knows%20percent20that%20percent20%20percent22knowledge%20percent20is,enlighten%20percent20the%20percent20people%20percent20generally%20percent2%200.2

11   Adam Barnes, "Fewer than half of Americans can name all three branches of government, survey finds," Changing America, September 13, 2022, https://thehill.com/changing-america/enrichment/education/3640520-less-than-half-of-americans-can-name-all-three-branches-of-government-survey-finds/.

12   Annenberg Public Policy Center, "Survey: Only 32 percent of Americans able to correctly name all 3 branches of government," YubaNet, September 17, 2018, https://yubanet.com/usa/survey-only-32-percent-of-americans-able-to-correctly-name-all-3-branches-of-government/.

13   Alexa Lardieri, "2 of 3 Americans Wouldn't Pass U.S. Citizenship Test," U.S. News, October 12, 2018, https://www.usnews.com/news/politics/articles/2018-10-12/2-of-3-americans-wouldnt-pass-us-citizenship-test#:~:text=About.

14   "Voter turnout, 2018–2022, Pew Research Center, July 12, 2023, https://www.pewresearch.org/politics/2023/07/12/voter-turnout-2018-2022/.

15   Oliver Wendall Holmes Jr., Quote Investigator, https://quoteinvestigator.com/author/garson/.

Chapter One

16   King, Martin Luther, Jr., 1963, The Negro Is Your Brother: The Atlantic Monthly (August 1963), v. 212, no. 2, p. 78–88. https://www.theatlantic.com/magazine/archive/1963/08/the-negro-is-your-brother/658583/

17   Kara Goldin, "Great Leaders Take People Where They May Not Want to Go," *Forbes*, October 1, 2018, https://www.pgpf.org/chart-archive/0053_defense-comparison.

18   Robert J. Samuelson, "Why We Don't Prepare for the Future," *The Washington Post*, September 9, 2018, accessed February 8, 2023, https://www.washingtonpost.com/opinions/why-we-dont-prepare-for-the-future/2018/09/09/cb91cc34-b2c3-11e8-aed9-001309990777_story.html.

19   Dennis Cauchon, "Some Federal Workers More Likely to Die Than Lose Jobs," *USA Today*, July 18, 2011, accessed February 8, 2023, http://usatoday30.usatoday.com/news/washington/2011-07-18-fderal-job-security_n.htm.

20   Stephen Rushin. "Police Arbitration." *Vanderbilt Law Review* 74 (2021): 1023.

21   Noam Scheiber, Farah Stockman, and J. David Goodman, "How Police Unions Became Such Powerful Opponents to Reform Efforts, *The New York Times*, April 2, 2021, https://www.nytimes.com/2020/06/06/us/police-unions-minneapolis-kroll.html.

22   John McCain, "Address to the Oklahoma State Legislature," accessed February 8, 2023, https://www.presidency.ucsb.edu/documents/address-the-oklahoma-state-legislature.

23   Franklin D. Roosevelt, "Letter on the Resolution of Federation of Federal Employees Against Strikes in Federal Service," accessed February 8, 2023, https://www.presidency.ucsb.edu/documents/letter-the-resolution-federation-federal-employees-against-strikes-federal-service.

24   "Steve Jobs Muses on What's Wrong with American Education, 1995," Open Culture. November 10, 2011, accessed February 8, 2023, https://www.openculture.com/2011/11/steve_jobs_muses_on_public_education_1995.html.

25   Author's recollection.

26   John Doerr, *Measure What Matters: How Google, Bono, and the Gates Foundation Rock the World with OKRs* (New York: Portfolio, 2018).

27   "How many people work for the federal government?" USAFacts, November 15, 2023, https://usafacts.org/articles/how-many-people-work-for-the-federal-government/.

Chapter Two

28   António Guterres, "Secretary-General's Remarks to High-Level Opening of COP27 as Delivered," November 7, 2022, accessed February 8, 2023, https://www.un.org/sg/en/content/sg/statement/2022-11-07/secretary-generals-remarks-high-level-opening-of-cop27-delivered-scroll-down-for-all-english-version.

29   White House, National Climate Task Force, accessed February 8, 2023, https://www.whitehouse.gov/climate/.

30   Oliver Milman, "Climate Bill Could Slash U.S. Emissions by 40 percent after Historic Senate Vote," *The Guardian*, August 7, 2022, accessed February 8, 2023, https://www.theguardian.com/environment/2022/aug/05/us-climate-bill-slash-emissions-analysis-biden.

31   Christopher Ingraham, "Houston Is Experiencing Its Third '500-year Flood' in 3 Years. How Is That Possible?," *The Washington Post*, August 29, 2017, accessed February 8, 2023, https://www.washingtonpost.com/news/wonk/wp/2017/08/29/houston-is-experiencing-its-third-500-year-flood-in-3-years-how-is-that-possible/.

32   Ian Livingston and Jason Samenow, "In Hot Water: South Florida Ocean Tops 100 Degrees," *The Washington Post*, July 25, 2023, accessed September 2, 2023, https://www.washingtonpost.com/weather/2023/07/25/florida-record-warm-ocean-climate/.

33   Jen Christensen, "It's so hot in Arizona, doctors are treating a spike of patients who were burned by falling on the ground," CNN, July 24, 2023, accessed September 25, 2023, https://edition.cnn.com/2023/07/24/health/arizona-heat-burns-er/index.html.

34   Zeke Hausfather, "I Study Climate Change. The Data Is Telling Us Something New, October 13, 2023, *The New York Times*, https://www.nytimes.com/2023/10/13/opinion/climate-change-excessive-heat-2023.html.

35   "Trends in Atmospheric Carbon Dioxide," National Oceanic and Atmospheric Administration, accessed February 8, 2023, https://gml.noaa.gov/ccgg/trends/.

36   Ibid.

37   Zeke Hausfather, "Explainer: How Scientists Estimate 'Climate Sensitivity,'" Carbon Brief, June 19, 2018, accessed February 8, 2023, https://www.carbonbrief.org/explainer-how-scientists-estimate-climate-sensitivity/.

38   "World of Change: Global Temperatures," NASA Earth Observatory, accessed February 8, 2023, https://earthobservatory.nasa.gov/world-of-change/global-temperatures.

39 Rebecca Lindsey, "2020 Was the United States' Fifth-Warmest Year on Record," National Oceanic and Atmospheric Administration, January 13, 2021, accessed February 8, 2023, https://www.climate.gov/news-features/understanding-climate/2020-was-united-states-fifth-warmest-year-record.

40 "2021 One of the Seven Warmest Years on Record, WMO Consolidated Data Shows," World Meteorological Organization, January 19, 2022, accessed February 8, 2023, https://public.wmo.int/en/media/press-release/2021-one-of-seven-warmest-years-record-wmo-consolidated-data-shows.

41 Saloni Gupta et al., "Did Climate Change Influence the Emergence, Transmission, and Expression of the COVID-19 Pandemic?," December 8, 2021, Frontiers in Medicine, https://doi.org/10.3389/fmed.2021.769208.

42 "68 percent Average Decline in Species Population Sizes Since 1970, Says New WWF Report," World Wildlife Fund, September 9, 2020, accessed February 8, 2023, https://www.worldwildlife.org/press-releases/68-average-decline-in-species-population-sizes-since-1970-says-new-wwf-report.

43 Rebecca Lindsey, "Climate Change: Global Sea Level," National Oceanic and Atmospheric Administration, April 9, 2022, accessed February 8, 2023, https://www.climate.gov/news-features/understanding-climate/climate-change-global-sea-level.

44 "Record-breaking Atlantic hurricane season draws to an end," National Oceanic and Atmospheric Administration, June 10, 2021, accessed September 29, 2021, https://www.noaa.gov/media-release/record-breaking-atlantic-hurricane-season-draws-to-end.

45 "National Hurricane Center Tropical Cyclone Report: Hurricane Laura," Richard J. Pasch et al., National Hurricane Center, May 26, 2021, accessed on September 29, 2023, https://www.nhc.noaa.gov/data/tcr/AL132020_Laura.pdf.

46 "Record number of billion-dollar disasters struck U.S. in 2020," National Oceanic and Atmospheric Administration, January 8, 2021, accessed on September 25, 2023, https://www.noaa.gov/stories/record-number-of-billion-dollar-disasters-struck-us-in-2020.

47 Adam B. Smith, "2020 U.S. Billion-Dollar Weather and Climate Disasters in Historical Context," National Oceanic and Atmospheric Administration, January 8, 2021, accessed February 8, 2023, https://www.climate.gov/disasters2020.

48 Douglas Soule, "Three months after Hurricane Ian landfill, Florida's official death toll at 144," *Tallahassee Democrat*, December 29, 2022, accessed September 25, 2023, https://www.tallahassee.com/story/news/politics/2022/12/29/hurricane-ian-florida-deaths-toll-three-months-later-category-4-storm/69762991007/.

49 Darreonna Davis, "U.S. Has Seen Four 1-in-1,000 Year Rainfall Events This Summer," *Forbes*, August 10, 2022, accessed February 8, 2023, https://www.forbes.com/sites/darreonnadavis/2022/08/10/us-has-seen-four-1-in-1000-year-rainfall-events-this-summer/?sh=25a41c985a40.

50 Kat Kerlin, "California's 2020 Wildfire Season: Report Summarizes Record-Breaking Fire Year and Calls for Shift in Strategy," May 4, 2022, UC Davis, accessed February 8, 2023, https://www.ucdavis.edu/climate/news/californias-2020-wildfire-season-numbers.

51 Ibid.

52 Ibid.

53 "High Winds and Marshall Fire on December 30th, 2021," National Weather Service, accessed February 8, 2023, https://www.weather.gov/bou/HighWinds12_30_2021.

54 Karin Brulliard, "Can they go home again?" *The Washington Post*, January 25, 2022, accessed September 25, 2023, https://www.washingtonpost.com/nation/interactive/2022/marshall-fire-colorado-rebuilding/.

55 Johnathan Oatis, "Maui fires: What to know about Hawaii's deadliest disaster, damage and death toll," August 21, 2023, Reuters, https://www.reuters.com/world/us/how-did-hawaii-wildfires-start-what-know-about-maui-big-island-blazes-2023-08-11

56 "Billion-Dollar Weather and Climate Disasters," National Oceanic and Atmospheric Administration, accessed February 8, 2023, https://www.ncei.noaa.gov/access/billions/.

57 "Climate Change Indicators: U.S. Greenhouse Gas Emissions," United States Environmental Protection Agency, accessed February 8, 2023, https://www.epa.gov/climate-indicators/climate-change-indicators-us-greenhouse-gas-emissions.

58 "CO2 Emissions (Metric Tons per Capita)," The World Bank, accessed February 8, 2023, https://data.worldbank.org/indicator/EN.ATM.CO2E.PC.

59 Alister Doyle, "Weather Extremes, Fossil Fuel Pollution, Cost U.S. $240 Billion: Study," September 27, 2017, Reuters, https://www.reuters.com/article/us-climatechange-usa-idUKKCN1C22AM.

60 "RMS Range of Insured Losses from Ian $53–74B, 'Best Estimate' of $67B," Insurance Journal, October 10, 2022, accessed February 8, 2023, https://www.insurancejournal.com/news/national/2022/10/10/688808.htm.

61 "World Population Projected to Reach 9.8 Billion in 2050, and 11.2 Billion in 2100," United Nations, accessed February 8, 2023, https://www.un.org/en/desa/world-population-projected-reach-98-billion-2050-and-112-billion-2100.

62 Thomas Friedman, *Thank You for Being Late: An Optimist's Guide to Thriving in the Age of Accelerations*, (New York: Farrar, Straus and Giroux, 2016).

63 Mark Fischetti, "Climate Change Hastened Syria's Civil War," *Scientific American*, March 2, 2015, accessed February 8, 2023, https://www.scientificamerican.com/article/climate-change-hastened-the-syrian-war/.

64 Ibid.

65 Josep Borrell, "Syria: Speech by High Representative/Vice-President Josep Borrell at the EP Debate on 10 Years of the Conflict," October 3, 2021, accessed February 8, 2023, https://www.eeas.europa.eu/eeas/syria-speech-high-representativevice-president-josep-borrell-ep-debate-10-years-conflict_en.

66   António Guterres, "U.N. Secretary General António Guterres Calls for Climate Leadership, Outlines Expectations for Next Three Years," United Nations Climate Change, accessed February 8, 2023, https://unfccc.int/news/un-secretary-general-antonio-guterres-calls-for-climate-leadership-outlines-expectations-for-next.

67   "The Four Pillars of Our Carbon Dividends Plan," Climate Leadership Council, updated September 2019, accessed February 8, 2023, https://clcouncil.org/our-plan/.

68   Al Gore, "The Climate Crisis is the Battle of Our Time and We Can Win," *The New York Times*, September 20, 2019, accessed February 8, 2023, https://www.nytimes.com/2019/09/20/opinion/al-gore-climate-change.html.

69   United Nations, "For a Livable Climate: Net-zero Commitments Must be Backed by Action," Accessed February 8, 2023, https://www.un.org/en/climatechange/net-zero-coalition.

70   Robert Swan, "The Greatest Threat to Our Planet is the Belief That Someone Else Will Save It," November 17, 2016, accessed February 8, 2023, https://www.youtube.com/watch?v=su0-8-yA-3M.

Chapter Three

71   Noam Chomsky, "Noam Chomsky: The Week the World Stood Still: The Cuban Missile Crisis and Ownership of the World," *Guernica*, October 16, 2012, accessed February 8, 2023, https://www.guernicamag.com/noam-chomsky-the-week-the-world-stood-still/.

72   António Guterres, "Secretary-General's Remarks to the Tenth Review Conference of the Parties to the Treaty on the Non-Proliferation of Nuclear Weapons," United Nations, August 1, 2022, accessed on February 8, 2023, https://www.un.org/sg/en/content/sg/speeches/2022-08-01/secretary-generals-remarks-the-tenth-review-conference-of-the-parties-the-treaty-the-non-proliferation-of-nuclear-weapons.

73   "Nuclear Weapons Worldwide," Union of Concerned Scientists, accessed on February 8, 2023, https://www.ucsusa.org/nuclear-weapons/worldwide.

74   Melissa Chan, "What Is the Difference Between a Hydrogen Bomb and an Atomic Bomb?," September 22, 2017, Truman Library, accessed February 8, 2023, https://www.trumanlibrary.gov/sites/default/files/2019-10/Development percent20of percent20the percent20Hydrogen percent20Bomb- percent20Document percent20Set.pdf?VersionId=Tlums5XoxSxXDVHA.MGW8aqOO6IZItZ2.

75   Richard Stone, "'National Pride is at Stake': Russia, China, United States Race to Build Hypersonic Weapons," *Science*, January 8, 2020, https://www.science.org/content/article/national-pride-stake-russia-china-united-states-race-build-hypersonic-weapons.

76   John Mecklin, "Closer than ever: It is 100 seconds to midnight," Bulletin of the Atomic Scientists, January 23, 2020, accessed February 8, 2023, https://thebulletin.org/doomsday-clock/2020-doomsday-clock-statement.

77   John Mecklin, "At doom's doorstep: It is 100 seconds to midnight," Bulletin of the Atomic Scientists, January 20, 2022, accessed on September 25, 2023, https://thebulletin.org/doomsday-clock/2022-doomsday-clock-statement/.

78   Ibid.

79   David E. Sanger, "Biden Warned of a Nuclear Armageddon. How Likely is a Nuclear Conflict with Russia?" *The New York Times*, October 9, 2022, accessed February 8, 2023, https://www.nytimes.com/2022/10/09/world/europe/russia-putin-nuclear-threat.html.

80   Ibid.

81   Sarah Starkey, "Press Release: Doomsday Clock remains at 90 seconds to midnight," Bulletin of the Atomic Scientists, January 23, 2024, https://thebulletin.org/2024/01/press-release-doomsday-clock-remains-at-90-seconds-to-midnight/.

82   "COVID-19 Coronavirus Pandemic," October 23, 2023, accessed February 9, 2023, https://www.worldometers.info/coronavirus/.

83   Ed Pilkington, "U.S. nearly detonated atomic bomb over North Carolina — secret document," Sept. 20, 2013, *The Guardian*, https://www.theguardian.com/world/2013/sep/20/usaf-atomic-bomb-north-carolina-1961.

84   Erik Sass, "8 Nuclear Weapons the U.S. Has Lost," *Mental Floss*, November 29, 2007, accessed February 9, 2023, https://www.mentalfloss.com/article/17483/8-nuclear-weapons-us-has-lost.

85   "The 3 a.m. phone call," The National Security Archive, George Washington University, quoting from Robert M. Gates, *From the Shadows: The Ultimate Insider's Story of Five Presidents and How They Won the Cold War*, Simon & Schuster, 2007 https://nsarchive2.gwu.edu/nukevault/ebb371/.

86   Martin E. Hellman, "On the Probability of Nuclear War," Stanford University Electrical Engineering website https://ee.stanford.edu/~hellman/opinion/inevitability.html. Originally an op-ed, "Arms race can only lead to one end: If we don't change our thinking, someone will drop the big one," *The Houston Post*, April 4, 1985.

87   Ibid.

88   Ibid.

89   "Status of World Nuclear Forces," Federation of American Scientists, March 31, 2023, accessed on February 9, 2023, https://fas.org/issues/nuclear-weapons/status-world-nuclear-forces/.

90   Martin E. Hellman, *Breakthrough: Emerging New Thinking: Soviet and Western Scholars Issue a Challenge to Build a World beyond War*, (New York: Walker and Company, 1988).

91   Anatoly Gromyko and Martin E. Hellman, "How Risky is Nuclear Optimism?" Bulletin of the Atomic Scientists, 67 no. 2, November 27, 2015, https://doi.org/10.1177/0096340211399873.

92   "Projected Costs of U.S. Nuclear Forces, 2019 to 2028," Congressional Budget Office, January 2019, accessed February 9, 2023, https://www.cbo.gov/system/files/2019-01/54914-NuclearForces.pdf.

93   Max Bergmann, "Colin Powell: 'Nuclear Weapons Are Useless,'" ThinkProgress, January 27, 2010, accessed February 8, 2023, https://archive.thinkprogress.org/colin-powell-nuclear-weapons-are-useless-4ab6657759c7/.

94   Dan Farber, "WikiLeaks: U.S. Diplomats Confront Black Market for Nuclear Bomb Material," CBS News, December 19, 2010, accessed February 8, 2023, https://www.cbsnews.com/news/wikileaks-us-diplomats-confront-black-market-for-nuclear-bomb-material/.

95   "Nuclear Tipping Point," Nuclear Threat Initiative, accessed February 8, 2023, https://www.nti.org/about/programs-projects/project/nuclear-tipping-point/.

96   Gary Schaub Jr. and James Forsyth Jr., "An Arsenal We Can All Live With," *The New York Times*, May 23, 2010, accessed February 8, 2023, https://www.nytimes.com/2010/05/24/opinion/24schaub.html.

97   "Decreasing the Operational Readiness of Nuclear Weapons Systems: Resolution, Adopted by the General Assembly," 2008, United Nations General Assembly, accessed February 8, 2023, https://digitallibrary.un.org/record/613116?ln=es.

98   Matthew Bunn, "Securing the Bomb 2010: Securing All Nuclear Materials in Four Years," April 2010, Project on Managing the Atom, Belfer Center for Science and International Affairs, Harvard University, age 69.

99   John F. Kennedy, "Address before the General Assembly of the United Nations," September 25, 1961, accessed February 8, 2023, https://www.jfklibrary.org/archives/other-resources/john-f-kennedy-speeches/united-nations-19610925.

Chapter Four

100   "The Mayo Clinic: Faith-Hope-Science," KQED, September 25, 2018, accessed September 25, 2023, https://video.kqed.org/video/the-mayo-clinic-faith-hope-science-czhdtb/.

101   "NHE Fact Sheet," Centers for Medicare & Medicaid Services, accessed February 8, 2023, https://www.cms.gov/research-statistics-data-and-systems/statistics-trends-and-reports/nationalhealthexpenddata/nhe-fact-sheet.

102   Lee J. Miller and Wei Lu, "Asia Trounces U.S. in Health-Efficiency Index Amid Pandemic," Bloomberg, December 17, 2020, https://www.bloomberg.com/news/articles/2020-12-18/asia-trounces-u-s-in-health-efficiency-index-amid-pandemic.

103   David U. Himmelstein et al., "Medical Bankruptcy: Still Common Despite the Affordable Care Act," *American Journal of Public Health*, 109, no. 3, (March 2019): 431–433.

104   "Life Expectancy in the U.S. Dropped for the Second Year in a Row in 2021," Centers for Disease Control, August 31, 2022, accessed February 8, 2023, https://www.cdc.gov/nchs/pressroom/nchs_press_releases/2022/20220831.htm.

105   Lee J. Miller and Wei Lu, "These Are the Economies With the Most (and Least) Efficient Health Care," Bloomberg News, Sept. 19, 2018, https://www.bloomberg.com/news/articles/2018-09-19/u-s-near-bottom-of-health-index-hong-kong-and-singapore-at-top?sref=zcBXJvHi.

106 Sources for the Canadian information: World Health Rankings, https://www.worldlifeexpectancy.com/canada-life-expectancy#:~:text=Canada percent20 percent3A percent20Life percent20Expectancy&text=According percent20to percent20the percent20latest percent20WHO,Life percent20Expectancy percent20ranking percent20of percent207.; Jason Miller, "Canadian spending on health care expected to increase by 4.2 percent over last year, report says," *Toronto Star*, Nov. 20, 2018, https://www.thestar.com/news/canada/2018/11/20/canadian-spending-on-health-care-expected-to-increase-by-42-per-cent-over-last-year-report-says.html; and "National Health Expenditure Trends, 1975 to 2019," Canadian Institute for Health Information.

107 Barack Obama, Remarks at the White House Health Care Forum, March 5, 2009, available via *The New York Times* https://www.nytimes.com/2009/03/05/us/politics/05obama-text.html.

108 Alex Kay, "ESPN Body Issue 2013: Gary Player Tees Off on America's Obesity Problem," Bleacher Report, July 11, 2013, accessed February 8, 2023, https://bleacherreport.com/articles/1700781-espn-body-issue-2013-gary-player-tees-off-on-americas-obesity-problem.

109 William Brangham and Jason Kane, "The U.S. Spends Nearly $4 Trillion on Health Care but Inequities Still Exist. Here's Why." *PBS News Hour*, April 21, 2021, accessed February 8, 2023, https://www.pbs.org/newshour/show/the-u-s-spends-nearly-4-trillion-on-health-care-but-inequities-still-exist-heres-why.

110 Atul Gawande, "Overkill," *The New Yorker*, May 11, 2015, accessed February 8, 2023, https://www.newyorker.com/magazine/2015/05/11/overkill-atul-gawande.

111 "Why Are Americans Paying More for Healthcare?" Peter G. Peterson Foundation, July 14, 2023, accessed February 8, 2023, https://www.pgpf.org/blog/2023/07/why-are-americans-paying-more-for-healthcare.

112 "Annual Family Premiums for Employer Coverage Average $22,463 This Year, with Workers Contributing an Average of $6,106, Benchmark KFF Employer Health Benefit Survey Finds," The Kaiser Family Foundation, October 27, 2022, accessed February 8, 2023, https://www.kff.org/private-insurance/press-release/annual-family-premiums-for-employer-coverage-average-22463-this-year/.

113 Micah Hartman et al., "National Health Care Spending in 2020: Growth Driven by Federal Spending in Response to the COVID-19 Pandemic," *Health Affairs*, 41, no. 1, (December 2021), https://doi.org/10.1377/hlthaff.2021.01763.

114 "CMS Office of the Actuary Releases 2021–2030 Projections of National Health Expenditures," Centers for Medicare & Medicaid Services, March 28, 2022, accessed February 9, 2023, https://www.cms.gov/newsroom/press-releases/cms-office-actuary-releases-2021-2030-projections-national-health-expenditures.

115 "NHE Fact Sheet 2021," Centers for Medicare & Medicaid Services, July 31, 2023, accessed September 25, 2023, https://www.cms.gov/Research-Statistics-Data-and-Systems/Statistics-Trends-and-Reports/NationalHealthExpendData/NHE-Fact-Sheet.

116   NHE Fact Sheet 2021, Centers for Medicare & Medicaid Services, July 31, 2023, Table 3, National Health Expenditures by Source of Funds, https://www.cms.gov/Research-Statistics-Data-and-Systems/Statistics-Trends-and-Reports/NationalHealthExpendData/NHE-Fact-Sheet.

117   "Testimony: Statement of Peter R. Orszag, Director: The Long-term Budget Outlook and Options for Slowing the Growth of Health Care Costs," Congressional Budget Office, June 17, 2008, accessed September 25, 2023.

118   "NQF-endorsed measures for surgical procedures: Technical report," National Quality Forum, February 13, 2015, accessed September 25, 2023, https://www.qualityforum.org/Publications/2015/02/NQF-Endorsed_Measures_for_Surgical_Procedures.aspx.

119   Steven Brill, "Bitter Pill: Why Medical Bills Are Killing Us," *Time*, April 4, 2013, https://time.com/198/bitter-pill-why-medical-bills-are-killing-us/.

120   Ibid.

121   Daniel Ward, "The Money Taboo in Health Reform Coverage," FAIR, November 1, 2009, accessed February 8, 2023, https://fair.org/home/the-money-taboo-in-health-reform-coverage/.

122   U.S. Debt Clock, accessed January 18, 2024, https://www.usdebtclock.org.

123   Steven Brill, "Bitter Pill: Why Medical Bills Are Killing Us," *Time*, April 4, 2013, https://time.com/198/bitter-pill-why-medical-bills-are-killing-us/.

124   "U.S. Surgical Procedure Volumes: New Technologies & Aging Demographics Having Impact," LSI, October 23, 2019, https://www.lifesciencemarketresearch.com/blog/u.s.-procedure-volume-trends-driven-by-new-technologies-demographics.

125   Steven Brill, "Bitter Pill: Why Medical Bills Are Killing Us," *Time*, April 4, 2013, accessed February 8, 2023, https://time.com/198/bitter-pill-why-medical-bills-are-killing-us/.

126   Christopher Ingraham, "The Average American Woman Now Weighs as Much as a 1960s Man," *The Washington Post*, June 12, 2015, accessed February 8, 2023, https://www.washingtonpost.com/news/wonk/wp/2015/06/12/look-at-how-much-weight-weve-gained-since-the-1960s/.

127   Peter Attia, *Outlive: The Science and Art of Longevity*, 2023, (New York: Harmony/Rodale, 2023).

128   "Overweight & Obesity Statistics," National Institute of Diabetes and Digestive and Kidney Diseases, n.d., https://www.niddk.nih.gov/health-information/health-statistics/overweight-obesity.

129   Priyanka Boghani, "Report: 50 Percent of Americans Will be Obese by 2030 at Current Rate," GlobalPost, September 18, 2012, accessed February 8, 2023, https://theworld.org/stories/2012-09-18/report-50-percent-americans-will-be-obese-2030-current-rate.

130 Jane E. Brody, "Half of Us Face Obesity, Dire Projections Show," *The New York Times*, February 10, 2020, accessed February 8, 2023, https://www.nytimes.com/2020/02/10/well/live/half-of-us-face-obesity-dire-projections-show.html.

131 "Obesity and Overweight," Centers for Disease Control and Prevention, accessed February 9, 2023, https://www.cdc.gov/nchs/fastats/obesity-overweight.htm.

132 "Health Effects of Overweight and Obesity," Centers for Disease Control and Prevention, accessed February 9, 2023, https://www.cdc.gov/healthyweight/effects/index.html.

133 David Sinclair and Matthew D. LaPlante, *Lifespan: Why We Age – and Why We Don't Have to*, (New York: Atria, 2019).

134 Centers for Disease Control and Prevention, "Overweight & Obesity: Why It Matters: Obesity is Common, Serious, and Costly," accessed February 9, 2023, https://www.cdc.gov/obesity/about-obesity/why-it-matters.html.

135 Centers for Disease Control and Prevention, "Body Mass Index and Risk for COVID-19–Related Hospitalization, Intensive Care Unit Admission, Invasive Mechanical Ventilation, and Death — United States, March–December 2020," March 12, 2021, accessed February 9, 2023, https://www.cdc.gov/mmwr/volumes/70/wr/mm7010e4.htm.

136 "COVID-19 and Obesity: The 2021 Atlas," World Obesity Federation, March 2021, accessed February 9, 2023, https://www.worldobesityday.org/assets/downloads/COVID-19-and-Obesity-The-2021-Atlas.pdf.

137 Andrew Jacobs, "Two Top Medical Groups Call for Soda Taxes and Advertising Curbs on Sugary Drinks," *The New York Times*, March 25, 2019, accessed February 9, 2023, https://www.nytimes.com/2019/03/25/health/soda-taxes-sugary-drinks-advertising.html.

138 "Denver: Sugary Drink Excise Tax," Denver Public Health and the CHOICES Project Team at the Harvard T.H. Chan School of Public Health, accessed February 9, 2023, https://www.phidenverhealth.org/-/media/dph-files-and-docs/community-health-promotion/heal/choices-denver-sugarydrinktax-report-2018-11-06.pdf.

139 Nathan Bomey, "Philadelphia soda tax caused 'substantial decline' in soda sales, study finds," *USA Today*, May 15, 2019, https://www.usatoday.com/story/money/2019/05/15/philadelphia-soda-tax-sales-study/3677713002/.

140 "CMS Releases Latest Enrollment Figures for Medicare, Medicaid, and Children's Health Insurance Program (CHIP)," Centers for Medicare & Medicaid Services, December 21, 2021, accessed February 9, 2023, https://www.cms.gov/newsroom/news-alert/cms-releases-latest-enrollment-figures-medicare-medicaid-and-childrens-health-insurance-program-chip.

141 Reed Abelson and Margot Sanger-Katz, "'The Cash Monster Was Insatiable': How Insurers Exploited Medicare for Billions," *The New York Times*, October 8, 2022, accessed February 9, 2023, https://www.nytimes.com/2022/10/08/upshot/medicare-advantage-fraud-allegations.html?searchResultPosition=1.

142 Ibid.

143 Ibid.

144 "Health Insurance Coverage in the United States: 2021," United States Census Bureau, September 13, 2022, accessed February 9, 2023, https://www.census.gov/library/publications/2022/demo/p60-278.html.

145 David Sinclair and Matthew D. LaPlante, *Lifespan: Why We Age – and Why We Don't Have to,* (New York: Atria, 2019).

146 Ibid.

147 Jon Gitlin, "What Is a Good Net Promoter Score? And How Does It Vary across Industries?," SurveyMonkey Curiosity at Work, accessed February 9, 2023, https://www.surveymonkey.com/curiosity/what-is-a-good-net-promoter-score/.

148 Ibid.

149 Elisabeth Rosenthal, "Those Indecipherable Medical Bills? They're One Reason Health Care Costs So Much," *The New York Times Magazine,* March 29, 2017, accessed February 9, 2023, https://www.nytimes.com/2017/03/29/magazine/those-indecipherable-medical-bills-theyre-one-reason-health-care-costs-so-much.html.

150 David Sinclair and Matthew D. LaPlante, *Lifespan: Why We Age – and Why We Don't Have to,* (New York: Atria, 2019).

151 Kimberly Leonard, Business Insider, October 30, 2020, chrome-extension://efaidnbmnnnibpcajpcglclefindmkaj/https://politicalaccountability.net/hifi/files/CPA—Business-Insider—We-combed-through-records-of-100-healthcare-companies-L-L—10-30-20—CPA-quoted.pdf.

152 Eliza Barclay, "Warning Labels Might Help Parents Buy Fewer Sugary Drinks, Study Finds," Eating and Health, January 14, 2016, https://www.npr.org/sections/thesalt/2016/01/14/463061869/warning-labels-might-help-parents-buy-fewer-sugary-drinks-study-finds.

Chapter Five

153 "Interstate Highway System – Quotables," U.S. Department of Transportation, Federal Highway Administration, accessed February 9, 2023, https://www.fhwa.dot.gov/interstate/quotable.cfm.

154 "Fact Sheet: Historic Bipartisan Infrastructure Deal," The White House, July 28, 2021, accessed February 9, 2023, https://www.whitehouse.gov/briefing-room/statements-releases/2021/07/28/fact-sheet-historic-bipartisan-infrastructure-deal/.

155 Ibid.

156 "2021 Report Card for America's Infrastructure," accessed February 9, 2023, https://infrastructurereportcard.org/infrastructure-categories/.

157 Ibid.

158 Anisha Kohli, "Jackson, Mississippi Has No Safe Tap Water for the Foreseeable Future. It's a Crisis Decades in the Making," Time, September 1, 2022, https://time.com/6209710/jackson-mississippi-water-crisis/.

159 "Motor Vehicle Deaths in 2020 Estimated to be Highest in 13 years, Despite Dramatic Drops in Miles Driven," National Safety Council, March 4, 2021, accessed February 9, 2023, https://www.nsc.org/newsroom/motor-vehicle-deaths-2020-estimated-to-be-highest.

160 Ibid.

161 "Motor Vehicle Crash Deaths — United States and 28 Other High-Income Countries, 2015 and 2019," "TABLE 1. Motor vehicle crash deaths and deaths per 100,000 population — 29 high-income countries, 2015 and 2019*," Centers for Disease Control and Prevention, July 1, 2022, accessed September 29, 2023, https://www.cdc.gov/mmwr/volumes/71/wr/mm7126a1.htm?s_cid=mm7126a1_w#T1_down.

162 "2021 Report Card for America's Infrastructure," "Assessing America's Infrastructure Gap," accessed February 9, 2023, https://infrastructurereportcard.org/resources/investment-gap-2020–2029/.

163 Kevin McCormally, "A Brief History of the Federal Gasoline Tax," Kiplinger Personal Finance, July 1, 2014, accessed February 9, 2023, https://www.kiplinger.com/article/spending/t063-c000-s001-a-brief-history-of-the-federal-gasoline-tax.html.

164 "The Gas Tax's Tortured History Shows How Hard It Is to Fund New Infrastructure," PBS New Hour, June 22, 2021, accessed February 9, 2023, https://www.pbs.org/newshour/politics/the-gas-taxs-tortured-history-shows-how-hard-it-is-to-fund-new-infrastructure.

165 "Value of $1 from 1993 to 2023," CPI Inflation Calculator, accessed February 9, 2023, https://www.in2013dollars.com/us/inflation/1993?amount=1.

166 "U.S. Population: 1950–2023," Macrotrends, accessed February 9, 2023, https://www.macrotrends.net/countries/USA/united-states/population.

167 "Number of motor vehicles registered in the United States from 1990 to 2021," Statista, https://www.statista.com/statistics/183505/number-of-vehicles-in-the-united-states-since-1990/.

168 Joseph Kile, "Testimony on Addressing the Long-Term Solvency of the Highway Trust Fund," Congressional Budget Office, April 14, 2021, https://www.cbo.gov/publication/57138.

169 U.S. Department of Energy, "Maps and Data – Fuel Taxes by Country," https://afdc.energy.gov/data/10327.

Chapter Six

170 Ronald Reagan, "Inaugural Address 1981," accessed February 9, 2023, https://www.reaganlibrary.gov/archives/speech/inaugural-address-1981.

171 "Anniversary of the Social Security Act of 1935," GovInfo, August 12, 2022, accessed February 9, 2023, https://www.govinfo.gov/features/ssa-anniversary-2022.

172 Frank Bane, "Problems of Social Security," Social Security Administration, December 10, 1936, accessed February 9, 2023, https://www.ssa.gov/history/banesp.html.

173 "Child Poverty in America," Children's Defense Fund, accessed February 9, 2023, https://www.childrensdefense.org/wp-content/uploads/2018/08/Child_Poverty_in_America_Sept_2007.pdf.

174 Kathleen Romig, "Social Security Lifts More People Above the Poverty Line Than Any Other Program," Center of Budget and Policy Priorities, April 19, 2022, accessed February 9, 2023, https://www.cbpp.org/research/social-security/social-security-lifts-more-people-above-the-poverty-line-than-any-other.

175 Ibid.

176 "Fact Sheet," Social Security Administration, accessed February 9, 2023, https://www.ssa.gov/news/press/factsheets/basicfact-alt.pdf.

177 Ibid.

178 Kate Davidson, "Social Security Costs to Exceed Income in 2020, Trustees Say; the Trust Fund to be Depleted by 2035, They Add," *The Wall Street Journal*, April 22, 2019, accessed February 9, 2023, https://www.wsj.com/articles/social-security-trust-fund-to-be-depleted-in-2035-trustees-say-11555946113.

179 "Fact Sheet," Social Security Administration, accessed February 9, 2023, https://www.ssa.gov/news/press/factsheets/basicfact-alt.pdf.

180 "Life Expectancy in the USA, 1990–98, Men and Women," accessed February 9, 2023, https://u.demog.berkeley.edu/~andrew/1918/figure2.html.

181 "Life Expectancy in the U.S. Dropped for the Second Year in a Row in 2021," Centers for Disease Control and Prevention, August 31, 2022, accessed February 9, 2023, www.cdc.gov/nchs/pressroom/nchs_press_releases/2022/20220831.htm.

182 "Social Security: Raising or Eliminating the Taxable Earnings Base," Congressional Research Service, December 22, 2021, https://sgp.fas.org/crs/misc/RL32896.pdf.

183 "Why is the U.S. Birth Rate Declining?" Population Reference Bureau, May 6, 2021, accessed February 9, 2023, https://www.prb.org/resources/why-is-the-u-s-birth-rate-declining/.

184 Aaron Keating, "7 Reforms to Strengthen Social Security," Economic Opportunity Institute, November 9, 2018, accessed February 9, 2023, https://www.opportunityinstitute.org/blog/post/7-ways-to-reform-social-security/.

185 Lorie Konish, "7 changes Americans are willing to make to fix Social Security – including one with 'overwhelming bipartisan support,'" CNBC, August 3, 2022, accessed September 25, 2023 https://www.cnbc.com/2022/08/03/changes-americans-are-willing-to-make-to-fix-social-security.html.

186 Ed Hornick, "Make more than $250k? Obama wants you to pay more in taxes, like it or not," CNN, April 14, 2011, http://www.cnn.com/2011/POLITICS/04/13/wealthy.taxes/index.html.

187 Lorie Konish, "7 changes Americans are willing to make to fix Social Security — including one with 'overwhelming bipartisan support,'" CNBC, August 3, 2022, accessed September 25, 2023, https://www.cnbc.com/2022/08/03/changes-americans-are-willing-to-make-to-fix-social-security.html.

188 Steve Kroft (produced by James Jacoby and Michael Karzis), "Disability, USA," *60 Minutes*, October 10, 2013, https://www.cbsnews.com/news/disability-usa/.

189 "Fiscal Year 2023 President's Budget," Social Security Administration, https://www.ssa.gov/budget/assets/materials/2023/2023BO.pdf.

190 Charles M. Blow, "Reducing Our Obscene Level of Child Poverty," *The New York Times*, January 28, 2015, accessed February 9, 2023, https://www.nytimes.com/2015/01/28/opinion/charles-blow-reducing-our-obscene-level-of-child-poverty.html.

191 "Brown v. Board of Education of Topeka, 347 U.S. 483," Justia U.S. Supreme Court, 1954, accessed February 9, 2023, https://supreme.justia.com/cases/federal/us/347/483/.

192 Alana Semuels, "Good School, Rich School; Bad School, Poor School," *The Atlantic*, August 25, 2016, accessed February 9, 2023, https://www.theatlantic.com/business/archive/2016/08/property-taxes-and-unequal-schools/497333/.

193 "Lawrence A. Cremin, Horace Mann," Britannica, accessed February 9, 2023, https://www.britannica.com/biography/Horace-Mann.

Chapter Seven

194 Ariane de Vogue, "Ginsburg Talks Partisan Rancor, Electoral College, and Kale," CNN, February 7, 2017, accessed February 9, 2023, https://edition.cnn.com/2017/02/07/politics/ruth-bader-ginsburg-electoral-college/index.html.

195 "Congressional Approval Sinks to 18 percent as Democrats Sour Further," Gallup, January 21, 2022, accessed February 9, 2023, https://news.gallup.com/poll/389096/congressional-approval-sinks-democrats-sour-further.aspx.

196 U.S. Debt Clock, accessed February 9, 2023, https://www.usdebtclock.org.

197 Ally J. Levine and Minami Funakoshi, "Financial Sinkholes," Reuters, November 24, 2020, https://www.reuters.com/graphics/USA-ELECTION/SENATE-FUNDRAISING/yxmvjeyjkpr/.

198 "The 2020 election was the most expensive in history, but campaign spending does not always lead to success," LSE, November 27, 2020, https://blogs.lse.ac.uk/usappblog/2020/11/27/the-2020-election-was-the-most-expensive-in-history-but-campaign-spending-does-not-always-lead-to-success/.

199 Alan Zibel, "Revolving Congress: The Revolving Door Class of 2019 Flocks to K Street," Public Citizen, May 30, 2019, accessed February 9, 2023, https://www.citizen.org/article/revolving-congress/.

200 Dan Friedman, "Former Congressmen Make Huge Salaries as Lobbyists While Still Collecting Congressional Pensions," *The New York Daily News*, May 24, 2014, accessed February 9, 2023, https://www.nydailynews.com/news/politics/congressman-bank-lobbyists-article-1.1804659.

201 "Representative W. J. (Billy) Tauzin," Congress.gov, accessed February 9, 2023, https://www.congress.gov/member/w-tauzin/T000058.

202 "Revolving Door: Former Members of the 115th Congress," OpenSecrets, accessed February 9, 2023, https://www.opensecrets.org/revolving/departing.php?cong=115.

203 Tim Lau, "The Filibuster Explained," Brennan Center for Justice, April 26, 2021, accessed February 9, 2023, https://www.brennancenter.org/our-work/research-reports/filibuster-explained.

204 Dominique Maria Bonessi, "This Pterodactyl-Shaped Maryland District to Have Its Day in High Court," WAMU, January 18, 2019, accessed February 9, 2023, https://wamu.org/story/19/01/18/this-pterodactyl-shaped-maryland-district-to-have-its-day-in-high-court/.

205 Wallace McKelvey, "Sailboats, lobsters and Donald Duck: Pennsylvania's most gerrymandered districts," *PennLive*, Sept. 27, 2017 https://www.pennlive.com/politics/2017/09/pennsylvania_gerrymandering_di.html.

206 "Retirement Benefits for Members of Congress," Congressional Research Service, accessed February 9, 2023, https://www.everycrsreport.com/reports/RL30631.html.

207 "Retirement Benefits for Members of Congress," Congressional Research Services, July 25, 2023, https://crsreports.congress.gov/product/pdf/RL/RL30631.

208 "Line-item Veto in the United States," Wikipedia, accessed February 9, 2023, https://en.wikipedia.org/wiki/Line-item_veto_in_the_United_States.

209 Stephen Moore, "The Line Item Veto," Cato Institute, March 23, 2000, accessed February 9, 2023, https://www.cato.org/testimony/line-item-veto.

210 "Clinton v. City of New York," Ballotpedia, accessed February 9, 2023, https://ballotpedia.org/Clinton_v._City_of_New_York.

Chapter Eight

211 Dwight D. Eisenhower, "Chance for Peace," UVA Miller Center, April 16, 1953, accessed February 9, 2023, https://millercenter.org/the-presidency/presidential-speeches/april-16–1953-chance-peace.

212 "Summary of the Fiscal Year 2023 National Defense Authorization Act," United States Senate Committee on Armed Services, https://www.armed-services.senate.gov/imo/media/doc/fy23_ndaa_agreement_summary.pdf.

213 CNN Wire Staff, "Mullen: Debt is Top National Security Threat," CNN, August 27, 2010, accessed February 10, 2023, http://edition.cnn.com/2010/US/08/27/debt.security.mullen/index.html.

214 Nick Routley, "Visualized: The World's Population at 8 Billion," Visual Capitalist, September 27, 2022, accessed February 10, 2023, https://www.visualcapitalist.com/visualized-the-worlds-population-at-8-billion/.

215 Niccolo Conte, "Ranked: Top 10 Countries by Military Spending," Visual Capitalist, August 18, 2022, accessed February 10, 2023, https://www.visualcapitalist.com/ranked-top-10-countries-by-military-spending/.

216 Ibid.

217 Doug Bandow, "750 Bases in 80 Countries Is Too Many for Any Nation: Time for the U.S. to Bring Its Troops Home," Cato Institute, October 4, 2021, accessed February 10, 2023, https://www.cato.org/commentary/750-bases-80-countries-too-many-any-nation-time-us-bring-its-troops-home.

218 Agnieszka Rogozińska & Aleksander Ksawery Olech, "The Russian Federation's Military Bases Abroad," Institute of New Europe, accessed February 10, 2023, https://ine.org.pl/wp-content/uploads/2020/12/THE-RUSSIAN-FEDERATIONS-MILITARY-BASES-ABROAD-1.pdf.

219 Doug Bandow, "750 Bases in 80 Countries Is Too Many for Any Nation: Time for the U.S. to Bring Its Troops Home," Cato Institute, October 4, 2021, accessed February 10, 2023, https://www.cato.org/commentary/750-bases-80-countries-too-many-any-nation-time-us-bring-its-troops-home.

220 Andrew Lautz, "Would You Pay $1.7 Trillion for a Plane That Couldn't Fly?" Responsible Statecraft, April 27, 2021, accessed February 10, 2023, https://responsiblestatecraft.org/2021/04/27/would-you-pay-1-7-trillion-for-a-plane-that-couldnt-fly/.

221 Ryan Browne, "John McCain: F-35 is 'a Scandal and a Tragedy,'" CNN, April 27, 2016, accessed February 10, 2023, https://edition.cnn.com/2016/04/26/politics/f-35-delay-air-force/index.html.

222 "Lockheed Martin," OpenSecrets, accessed February 10, 2023, https://www.opensecrets.org/orgs/lockheed-martin/recipients?id=D000000104.

223 Taylor Giorno, "Defense Sector Donors Contributed $3.4 Million to House Armed Services Committee Members in the 2022 Election Cycle," OpenSecrets, July 13, 2022, accessed February 10, 2023, https://www.opensecrets.org/news/2022/07/defense-sector-donors-contributed-3-4-million-to-house-armed-services-committee-members-in-the-2022-election-cycle/.

224 Dan Auble, "Capitalizing on Conflict: How defense contractors and foreign nations lobby for arms sales," OpenSecrets, February 25, 2021, https://www.opensecrets.org/news/reports/capitalizing-on-conflict/defense-contractors.

225 Eloise Lee, "Congress Is Forcing the Army to Buy 33 Battle Tanks It Doesn't Even Want," Business Insider, May 25, 2012, accessed February 10, 2023, https://www.businessinsider.com/congressmen-want-to-force-the-army-to-buy-33-battle-tanks-it-says-it-doesnt-even-need-2012-5?r=MX&IR=T.

226 Eric Lipton, "The Pentagon Saw a Warship Boondoggle. Congress Saw Jobs." *The New York Times*, February 4, 2023, accessed September 25, 2023, https://www.nytimes.com/2023/02/04/us/politics/littoral-combat-ships-lobbying.html.

227 Elliott Negin, "It's Time to Rein in Inflated Military Budgets," Scientific American, September 14, 2020, accessed February 10, 2023, https://www.scientificamerican.com/article/its-time-to-rein-in-inflated-military-budgets/.

228 Sarah Miller Caldicott, "Why Ford's Alan Mulally Is an Innovation CEO for the Record Books," *Forbes*, June 25, 2014, https://www.forbes.com/sites/sarahcaldicott/2014/06/25/why-fords-alan-mulally-is-an-innovation-ceo-for-the-record-books/?sh=5cf031b47c04.

229 "List of Active United States Military Aircraft," Wikipedia, accessed February 10, 2023, https://en.wikipedia.org/wiki/List_of_active_United_States_military_aircraft#.

230 Ibid.

231 Ibid.

232 "Armed forces of the United States – Statistics & Facts," Statista, July 14, 2023, https://www.statista.com/topics/2171/armed-forces-of-the-united-states/#topicOverview.

233 "Number of Personnel in the Armed Forces of the United Kingdom between 2012 and 2023, by Military Branch," Statista, accessed February 10, 2023, https://www.statista.com/statistics/579991/1number-of-uk-armed-forces-by-military-branch/.

234 Doug Bandow, "750 Bases in 80 Countries Is Too Many for Any Nation: Time for the U.S. to Bring Its Troops Home," Cato Institute, October 4, 2021, accessed February 10, 2023, https://www.cato.org/commentary/750-bases-80-countries-too-many-any-nation-time-us-bring-its-troops-home.

235 Phil Miller, "Revealed: The U.K. Military's Overseas Base Network Involves 145 Sites in 42 Countries," Declassified UK, November 24, 2020, accessed February 10, 2023, https://declassifieduk.org/revealed-the-uk-militarys-overseas-base-network-involves-145-sites-in-42-countries/.

236 Mark F. Cancian, "U.S. Military Forces in FY 2022: Army," Center for Strategic & International Studies, October 2021, accessed February 10, 2023, http://defense360.csis.org/wp-content/uploads/2021/10/211021_Cancian_MilitaryForcesFY2022_Army_v2.pdf.

237 "Projected Costs of U.S. Nuclear Forces, 2021 to 2030," Congressional Budget Office, May 2021, accessed February 10, 2023, https://www.cbo.gov/publication/57240.

238 Hans Kristensen et al., "Status of World Nuclear Forces," Federation of American Scientists, accessed February 10, 2023, https://fas.org/issues/nuclear-weapons/status-world-nuclear-forces/.

239 Taylor Giorno, "Defense Sector Donors Contributed $3.4 Million to House Armed Services Committee Members in the 2022 Election Cycle," OpenSecrets, July 13, 2022, accessed February 10, 2023, https://www.opensecrets.org/news/2022/07/defense-sector-donors-contributed-3-4-million-to-house-armed-services-committee-members-in-the-2022-election-cycle/.

240 "Lobbying," OpenSecrets, accessed February 10, 2023, https://www.opensecrets.org/industries/lobbying.php?ind=D.

241 Dwight D. Eisenhower, "Farewell Address," National Archives, January 17, 1961, accessed February 10, 2023, https://www.archives.gov/milestone-documents/president-dwight-d-eisenhowers-farewell-address.

242 "Lobbying," OpenSecrets, accessed February 10, 2023, https://www.opensecrets.org/industries/lobbying.php?ind=D.

Chapter Nine

243 Craig E. Johnson and Michael Z. Hackman, *Leadership: A Communication Perspective*, (Long Grove, IL: Waveland Press, Inc., 2018).

244 "Our Mission Statement," U.S. Department of State, May 10, 2010, https://2009–2017.state.gov/s/d/rm/rls/perfrpt/2009 performancesummary/html/139613.htm.

245 "International Trade in Merchandise and Services," UNCTAD, accessed February 10, 2023, https://unctad.org/system/files/official-document/gdscsir20041c4_en.pdf.

246 "U.S. Trade in Goods and Services – Balance of Payments Basis," U.S. Census Bureau, Economic Analysis Division, accessed February 10, 2023, https://www.census.gov/foreign-trade/statistics/historical/gands.pdf.

247 "Total value of international U.S. exports of goods and services from 2000 to 2022," Statista, April 24, 2023, https://www.statista.com/statistics/219691/value-of-international-us-exports-of-goods-and-services-since-2000/.

248 David Brooks, "Voters, Your Foreign Policy Views Stink!" *The New York Times*, June 13, 2019, accessed February 10, 2023, https://www.nytimes.com/2019/06/13/opinion/foreign-policy-populism.html.

249 John McCain, "Farewell Statement," CNN, August 27, 2018, accessed February 10, 2023, https://edition.cnn.com/2018/08/27/politics/john-mccain-farewell-statement/index.html.

250 "Economic Costs of War," Watson Institute of International and Public Affairs, accessed February 10, 2023, https://watson.brown.edu/costsofwar/costs/economic.

251 James Mattis, *Call Sign Chaos: Learning to Lead*, (New York: Random House, 2019).

252 Jonathan Pearson, "Peace Corps Budget Update: Congress Votes for Flat Funding for Seventh Year in a Row," National Peace Corps Association, accessed February 10, 2023, https://www.peacecorpsconnect.org/articles/congress-votes-for-seventh-year-of-flat-peace-corps-funding.

253 Thomas L. Friedman, *Thank You for Being Late: An Optimist's Guide to Thriving in the Age of Accelerations*, (New York: Farrar, Straus and Giroux, 2016).

254 Thomas L. Friedman, "Tanks, Jets or Scholarships?" *The New York Times*, May 1, 2012, accessed February 10, 2023, https://www.nytimes.com/2012/05/02/opinion/friedman-tanks-jets-or-scholarships.html.

255 "U.S. Leads in Greenhouse Gas Reductions, but Some States are Falling Behind," Environmental and Energy Study Institute, March 27, 2018, accessed February 10, 2023, https://www.eesi.org/articles/view/u.s.-leads-in-greenhouse-gas-reductions-but-some-states-are-falling-behind.

256 "Prison Populations Continue to Rise in Many Parts of the World, New Report Published by the Institute for Crime & Justice Policy Research Shows," Institute for Crime and Justice Policy Research, December 1, 2021, accessed February 10, 2023, https://www.icpr.org.uk/news-events/2021/prison-populations-continue-rise-many-parts-world-new-report-published-institute.

257 Stephen Feller, "U.S. Ranks Near Bottom Among Countries for Youth Fitness, Study Says," UPI, September 22, 2016, accessed February 10, 2023, https://www.upi.com/Health_News/2016/09/22/US-ranks-near-bottom-among-countries-for-youth-fitness-study-says/3581474552993/.

258 "Poverty Facts and Myths," Confronting Poverty, accessed February 9, 2023, https://confrontingpoverty.org/poverty-facts-and-myths/americas-poor-are-worse-off-than-elsewhere/.

259 "Murder Rate by Country 2023," World Population Review, accessed February 9, 2023, https://worldpopulationreview.com/country-rankings/murder-rate-by-country.

Chapter Ten

260 Cameron Kasky, "My Generation Won't Stand for This," CNN, February 20, 2018, accessed on February 10, 2023, https://edition.cnn.com/2018/02/15/opinions/florida-shooting-no-more-opinion-kasky/index.html.

261 Caitlin Hoffman, "Report: CDC Records Highest-Ever Number of Gun-related Deaths in 2020," Hub, May 2, 2022, accessed February 10, 2023, https://hub.jhu.edu/2022/05/02/highest-number-of-gun-related-deaths-in-2020-report/.

262 John Gramlich, "What the data says about gun deaths in the U.S.," Pew Research Center, April 26, 2023, https://www.pewresearch.org/short-reads/2023/04/26/what-the-data-says-about-gun-deaths-in-the-u-s/.

263 "By the Numbers: Stark Contrast in Australian, U.S. Gun Deaths," United States Studies Centre, June 1, 2022, accessed February 10, 2023, https://www.ussc.edu.au/analysis/by-the-numbers-stark-contrast-in-australian-us-gun-deaths.

264 Nurith Aizenman, "Deaths from Gun Violence: How the U.S. Compares with the Rest of the World," NPR, November 9, 2018, accessed February 10, 2023, https://www.npr.org/sections/goatsandsoda/2018/11/09/666209430/deaths-from-gun-violence-how-the-u-s-compares-with-the-rest-of-the-world.

265 Jason E. Goldsticketal, "Letter to the Editor: Current Causes of Death of Children and Adolescents in the United States," *The New England Journal of Medicine*, 386 (May 2022): 1955–1956.

266 Angel Adegbesan, "Caring for U.S. Victims of Gun Violence Costs $2.5 Billion in the Year After Shooting," Bloomberg, April 2, 2022, https://www.bloomberg.com/news/articles/2022-04-04/u-s-gun-victims-care-costs-2-5-billion-in-year-after-shooting?utm_source=website&utm_medium=share&utm_campaign=email.

267 Rajeev Ramchand and Jessica Saunders, "The Effects of the 1996 National Firearms Agreement in Australia on Suicide, Homicide, and Mass Shootings," RAND Corporation, April 15, 2021, accessed February 10, 2023, https://www.rand.org/research/gun-policy/analysis/essays/1996-national-firearms-agreement.html.

268 "The Economic Cost of Gun Violence," Everytown for Gun Safety, July 19, 2022, accessed February 10, 2023, https://everytownresearch.org/report/the-economic-cost-of-gun-violence/.

269 Ibid.

270 Charlotte Morabito, "The School Security Industry Is Valued at $3.1 Billion. Here's Why That May Not Be Enough," CNBC, July 6, 2022, accessed February 11, 2023, https://www.cnbc.com/2022/07/06/the-school-security-industry-was-valued-at-3point1-billion-in-2021.html.

271 Siladitya Ray, "More Than 300 U.S. Mass Shootings Recorded Halfway into 2023—This Year Is on Pace to Be Deadliest Ever," Forbes, June 19, 2023, https://www.forbes.com/sites/siladityaray/2023/06/19/more-than-300-us-mass-shootings-recorded-halfway-into-2023-this-year-is-on-pace-to-be-deadliest-ever/?sh=713c7ef774ee.

272 "A Partial List of U.S. Mass Shootings in 2023," *The New York Times*, July 3, 2023, https://www.nytimes.com/article/mass-shootings-2023.html.

"More Than 300 U.S. Mass Shootings Recorded Halfway Into 2023 – This Year Is on Pace to be Deadliest Ever, *Forbes*, June 19, 2023, https://www.forbes.com/sites/siladityaray/2023/06/19/more-than-300-us-mass-shootings-recorded-halfway-into-2023-this-year-is-on-pace-to-be-deadliest-ever/?sh=6b66b05274ee.

273 Scott Pelley, "Ukraine's First Lady Olena Zelenska: The 60 Minutes Interview," *60 Minutes*, October, 2, 2022, accessed September 25, 2023, https://www.cbsnews.com/news/ukraine-first-lady-olena-zelenska-60-minutes-transcript-2022-10-02/.

274 Ezra Klein, "Twelve Facts About Guns and Mass Shootings in the United States," *The Washington Post*, December 14, 2012, accessed February 11, 2023, https://www.washingtonpost.com/news/wonk/wp/2012/12/14/nine-facts-about-guns-and-mass-shootings-in-the-united-states/.

275 "Amendment II to the U.S. Constitution," accessed February 11, 2023, https://www.senate.gov/civics/constitution_item/constitution.htm#amdt_2_(1791).

276 Nina Totenberg, "From 'Fraud' to Individual Right, Where Does the Supreme Court Stand on Guns?" NPR, March 5, 2018, accessed February 11, 2023, https://www.npr.org/2018/03/05/590920670/from-fraud-to-individual-right-where-does-the-supreme-court-stand-on-guns.

277 Aliza Vigderman and Gabe Turner, "A Timeline of School Shootings Since Columbine," January 23, 2023, accessed February 11, 2023, https://www.security.org/blog/a-timeline-of-school-shootings-since-columbine/.

278 Hannah Dellinger, "New Law Asks Texas Schools to Distribute Kits to Students to Keep DNA Samples in Case of Emergencies Like Uvalde," *Houston Chronicle*, October 21, 2022, accessed February 11, 2023, https://www.houstonchronicle.com/news/houston-texas/education/article/Texas-school-districts-DNA-kits-HISD-Uvalde-17510329.php.

279 "'Pass These Bills': New Polling Shows Overwhelming Support for Universal Background Checks," Brady Campaign to Prevent Gun Violence, March 10, 2021, accessed February 11, 2023, https://www.bradyunited.org/press-releases/new-polling-overwhelming-support-for-universal-background-checks.

280 Sari Horwitz, "Glock semiautomatic pistol links recent mass shootings," *The Washington Post*, July 20, 2012, https://www.washingtonpost.com/national/glock-semiautomatic-pistol-links-recent-mass-shootings/2012/07/20/gJQAINYwyW_story.html.

281 Mary B. Pasciak, "Tops Markets Shooter Chose AR-15 to Stoke Controversy," *Buffalo News*, December 20, 2022, accessed February 11, 2023, https://buffalonews.com/news/local/crime-and-courts/tops-markets-shooter-chose-ar-15-to-stoke-controversy/article_28ed09a0-d54f-11ec-841c-6f77fed17035.html.

282 Julia Jacobo and Nadine El-Bawab, "Timeline: How the Shooting at a Texas Elementary School Unfolded," ABC News, December 12, 2022, accessed February 11, 2023, https://abcnews.go.com/US/timeline-shooting-texas-elementary-school-unfolded/story?id=84966910.

283 Frank Main, "Dad of Suspect in Highland Park Fourth of July Massacre OK'd His Seeking Gun Permit, State Police Say," *Chicago Sun-Times*, July 5, 2022, accessed February 11, 2023, https://chicago.suntimes.com/2022/7/5/23195378/highland-park-mass-shooting-fourth-july-parade-gun-robert-crimo-rifle.

284 Ko Lyn Cheang, "Greenwood Gunman Used AR-15 Style Rifle That's behind Deadliest Mass Shootings," *Indy Star*, July 18, 2022, accessed February 11, 2023, https://www.indystar.com/story/news/crime/2022/07/18/greenwood-mass-shooting-ar-15-style-rifle-used/65376399007/.

285 Troy Closson, "Subway Victim Sues Gun Maker Over Attack That 'Changed My Life Forever,'" *The New York Times*, May 31, 2022, accessed February 11, 2023, https://www.nytimes.com/2022/05/31/nyregion/subway-shooting-victim-sues-gun-maker-glock.html.

286 Gun Violence Archive, "Incident," November 19, 2022, accessed September 29, 2023, https://www.gunviolencearchive.org/incident/2463465.

287 Ibid.

288 Rajeev Ramchand and Jessica Saunders, "The Effects of the 1996 National Firearms Agreement in Australia on Suicide, Homicide, and Mass Shootings," RAND Corporation, April 15, 2021, accessed February 10, 2023, https://www.rand.org/research/gun-policy/analysis/essays/1996-national-firearms-agreement.html.

289 "Universal Background Checks," Giffords Law Center to Prevent Gun Violence, accessed February 11, 2023, https://giffords.org/lawcenter/gun-laws/policy-areas/background-checks/universal-background-checks/.

290 "Guns," Gallup, accessed February 11, 2023, https://news.gallup.com/poll/1645/guns.aspx.

291 Brandon Formby, "Reports: Odessa Shooter Bought Gun via Private Sale Without Background Check," September 3, 2019, accessed February 11, 2023, https://www.texastribune.org/2019/09/03/odessa-texas-shooter-bought-gun-private-sale-without-background-check/.

292 Jeanne Marie Laskas, "Inside the Federal Bureau of Way Too Many Guns," *GQ*, August 30, 2016, https://www.gq.com/story/inside-federal-bureau-of-way-too-many-guns.

293 Andrew Blankstein et al., "Las Vegas Shooting: 59 Killed and More Than 500 Hurt Near Mandalay Bay," NBC News, October 2, 2017, accessed February 11, 2023, https://www.nbcnews.com/storyline/las-vegas-shooting/las-vegas-police-investigating-shooting-mandalay-bay-n806461.

294 "S.397 – Protection of Lawful Commerce in Arms Act," Congress.Gov, accessed February 11, 2023, https://www.congress.gov/bill/109th-congress/senate-bill/397/text.

295 "Guns," Gallup, accessed February 11, 2023, https://news.gallup.com/poll/1645/guns.aspx.

296 Holly Yan, "This mom's son died in the California massacre, but she doesn't want your thoughts and prayers," CNN, November 9, 2018, accessed September 25, 2023, https://www.cnn.com/2018/11/09/us/california-victim-mom-gun-control/index.html.

Chapter Eleven

297 Lewis F. Powell, Jr., as quoted in numerous books and publications, including on the University of Virginia School of Law website https://www.law.virginia.edu/public-service/powell-fellowship-legal-services.

298 Ram Subramanian et al., "A Federal Agenda for Criminal Justice Reform," Brennan Center for Justice, December 9, 2020, https://www.brennancenter.org/our-work/policy-solutions/federal-agenda-criminal-justice-reform.

299 Jeff Jacoby, "U.S. Legal Bubble Can't Pop Soon Enough," *The Boston Globe*, May 9, 2014, accessed February 11, 2023, https://www.bostonglobe.com/opinion/2014/05/09/the-lawyer-bubble-pops-not-moment-too-soon/qAYzQ823qpfi4GQl2OiPZM/story.html.

300 "Lawyers per Capita by Country 2023," World Population Review, n.d., https://worldpopulationreview.com/country-rankings/lawyers-per-capita-by-country.

301 Helen Fair and Roy Walmsley, "World Prison Population List," World Prison Brief, accessed February 11, 2023, https://www.prisonstudies.org/sites/default/files/resources/downloads/world_prison_population_list_13th_edition.pdf.

302 Ibid.

303 Peter Wagner and Bernadette Rabuy, "Following the Money of Mass Incarceration," Prison Policy Initiative, January 25, 2017, accessed February 11, 2023, https://www.prisonpolicy.org/reports/money.html.

304 Helen Fair and Roy Walmsley, "World Prison Population List," World Prison Brief, https://www.prisonstudies.org/sites/default/files/resources/downloads/world_prison_population_list_13th_edition.pdf.

305 "1 in 5 People Locked up for a Drug Offense," Prison Policy Initiative, accessed February 12, 2023, https://www.prisonpolicy.org/graphs/pie2022_drugs.html.

306 Kayla James, "How the Bail Bond Industry Became a $2 Billion Business," Global Citizen, January 31, 2019, accessed February 11, 2023, https://www.globalcitizen.org/en/content/bail-bond-industry-2-billion-poverty/.

307 Eve Tushnet, "Fifteen to Life: 15 Ways to Fix the Criminal Justice System," *Crisis Magazine*, March 1, 2003, https://www.crisismagazine.com/2003/fifteen-to-life-15-ways-to-fix-the-criminal-justice-system.

308 Ibid.

309 Morris Hoffman, "A Judge on the Injustice of America's Extreme Prison Sentences," *The Wall Street Journal*, February 7, 2019, accessed February 12, 2023, https://www.wsj.com/articles/a-judge-on-the-injustice-of-americas-extreme-prison-sentences-11549557185.

310 Ibid.

311 "The Punishment Rate: New Metric Evaluates Prison Use Relative to Reported Crime," The Pew Charitable Trusts, March 2016, accessed February 12, 2023, https://www.pewtrusts.org/~/media/assets/2016/03/the_punishment_rate.pdf.

Chapter Twelve

312 Madeleine Albright, in Congressional Record: Proceedings and Debates of the 113th Congress, Second Session, Volume 160, Part 4, 2014, 4852.

313 Ronald Reagan, "Statement on United States Immigration and Refugee Policy," July 30, 1981, accessed February 12, 2023, https://www.reaganlibrary.gov/archives/speech/statement-united-states-immigration-and-refugee-policy.

314 Vanessa Brown Calder, "Some Historical Perspective on U.S. Fertility Decline," Cato Institute, October 4, 2022, accessed February 12, 2023, https://www.cato.org/blog/some-historical-context-fertility-decline.

315 Stephanie H. Murray, "How Low Can America's Birth Rate Go Before It's a Problem?" FiveThirtyEight, June 9, 2021, accessed February 12, 2023, https://fivethirtyeight.com/features/how-low-can-americas-birth-rate-go-before-its-a-problem/.

316 "Job Openings Decreased to 10.7 Million in June 2022," U.S. Bureau of Labor Statistics, August 4, 2022, accessed February 12, 2023, https://www.bls.gov/opub/ted/2022/job-openings-decreased-to-10-7-million-in-june-2022.htm.

317 Curtis Dubay, Stephanie Ferguson, and Isabella Lucy, "The State of American Business Data Center 2024," U.S. Chamber of Commerce, January 9, 2024, https://www.uschamber.com/economy/state-of-american-business-data-center-2024.

318 "Monthly number of unemployed person in the United States from January 2022 to January 2024," Statista, https://www.statista.com/statistics/193256/unadjusted-monthly-number-of-unemployed-persons-in-the-us/.

319 "Fact Sheet: Immigration Facts: The Positive Economic Impact of Immigration," FWD.us, July 1, 2020, accessed February 12, 2023, https://www.fwd.us/news/immigration-facts-the-positive-economic-impact-of-immigration/.

320 Ibid.

321 Stuart Anderson, "Immigrants and Billion Dollar Startups," NFAP Policy Brief, March 2016, https://nfap.com/wp-content/uploads/2016/03/Immigrants-and-Billion-Dollar-Startups.NFAP-Policy-Brief.March-2016.pdf.

322 "Fact Sheet: Immigration Facts: The Positive Economic Impact of Immigration," FWD.us, July 1, 2020, accessed February 12, 2023, https://www.fwd.us/news/immigration-facts-the-positive-economic-impact-of-immigration/.

323 George W. Bush, "Address to the Nation on Immigration Reform," The American Presidency Project, May 15, 2006, accessed February 12, 2023, https://www.presidency.ucsb.edu/documents/address-the-nation-immigration-reform.

324 Derek Thompson, "Why U.S. Population Growth is Collapsing," *The Atlantic*, March 28, 2022, accessed February 12, 2023, https://www.theatlantic.com/newsletters/archive/2022/03/american-population-growth-rate-slow/629392/.

325 "Naturalization Statistics," U.S. Citizenship and Immigration Services, accessed February 12, 2023, https://www.uscis.gov/citizenship-resource-center/naturalization-statistics.

326 "N-400 Application for Naturalization," U.S. Citizenship and Immigration Services, accessed February 12, 2023, https://www.uscis.gov/n-400.

327 "Immigration Court Case Backlog Nears Two Million!" LexisNexis, July 15, 2022, https://www.lexisnexis.com/LegalNewsRoom/immigration/b/outsidenews/posts/immigration-court-case-backlog-nears-two-million.

328 "Profile of the Unauthorized Population: United States," Migration Policy Institute, accessed February 12, 2023, https://www.migrationpolicy.org/data/unauthorized-immigrant-population/state/US.

329 "Public Opinion on a Path to Legal Status for Undocumented Immigrants in the United States in 2020," Statista, accessed February 12, 2023, https://www.statista.com/statistics/367872/public-opinion-on-a-path-to-legal-status-for-illegal-immigrants-in-the-us/.

Chapter Thirteen

330 Alan Simpson, "Special Interests Distort Elections," Politico, April 25, 2011, accessed February 11, 2023, https://www.politico.com/story/2011/04/special-interests-distort-elections-053597.

331 Bradley Jones, "Most Americans Want to Limit Campaign Spending, Say Big Donors Have Greater Political Influence," Pew Research Center, May 8, 2018, accessed February 12, 2023, https://www.pewresearch.org/fact-tank/2018/05/08/most-americans-want-to-limit-campaign-spending-say-big-donors-have-greater-political-influence/.

332 "Did Money Win?" OpenSecrets, accessed September 25, 2023, https://www.opensecrets.org/elections-overview/did-money-win.

333 Taylor Giorno and Pete Quist, "Total Cost of 2022 State and Federal Elections Projected to Exceed $16.7 Billion," OpenSecrets, November 3, 2022, accessed February 12, 2023, https://www.opensecrets.org/news/2022/11/total-cost-of-2022-state-and-federal-elections-projected-to-exceed-16-7-billion/.

334 Ken Bensinger and Alyce McFadden, "Georgia Senate Race Again Draws Huge Spending: 'There's Never Been Anything Like It,'" *The New York Times*, December 6, 2022, accessed February 12, 2023, https://www.nytimes.com/2022/12/06/us/politics/georgia-runoff-election-cost-funding.html.

335 Kim Strong, "'Watching People Throw Poo at Each Other': Oz, Fetterman Ads Set Campaign Spending Record," *York Daily Record*, November 9, 2022, accessed February 12, 2023, https://www.ydr.com/story/news/2022/11/09/fetterman-and-oz-break-spending-records-for-a-federal-election-race/69630358007/.

336 "Data Points: Presidential Campaign Spending," U.S. News and World Report, October 21, 2008, accessed February 12, 2023, https://www.usnews.com/opinion/articles/2008/10/21/data-points-presidential-campaign-spending.

337 "Billionaire Political Influence," Americans for Tax Fairness, accessed February 12, 2023, https://americansfortaxfairness.org/billionaire-politics/.

338 Kenneth P. Vogel and Shane Goldmacher, "Democrats Decried Dark Money. Then They Won with It in 2020," *The New York Times*, January 29, 2022, accessed February 12, 2023, https://www.nytimes.com/2022/01/29/us/politics/democrats-dark-money-donors.html.

339 Nick Penniman, "Time Spent Fundraising in Congress," C-SPAN, January 4, 2018, accessed February 12, 2023, https://www.c-span.org/video/?c4706765/time-spent-fundraising-congress.

340 "Fundraising Remains Predictive of Success in Congressional Elections," *The Economist*, September 1, 2022, accessed February 12, 2023, https://www.economist.com/graphic-detail/2022/09/01/fundraising-remains-predictive-of-success-in-congressional-elections.

Chapter Fourteen

341 Francine J. lipman, "The Hardest Thing in the World to Understand is the Income Tax." Pro Bono Matters, Winter 2013, https://www.americanbar.org/content/dam/aba/publishing/aba_tax_times/13win/06-pbm.pdf.

342 "Tax Cuts and Jobs Act: A Comparison for Business," Internal Revenue Service, accessed February 12, 2023, https://www.irs.gov/newsroom/tax-cuts-and-jobs-act-a-comparison-for-businesses.

343 "CBO Confirms GOP Tax Law Contributes to Darkening Fiscal Future," House Committee on the Budget, February 5, 2019, accessed February 12, 2023, https://democrats-budget.house.gov/publications/report/cbo-confirms-gop-tax-law-contributes-darkening-fiscal-future.

344 Amy Fontinelle, "How the TCJA Tax Law Affects Your Personal Finances," Investopedia, December 27, 2022, https://www.investopedia.com/taxes/how-gop-tax-bill-affects-you/#:~:text=The percent20nearly percent20200 percent2Dpage percent20Act,lowering percent20the percent20corporate percent20tax percent20rate.

345 Ben Casselman and Jim Tankersley, "Face It: You (Probably) Got a Tax Cut," *The New York Times*, April 14, 2019, https://www.nytimes.com/2019/04/14/business/economy/income-tax-cut.html.

346 John Hamilton, "No City Would Ever Pass This Tax Bill," *The Washington Post*, December 7, 2017, accessed February 12, 2023, https://www.washingtonpost.com/opinions/no-city-would-ever-pass-this-tax-bill/2017/12/07/899216ac-dad5-11e7-b859-fb0995360725_story.html.

347 Emmanuel Saez and Gabriel Zucman, "The Rise of Income and Wealth Inequality in America: Evidence from Distributional Macroeconomic Accounts," *Journal of Economic Perspectives*, 34, no. 4, (2020), 3–26.

348 Christopher Ingraham, "For the First Time in History, U.S. Billionaires Paid a Lower Tax Rate Than the Working Class Last Year," *The Washington Post*, October 8, 2019, accessed February 12, 2023, https://www.washingtonpost.com/business/2019/10/08/first-time-history-us-billionaires-paid-lower-tax-rate-than-working-class-last-year/.

349 Susan Davis, "The 42 Million Americans Who Receive SNAP Benefits Are Set to Get $36 More a Month," NPR, August 22, 2021, accessed February 12, 2023, https://www.npr.org/2021/08/22/1030099959/the-42-million-americans-who-receive-snap-benefits-are-set-to-get-36-more-a-mont.

350 "Fact Sheet: Social Security," Social Security Administration, accessed February 12, 2023, https://www.ssa.gov/news/press/factsheets/basicfact-alt.pdf.

351 Maya Riser-Kositsky, "Education Statistics: Facts about American Schools," Edweek, January 3, 2019, accessed February 12, 2023, https://www.edweek.org/leadership/education-statistics-facts-about-american-schools/2019/01.

352 "50 Ways Government Works for Us," Securities and Exchange Commission, accessed February 12, 2023, https://www.sec.gov/spotlight/sec-employees/psrw50ways.pdf.

353 "Air Traffic Organization," Federal Aviation Administration, accessed February 12, 2023, https://www.faa.gov/about/office_org/headquarters_offices/ato.

354 "Postal Facts," United States Postal Service, accessed February 12, 2023, https://facts.usps.com/one-day/.

355 "Go Take a Hike," National Park Service, accessed February 12, 2023, https://www.nps.gov/subjects/trails/index.htm.

356 "List of Diplomatic Missions in United States and American Diplomatic Missions abroad," Embassy Worldwide, accessed February 12, 2023, https://www.embassy-worldwide.com/country/united-states/.

357 Jennie W. Wenger and Jason M. Ward, "The Role of Education Benefits in Supporting Veterans as They Transition to Civilian Life," RAND Corporation, accessed February 12, 2023, https://www.rand.org/pubs/perspectives/PEA1363-4.html.

358 Safi R. Bahcall, *Loonshots: How to Nurture the Crazy Ideas that Win Wars, Cure Diseases, and Transform Industries*, (New York: St. Martin's Press, 2019).

359 Jeffrey D. Sachs, The Price of Civilization: Reawakening American Virtue and Prosperity, (New York: Random House, 2012).

360 "How Many Pages Is the Tax Code (& How Long Does It Take to Read It)," Iris, n.d., https://irisreading.com/how-long-would-it-take-to-read-the-entire-u-s-tax-code/.

361 "Fact Sheet," CCH, 2013, https://www.cch.com/wbot2013/factsheet.pdf.

362 "2022 Tax Filing: Backlogs and Ongoing Hiring Challenges Led to Poor Customer Service and Refund Delays," Government Accountability Office, December 15, 2022, accessed February 12, 2023, https://www.gao.gov/products/gao-23-105880.

363 Eric Maus, "Tax Processing Issues Continue to Plague IRS," Citizens against Government Waste, April 18, 2022, accessed February 12, 2023, https://www.cagw.org/thewastewatcher/tax-processing-issues-continue-plague-irs.

364 Jacob Bogage, "Democrats' $80 Billion Wager: A Bigger IRS Will Be a Better IRS," August 6, 2022, accessed February 12, 2023, www.washingtonpost.com/business/2022/08/06/inflation-reduction-act-irs/.

365 David Kocieniewski, "G.E.'s Strategies Let it Avoid Taxes Altogether," *The New York Times*, March 24, 2011, accessed February 12, 2023, https://www.nytimes.com/2011/03/25/business/economy/25tax.html?_r=3&ref=business.

366 "Study: 73 percent of Fortune 500 Companies Used Offshore Tax Havens in 2016," Public Interest Research Group, October 17, 2017, accessed February 12, 2023, https://pirg.org/media-center/study-73-of-fortune-500-companies-used-offshore-tax-havens-in-2016/.

367 Adam Kazda, "The More Complex the Tax Code, the More the Wealthy Benefit," *The Hill*, July 25, 2017, accessed February 12, 2023, https://thehill.com/blogs/pundits-blog/economy-budget/343645-the-more-complex-the-tax-code-the-more-the-rich-benefit/.

368 Nina Olson, National Taxpayer Advocate, reported in Ellen Kant, "A Stark Reminder of the Excessive Cost of Complying with the Tax Code," Tax Foundation, Jan. 15, 2013 https://taxfoundation.org/stark-reminder-excessive-cost-complying-tax-code/.

369 Caroline Baum, "For $168 Billion, We Should Get a Better Return," Bloomberg, April 10, 2013, accessed February 12, 2023, https://www.bloomberg.com/opinion/articles/2013-04-10/for-168-billion-we-should-get-a-better-return-caroline-baum?leadSource=uverify percent20wall.

370 Michael Weisskopf, "Exxon Settles Spill for $1.1 Billion," *The Washington Post*, March 13, 1991, accessed February 12, 2023, https://www.washingtonpost.com/archive/politics/1991/03/13/exxon-settles-spill-for-11-billion/550c4390-1172-45fe-966b-c501805ae5e6/.

371 Jay Busbee, "NASCAR Tracks Get Part of a Nice Little $70 Million Perk in the Fiscal Cliff Deal," Yahoo Sports, January 2, 2013, accessed February 12, 2023, https://sports.yahoo.com/blogs/nascar-from-the-marbles/nascar-gets-nice-little-70-million-perk-fiscal-203238580-nascar.html?guccounter=1.

372 Robert W. Wood, "20 Really Stupid Things in the U.S. Tax Code," *Forbes*, December 16, 2014, accessed February 12, 2023, https://www.forbes.com/sites/robertwood/2014/12/16/20-really-stupid-things-in-the-u-s-tax-code/#ae88abb14b60.

373 "60 Fortune 500 Companies Avoided All Federal Income Tax in 2018 Under New Tax Law," Institute on Taxation and Economic Policy, April 11, 2019, accessed February 12, 2023, https://itep.org/60-fortune-500-companies-avoided-all-federal-income-tax-in-2018-under-new-tax-law/.

374 Jay MacDonald, "5 Tax Deductions That Favor the Rich," Bankrate, December 7, 2011, accessed February 12, 2023, https://www.bankrate.com/finance/taxes/tax-deductions-favor-rich-1.aspx.

375 David Floyd, "Explaining the Trump Tax Reform Plan," Investopedia, January 23, 2023, accessed February 12, 2023, https://www.investopedia.com/taxes/trumps-tax-reform-plan-explained.

376 John Buhl, "The Inflation Reduction Act Primarily Impacts Top 1 Percent of Taxpayers," Tax Policy Center, August 11, 2022, accessed February 12, 2023, https://www.taxpolicycenter.org/taxvox/inflation-reduction-act-primarily-impacts-top-1-percent-taxpayers.

377 Kimberly Amadeo, "Simpson-Bowles Plan Summary, History, and Whether it Would Work," The Balance, November 28, 2021, accessed February 12, 2023, https://www.thebalancemoney.com/simpson-bowles-plan-summary-history-would-it-work-3306323.

378 David Floyd, "Explaining the Trump Tax Reform Plan," Investopedia, January 23, 2023, accessed February 12, 2023, https://www.investopedia.com/taxes/trumps-tax-reform-plan-explained.

379 "60 Fortune 500 Companies Avoided All Federal Income Tax in 2018 Under New Tax Law," Institute on Taxation and Economic Policy, April 11, 2019, accessed February 12, 2023, https://itep.org/60-fortune-500-companies-avoided-all-federal-income-tax-in-2018-under-new-tax-law/.

380 Cass Sunstein, "How to Simplify the Tax Code. Simply," *Time*, May 31, 2013, accessed February 12, 2023, https://ideas.time.com/2013/05/31/how-to-simplify-the-tax-code-simply/.

381 "From Health Affairs: National Health Spending Projected to Hit $6.8 Trillion by 2030," Health Affairs, March 28, 2022, accessed February 12, 2023, https://www.healthaffairs.org/do/10.1377/forefront.20220328.49033/.

382 "Total Expenditure on Health as a Share of Gross Domestic Product (GDP) in Germany from 1980 to 2022," Statista, accessed February 12, 2023, https://www.statista.com/statistics/429202/healthcare-expenditure-as-a-share-of-gdp-in-germany/.

383 "The Economic Cost of Gun Violence," Everytown for Gun Safety, July 19, 2022, accessed February 23, 2023, https://everytownresearch.org/report/the-economic-cost-of-gun-violence/.

384 "World Prison Brief," Institute for Crime and Justice Policy Research, accessed February 12, 2023, https://www.prisonstudies.org.

385 "Policy Basics: Social Security Disability Insurance," Center on Budget and Policy Priorities, March 17, 2022, accessed February 12, 2023, https://www.cbpp.org/research/social-security/social-security-disability-insurance.

386 Centers for Disease Control and Prevention, "Adult Obesity Facts," accessed February 12, 2023, https://www.cdc.gov/obesity/data/adult.html.

Conclusion

387 Malala Yousafzai, *He Named Me Malala*, 2015, accessed February 12, 2023, https://www.imdb.com/title/tt3065132/characters/nm5324796.

Printed in the USA
CPSIA information can be obtained
at www.ICGtesting.com
JSHW012014060324
58373JS00001B/1/J

9 781955 656597